deal with unfinished suffrage reform on the eve of the Civil War and report the unpopular opinions of that minority at home or abroad who were critical of or opposed to reform.

Throughout the book, attention is given not only to the particular circumstances which led to reform in each state, but also to such general factors generating reform as intellectual currents, wars and rumors of wars, partisan politics, the uniqueness of the American environment.

CHILTON WILLIAMSON is an associate professor of history at Barnard College.

"This work will be used and cited by all scholars in the field of American history before 1860. The author has made a thoroughly reliable investigation of property qualifications for voting in the period, utilizing an admirable range of sources. It presents a great deal of new and important information about suffrage conditions in the century before 1860."— RICHARD P. McCORMICK

James J. Polk, Jacksonian
1795-1843

BY CHARLES GRIER SELLERS, JR.

The first full account of Polk's important pre-presidential career. Since Polk was immersed in so many of the major political developments of his day—the rise of popular democracy, the conflicts over the national bank and other crucial issues of Jackson's administration—this biography is a history of his generation's political experience.

AMERICAN SUFFRAGE
FROM PROPERTY TO DEMOCRACY
1760-1860

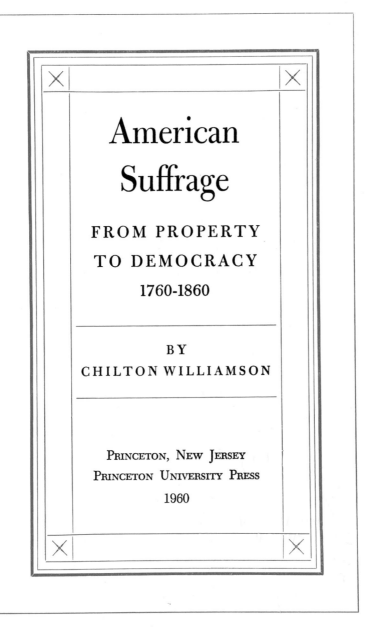

American Suffrage

FROM PROPERTY TO DEMOCRACY
1760-1860

BY
CHILTON WILLIAMSON

Princeton, New Jersey
Princeton University Press
1960

FOR MY FATHER,

ROBERT DAWSON WILLIAMSON

ALL comprehensive surveys of American history before the Civil War devote attention, in some fashion, to such important themes as nationalism, expansion, industrialism, sectionalism, and, last but not least, the accelerated tempo of democratization. By the time Tocqueville visited the United States, the outstanding characteristic of our polity was its democratic bias and content. Negro slavery was the great exception which in a perverse sense proved the rule.

Among the democratic achievements of the period between the Revolution and the Civil War, universal white manhood suffrage stands out as a reform of considerable magnitude in the context of the history of the United States and also of the world. In Europe, for example, suffrage democracy was almost wholly an achievement of the last quarter of the nineteenth century. Italy actually did not adopt it until 1912. Often suffrage democracy was achieved without the superstructure of liberal or democratic parliamentary institutions, as was the case of the North German Confederation of 1867 and the German Empire of 1871. In America, however, what Bismarck called his "drop of democratic oil" provided lubrication for a genuinely democratic machine.

The precise circumstances in which the suffrage qualifications of the colonial period, particularly the freehold, were swept away have never before been examined in the light of the considerable manuscript material on deposit in the archives and historical societies of the pertinent states. This material, together with printed sources, both primary and secondary, provides the historian with a fairly clear picture, state by state, of the extent of the denial of franchise under the old property tests and the circumstances, political and otherwise, under which suffrage reform was finally carried. Because suffrage reform was effected in all the states, albeit in

vii

different circumstances, by different methods and at different times, it may be considered in one sense a national movement, although not in the same sense in which abolitionism or woman's rights were national movements. The issue of universal white manhood suffrage divided the American people far less than did other significant issues in the history of the United States before the Civil War. Partly for this reason, the creation of a national organization was not required to achieve reform. To understand the reasons for this phenomenon, it is necessary to take into account the factors, environmental and intellectual, common to all or to some of the states, which often worked sight unseen to effect suffrage reform and to create an atmosphere congenial to its acceptance. Certainly it would have been extraordinary if suffrage reform had not been influenced by intellectual and political currents, European as well as American, which flowed without hindrance across interstate boundaries. In short, suffrage reform must be understood as a product of local, state, and national history, and even to some extent of European history.

Considered in this way, American suffrage history is a subject of great complexity. I am convinced that fundamental forces were at work, including widespread diffusion of land, natural rights philosophy, wars or rumors of war, as well as politics. I am convinced also that suffrage reform came when the right people in the right situations made reform of the suffrage qualifications an issue. There is abundant evidence for the fact that certain individuals at particular times in the various states attacked the existing property tests. There is less convincing evidence that fundamental forces dictated that the issue should arise when it did. For this reason, this study emphasizes state more than national history, and the particular as much as the general. Perhaps he who has studied the atom knows as much which is fundamental as he who peers at the stars.

It is a pleasant duty to extend my thanks to the staffs of the various archives and historical societies of all the seaboard states, save Florida and Delaware, as well as to officials of these same institutions in the Mississippi Valley who answered my requests for information with care and attention. I am very grateful for grants from the Columbia University Council for Research in the Social Sciences and from the Barnard College Faculty Research Committee to meet travel expenses and for release from summer teaching in order to bring the work to completion. I should like to thank also Miss R. Miriam Brokaw of the Princeton University Press for her interest and help. My wife cheerfully assumed the tasks of being my severest critic and of typing the various drafts of the manuscript. She has, I must add, lost her amateur standing in both roles. For any sins of omission and commission I assume all responsibility.

Barnard College   CHILTON WILLIAMSON
Columbia University
Sept. 21, 1960

ACKNOWLEDGMENTS

Acknowledgment is hereby made for permission to quote from the following works and manuscript collections.

Charles F. Adams (ed.). *The Works of John Adams.* Lyman H. Butterfield.

Edward W. Emerson (ed.). *The Complete Works of Ralph Waldo Emerson.* Houghton Mifflin Company.

Max Farrand (ed.). *The Records of the Federal Convention.* Yale University Press.

The Federalist. Everyman Edition, E. P. Dutton & Co., Inc.

Richard J. Hooker (ed.). *Charles Woodmason. Carolina Backcountry on the Eve of the Revolution: Being the*

Journal and other Writings of Charles Woodmason, Anglican Itinerant. The University of North Carolina Press.

P. H. Johnstone. "Turnips and Romanticism." *Agricultural History.* July 1938.

Benjamin H. Latrobe Papers. Maryland Historical Society.

Frederick W. Maitland. *The Constitutional History of England.* Cambridge University Press.

Samuel E. Morison. *Life and Letters of Harrison Gray Otis.* Houghton Mifflin Company.

Franz Neumann (ed.). *Baron de Montesquieu. The Spirit of the Laws.* Hafner Publishing Company.

Sir Lewis Namier. *The Structure of British Politics at the Accession of George III.* Macmillan & Company Ltd. of London and St. Martin's Press.

John G. Nicolay and John Hay. *The Complete Works of Abraham Lincoln.* Appleton-Century-Crofts, Inc.

Kate Rowland. *Life of George Mason.* G. P. Putnam's Sons.

A. J. P. Taylor (ed.). *Essays Presented to Sir Lewis Namier.* Macmillan & Co. Ltd. and St. Martin's Press.

Frederick J. Turner. *The Frontier in American History.* Henry Holt and Company, Inc.

———. *The Rise of the New West.* Harper & Brothers.

Charles Warren. *Jacobin and Junto.* Harvard University Press.

Albert B. White. *Self-Government at the King's Command.* University of Minnesota Press. Copyright, 1933.

A. S. P. Wodehouse. *Puritanism and Liberty.* University of Chicago Press.

CONTENTS

AMERICAN SUFFRAGE
FROM PROPERTY TO DEMOCRACY
1760-1860

CHAPTER 1

THE AGE OF PROPERTY TESTS

AN OBSCURE American pamphleteer of the late nineteenth century, William A. MacCorkle, asserted that the mother country was responsible for the undemocratic suffrage in the American colonies before the American Revolution. It was, he wrote, the "result of the commands of the King of England."[1] In the strict sense, MacCorkle was correct. Since the Stuart restoration, any but a freehold qualification for the suffrage represented a violation of royal instructions.

If MacCorkle meant to imply, however, that property tests for voting were foisted upon the American colonists against their will, he was mistaken. Actually, the thinking about property tests derived from an inheritance common to both colonists and Britons: the concept that the freeholders were and should remain the backbone of state and society because they were the repository of virtues not found in other classes. Trust in the freeholder was not confined to any age, to any particular school of political theory, or to any one country. It was, however, particularly strong in balanced or mixed government. From such classical thinkers as Plato, Polybius, and Cicero to the eighteenth-century philosopher, Montesquieu, government composed of a balance between monarchy, aristocracy, and democracy had been considered one of the grand contrivances of the western political mind.[2] When separated, monarchy,

---

[1] MacCorkle, William A., *Does the Experience of this Republic . . . Justify Universal Manhood Suffrage or shall the Elective Franchise be limited . . . ?* (Cincinnati, 1900), p. 5.

[2] See Pargellis, Stanley, "The Theory of Balanced Government," in Read, Conyers (ed.), *The Constitution Reconsidered* (New York, 1938), pp. 37-49; Weston, Corinne, *The House of Lords, Mixed Government and Democracy: 1556-1832* (unpub. Ph.D. thesis, Columbia University, 1951); Chinard, G., "Polybius and the American Constitution," *Journal*

aristocracy, and democracy had grave defects. As John Calvin explained, monarchy became despotic, aristocracies oligarchical, and democracies seditious.[3] In a judicious mixture or combination, the dangers in each were obviated. When accompanied by a separation of executive, legislative, and judicial powers, mixed government was considered superior to any other.

Political theorists who advocated mixed government found it necessary to concern themselves with the question of how democratic should be the democratic element in government. A good deal of confusion resulted from discussion of this problem because the meaning of the words employed was not always clear. Did democracy refer to a form of government with a strong representative element, or to a government in which the people directly exercised the power to legislate? Did it refer to a government, of whatever form, in which the most numerous and poorest class was the ultimate power or to one in which the middle class predominated? If the latter, how was one to define the middle class? Did it refer to agricultural, manufacturing, or commercial groups?

Undoubtedly, some of the confusion resulted from the social biases and convictions of the various writers. Aristotle preferred a government resting upon the middle classes but was hesitant, in certain circumstances, to admit artisans and tradesmen to citizenship, for which timidity and conservatism John Adams reproved him.[4] The agrarian policies of the Roman Gracchi were a fearsome example to those who considered their program inseparable from the growth of a landless urban proletariat. Many political thinkers remained uncon-

---

of the History of Ideas (I, 1940), pp. 39-58; Barker, Sir Ernest (ed.), *The Politics of Aristotle* (Oxford, 1946), pp. 107-109, 111, 111n, 214-216, 263-265.

[3] Calvin, John, *The Institutes of the Christian Religion* (Philadelphia, n.d., 2 vols.), II, pp. 770-782.

[4] Adams, Charles F. (ed.), *The Writings of John Adams* (Boston, 1850-1856, 10 vols.), V, p. 457.

vinced that even the town merchants and well-to-do artisans could be trusted with more than a token share in government.

Generally speaking, political theorists, particularly of the eighteenth century, agreed that the freeholders should comprise the bulk of the electorate of governments with a democratic element.[5] It was the freeholders who would have, in a phrase as old as Aristotle, a common interest in and a permanent attachment to society and the state. They cited Cato, Cicero, and Pliny as well as men of the Renaissance who had extolled the virtues of rural life, particularly when associated with the small landowner.[6] Farming virtues became political virtues—independence, stability, good character, and respect for the personal and property rights of others.

In early eighteenth-century Britain, Whigs and Tories, whatever their differences, did not quarrel over the merits of the suffrage qualifications which had existed since the famous statute of 1430. This statute confined the right to vote for members of Parliament to the 40-shilling freeholders, that is, to owners of land worth 40 shillings a year in rental value or in income, or the lawful or customary equivalents.

The origins of this statute remain obscure.[7] Probably the explanation contained in the statute should be taken at face value: namely, that a restriction of the electorate to the freeholders was desirable in the light of the disorder and confusion which the poorer and meaner sort of person had caused at the polls. Implicit also in English suffrage theory was the belief, as old as the emergence of the House of Com-

[5] Griswold, A. Whitney, *Farming and Democracy* (New York, 1948), pp. 19-29; Sydney, Algernon, *Political Classics* (London, 1790, 2 vols.), I, pp. 567-568; Namier, Lewis B., *England in the Age of the American Revolution* (London, 1930), pp. 20-21.

[6] Johnstone, Paul, "In Praise of Husbandry," *Agricultural History* (XI, April 1937), pp. 80-95.

[7] Porritt, E., *The Unreformed House of Commons* (Cambridge, 1903, 2 vols.), I, pp. 20-28. See also Gross, Charles A., "The Early History of the Ballot in England," *American Historical Review* (III, April 1898), pp. 456-463.

mons itself, that so long as the landowners directly paid the bulk of public taxes it was not inequitable or unjust to confine Commons' elections to them. This would be especially true at a time when one of the major functions of this body was the voting of funds to pay for the extraordinary expenses of government, occasioned in particular by the waging of continental wars. As A. B. White has said, it is the general consensus of historians that popular elections came about in this fashion.[8]

In all these matters, American opinion and practice mirrored those of Britain. "A Civil Society or State," declared a Pennsylvanian in 1775, "is a number of proprietors of land within certain limits, united by compact or mutual agreement, for making laws and appointing persons to execute these laws for their common benefit."[9] The Maryland Upper House in more succinct fashion stated flatly: "The freeholders are the strength of this province not the freemen. It is their persons, purses and stocks [which] must bear the burden of government, and not the freemen who can easily abandon us."[10] When in 1745 the governor's council of South Carolina recommended that voting be confined to freeholders, it rested its case squarely upon royal instructions and upon British precedents.

The crucial role of the freeholder in the payment of taxes and the holding of office in local and central government, at a time when government was a kind of non-partisan, public service device, made the suffrage theory of the times understandable. By and large, that element of the population which was relatively poor and lacked education and standing in the

[8] White, Albert B., *Self-Government at the King's Command* (Minneapolis, 1933), p. 88. See also Haskins, George L., *The Growth of English Representative Government* (Philadelphia, 1948).

[9] Force, Peter, *American Archives* (Washington, D.C., 1837-1853, 9 vols.), 4th Series, II, p. 962.

[10] Quoted in Seymour, Charles, and Frary, Donald P., *How the World Votes* (Springfield, Mass., 1918, 2 vols.), I, p. 210.

community was not likely to develop an active interest in the affairs of state. In this light, the freehold qualification of late medieval and early modern times was by no means unreasonable, no matter how undemocratic it may appear to modern eyes.

Historians of the law have given considerable attention to determining who qualified as a freeholder and what constituted a freehold. "A freeholder," writes Frederick W. Maitland, "must hold land for the life of himself or of some other person. . . . He who holds for a fixed term of years is no freeholder."[11] It is clear, therefore, that some leaseholders were deemed freeholders in English law. An English statute of 1540 conferred upon certain owners of land the right to make leases for the life of the lessee and the lives of other persons designated in the lease. Such tenancies were deemed freeholds. The leaseholder was qualified to vote in parliamentary elections if the annual income from his holding reached 40 shillings.[12] That eminent legal authority, Sir William Blackstone, referred to these leases as freeholds and designated them as forms of real property. On the other hand, leases for a definite number of years, even for a thousand, were not so designated according to his definition.[13] Other interpretations of the meaning of real property enabled recipients of annuities, rents from freeholds, dowries, or even the owners of church pews to vote.[14]

In addition to the freehold qualification for voting in the counties, there existed numerous borough qualifications, which

[11] Maitland, Frederick W., *The Constitutional History of England* (Cambridge, 1908), p. 36.

[12] Seligman, E. R. A. (ed.), *Encyclopedia of the Social Sciences* (New York, 1930-1935, 15 vols.), vi, pp. 461-465; Holdsworth, W. S., *A History of English Law* (London, 1903-1938, 12 vols.), vii, pp. 238-245.

[13] Blackstone, Sir William, *Commentaries on the Laws of England* (Philadelphia, 1771-1773, 4 vols.), ii, pp. 120-129, 140-149. See also Noyes, C. R., *The Institution of Property* (New York and Toronto, 1936), pp. 286-287, 312.

[14] Seymour, *op.cit.*, i, p. 68.

became increasingly important over the centuries. It was almost inevitable that the monarchy should look to the trading and entrepreneurial classes of the towns and cities as the source for further refreshment of royal income and, as such, entitled to parliamentary representation. "When the nation became more polished," wrote Algernon Sydney, "to inhabit cities and towns, and to set up arts and trades, those who exercised them were thought to be as useful to the commonwealth, as the freeholders in the country, and to deserve the same privileges."[15]

The crown responded to this new situation by chartering boroughs, partly for purposes of parliamentary taxation, partly to provide for more effective, urban-oriented local government. Some boroughs were known as close boroughs because the officials filled vacancies in local government and selected the parliamentary representatives. Most boroughs, however, were open boroughs in which persons legally qualified could vote to elect officials at the levels of local and central government. Some permitted all persons admitted to the freedom of the borough (i.e., to engage in trade and otherwise enjoy the privileges of freemanship) to vote; others allowed all inhabitants who were not paupers to vote. In some boroughs all persons who had paid scot and lot—roughly the equivalent of a tax-paying qualification—could participate in elections and, in still others, those who held land or dwellings by what was known as burgage tenure were qualified.[16]

Sometimes overlooked by American historians of the suffrage

[15] Quoted in Fink, Zera S., *The Classical Republicans* (Evanston, 1945), p. 166.

[16] See Griffith, Ernest S., *History of American City Government* (New York, 1938); Thomas, J. H., *Town Government in the Sixteenth Century* (London, 1930); Notestein, Wallace S., *The English People on the Eve of Colonization: 1603-1630* (New York, 1954); Walcott, Robert Jr., *English Politics in the Early Eighteenth Century* (Cambridge, 1956), pp. 8-23; Plumb, J. H., *Sir Robert Walpole* (London, 1956), pp. 56-57; Henderson, A. J., *London and the National Government, 1721-1742* (Durham, 1942), pp. 1-16.

was another form of electoral institution at the level of local government—the vestry. Since Tudor times the vestry had been charged not only with ecclesiastical duties but also with the responsibility of assessing on the rate-payers the levies necessary to meet the bills for poor relief. Like some of the boroughs, some vestries filled vacancies by co-optation, as was the case in the so-called close or ordinary vestries. In the case of select vestries, all householders, male rate-payers, or inhabitants were qualified to fill vacancies by election, illustrating once more the implicit assumption that taxation and voting privileges should go hand in hand.[17]

Although as late as the beginning of the seventeenth century England's electoral institutions were by no means exceptional in Europe as a whole, it remains a fact of great importance in American history that the English people, as A. B. White has written, were very familiar with elections of one kind or another, although, as he points out elsewhere, a voice "in government was not a boon but a duty that some must do; and it had been the king's will that very many should do it."[18]

Because of the emphasis in English electoral history upon the county and borough franchises, other qualifications have sometimes been overlooked. For example, an act of 1432 required that electors be resident of the county in which they voted. Seventeenth-century legislation imposed oaths on Catholics which no sincere member of that faith could conscientiously take; denied the vote to every person, obviously male, who was not twenty-one years of age; and made assessment for taxes twelve months prior to an election a prerequisite for voting. Persons not the natural-born subjects of the king could be naturalized by parliamentary act and, if otherwise qualified, gain admission to the polls. Otherwise, they could be granted rights of denization which conferred

[17] Keith-Lucas, Bryan, *English Local Government Franchise* (Oxford, 1952), pp. 13-24.
[18] White, *op.cit.*, I, p. 129.

9

certain legal rights and business privileges enjoyed by all natural-born subjects.[19]

Because of rather than in spite of these legal restrictions upon voting privilege, British electoral institutions were applauded on the continent by those who, during the eighteenth century, were increasingly impatient with divine-right monarchy and feudal aristocracies. This was particularly true among French critics of the ancien régime who, viewing British institutions from the continent, found them good and worthy of imitation. Voltaire, for one, had an extravagant admiration for them. Equally famous, perhaps, was Montesquieu's Anglophilism. Although he discerned a separation of power between the various branches of the British government which historians have been unable to see, Montesquieu rightly considered England a prime example of mixed government and, as such, praiseworthy.

Furthermore, there was nothing in the major voting qualifications in England contrary to Montesquieu's own theories on the subject as revealed in *The Spirit of the Laws*. In this celebrated work, Montesquieu wrote that suffrage laws were among the fundamental laws of any government containing a non-feudal representation. All "inhabitants" (meaning, one surmises, adult male citizens) should be permitted to vote "except such as are in so mean a situation as to be deemed to have no will of their own."[20] When William Blackstone digressed from his chief work at hand, his *Commentaries on the Laws of England*, to discuss the suffrage laws of his country, he was already acquainted with Montesquieu's dictum and incorporated it in his work without benefit of a footnote citation of his authority, a practice more prevalent then than now. As a writer in the *Virginia Gazette* declared in another

[19] See Troward, Richard, *A Collection of Statutes Now in Force Relative to Elections Down to the Present Time* . . . (London, 1790). Also Blackstone, *op.cit.*, i, pp. 366-374.

[20] Montesquieu, Baron de, *The Spirit of the Laws* (New York, 1949, 2 vols. in one), i, p. 155.

connection, "the trifling charge of pillaging from eminent writers is scarce worthy of notice. . . ."[21]

The "true reason of requiring any qualification with regard to property in voters," wrote Blackstone, "is to exclude such persons as are in so mean a situation as to be esteemed to have no will of their own."[22] Blackstone did not say that to do so was just or right but that it was expedient. He argued that a large number of country folk were tenants who could easily be coerced to vote as they were told. The same was true of urban working people. Blackstone saw that the rise of a new kind of tenantry with short-term, capitalist-type leaseholds in rural areas was paralleled by the growth in cities and towns of a working-class population which was often dependent exclusively upon employers for its livelihood. These working people were as vulnerable, if not more so, to the blandishments and threats of their employers as were tenants to those of their landlords. He believed that the population would be composed increasingly of a large number of persons unfortunately dependent upon others. To enfranchise them would be to increase the power of wealth in elections and reduce the effectiveness and honesty of government officials just as, for example, before the creation of property tests for justices of the peace their poverty had made them "covetous and contemptible."[23] If, as James Harrington had suggested, a secret ballot were used to prevent an increase in the power of wealth in elections, the cure might prove worse than the disease. The poor of both town and country might combine to attack property rights and pull down the pillars of the established order. History, so Blackstone thought, proved that this was the lesson to be learned from the fall of the classical republics. Montesquieu also was averse to secrecy at the polls, averring that,

[21] *Virginia Gazette* (Pinkney) Nov. 17, 1774.
[22] Blackstone, *op.cit.*, I, p. 171.
[23] Williamson, C., "American Suffrage and Sir William Blackstone," *Political Science Quarterly* (LXVIII, Dec. 1953), pp. 552-557; Blackstone, *op.cit.*, I, p. 341.

next to deciding who should be allowed to vote, the manner of voting was the most important decision facing practical statesmen. Public voting, amounting in form to viva voce, was desirable, Montesquieu said, because the "lower class ought to be directed by those of higher rank, and restrained within bounds by the gravity of eminent personages."[24] The publication of the *Commentaries* in Britain, by 1769, and in America, in 1771, was a landmark not only in American legal history but also in the defense of existing property rights for voting. It was invoked almost as often in the American colonies as in Britain. On this side of the Atlantic it was cited for partisan purposes as late as the debates in the Louisiana Constitutional Convention of 1845.

Nevertheless, a freehold qualification for voting in colony elections was not the only one, despite half-hearted efforts by the British government to encourage its adoption everywhere.[25] Only New Hampshire, Rhode Island, New York, Virginia, North Carolina, Georgia, and probably New Jersey required that colony voters, when not residents of certain boroughs and cities subject to special legislation, be the owners of freeholds. The freehold qualification differed from colony to colony in its specific terms. For example, New Hampshire required that the freehold be worth 50 pounds, Rhode Island

[24] Montesquieu, *op.cit.*, I, p. 12.

[25] This analysis is drawn from the statutes available in the splendid collection of the Library of the Law School, Columbia University. Standard treatises (to be used with some caution) are: McKinley, Albert E., *The Suffrage Franchise in the Thirteen English Colonies in America* (Philadelphia, 1905); Bishop, Cortlandt F., *History of Elections in the American Colonies* (New York, 1893); Howard, George E., *An Introduction to the Local Constitutional History of the United States* (Baltimore, 1889). Outstanding special studies are Brown, Robert E., "Democracy in Colonial Massachusetts," *New England Quarterly* (xxv, September 1952), pp. 291-313, and his *Middle Class Democracy and the Revolution in Massachusetts, 1691-1780* (Ithaca, 1955); Sydnor, Charles S., *Gentlemen Freeholders* (Chapel Hill, 1952); McCormick, Richard P., *The History of Voting in New Jersey: a Study of the Development of Election Machinery, 1664-1911* (New Brunswick, 1953).

that it be worth 40 pounds or at least 40 shillings per year in rental value, and New York required that it be worth 40 pounds. Other colonies with only a freehold qualification couched theirs in terms of acres. Virginia required the ownership of 100 acres, unsettled, or 25 acres, improved; North Carolina and Georgia had a simple qualification of 50 acres. In the remaining colonies, one of the qualifications for voting was ownership of a freehold, couched in terms of acreage, as in the cases of South Carolina, Maryland, Delaware, and Pennsylvania with a 50-acre requirement; or in terms of income, as in Massachusetts and Connecticut. Massachusetts required ownership of a freehold worth 40 shillings in sterling. Connecticut's qualification was the same but not in sterling. New Jersey had so many different laws regulating the suffrage as to make it impossible to say more than that the only requirement common to them all was ownership of a freehold.

At least two colonies in America defined the freehold qualification, as did Britain, in such a way as to permit those who held leases for an indefinite number of years to vote, if otherwise qualified. In 1701 New York passed an act permitting all those who had an "estate freehold during his life or for the life of his wife" to vote.[26] Four years later Virginia passed an act stating that "every person who hath an estate real for his own life, or the life of another, or any estate of greater dignity, shall be accounted a freeholder. . . ."[27] Whether or not other colonies permitted similarly situated residents to vote has not been determined.

So far as the statutes can be relied upon to give an accurate picture, they show that in other colonies the only legal alternative to the freehold qualification was a property (real and/or personal) or a tax-paying qualification.

[26] *Laws of New York from the Year 1691, to 1773, Inclusive* (New York, 1774, 2 vols.), I, pp. 40-41.
[27] Hening, William W. (ed.), *The Statutes at Large . . . [of Virginia] . . .* (New York, etc., 1809-1823, 13 vols.), III, p. 240.

During the colonial period, personal property undoubtedly was deemed to consist of those items which Blackstone designated as "chattels personal," such as "animals, house-hold stuff, money, jewels, corn, garments, and everything else that can be properly put in motion, and transferred from place to place."[28]

One colony in which a non-freehold qualification was very significant was Massachusetts. It extended the vote to all persons, otherwise qualified, worth 40 pounds sterling or possibly 50 pounds sterling, the difference arising from a discrepancy between the charter itself and the copy despatched to Massachusetts. Connecticut established an alternative to the freehold qualification by extending the franchise to possessors of personal estates assessed for 40 pounds on the tax books. Yet this qualification was not a practical alternative to the freehold qualification because until almost the eve of the Revolution the only form of personal property assessed for taxes was cattle.[29] In Pennsylvania, the alternative in the counties was the possession of a 50-pound clear estate. Although the strict definition of estate was estate in land, possibly non-freeholders with 50 pounds property (if indeed they existed) could qualify by a loose interpretation of the meaning of the word. In the city of Philadelphia, the vote was open to freeholders, meaning all those who owned tenements, and to those who owned a 50-pound personal estate, if otherwise qualified. This latter requirement underscored the deliberate intention of the colony to extend the vote to non-freeholders and also prevented confusion over the meaning of the phrase "clear estate." Delaware offered the vote to possessors of 40 pounds clear estate, and Maryland to possessors of visible estates of 40 pounds sterling at the least. South Carolina was exceptional in permitting persons to vote, if otherwise qualified, if they had been resident in the colony for two years and had paid

[28] Blackstone, op.cit., II, pp. 384-386.
[29] Grant, Charles S., A History of Kent, 1738-1796 (unpub. Ph.D. thesis, Columbia University, New York, 1957), pp. 208-209, 209n.

a tax of 20 shillings during the year in which they wished to vote, or in the previous year. Also exceptional was the extension of the vote in Rhode Island to the eldest sons of free-holders, a practice followed by at least one English borough and the famous Company of Merchant Adventurers.

Colonial solons did not exercise as much care as they might have in establishing qualifications for voting other than the ownership of property. Only three colonies, Pennsylvania, Delaware, and South Carolina, confined the vote to males either specifically or by employing the pronoun "he." Only Pennsylvania, South Carolina, Virginia, Connecticut, New York, and North Carolina stated that the voter must be twenty-one years of age. Residence or inhabitance was not required in four of the colonies: Delaware, Massachusetts, New Hampshire, and Virginia. The remainder required that voters be inhabitants or residents with or without a specific time limit. Pennsylvania's two years' residence requirement was unusually strict. More typical was a requirement of six months' residence in the colony or in the county. Proof of naturalization was required, not surprisingly, in Pennsylvania, where so many persons of non-British stock settled in the eighteenth century.[30]

A number of specific restrictions are significant in the light of the subsequent history of American suffrage. Among these was the denial of the vote to free Negroes in the Carolinas, Georgia, and Virginia. There were legal discriminations against Catholics in some colonies even where there were no Catholics, or very few. These discriminations were largely a reflection of anti-Catholic feeling in England both before and after the Glorious Revolution. Indeed, it has been said that Catholics were disfranchised and ineligible to vote in all the colonies before the Revolution.[31] If this was so, it did not result from

[30] These generalizations rest upon tables prepared from the colonial laws.

[31] Ray, Sister Mary Augustina, *American Catholic Opinion of Roman Catholicism in the Eighteenth Century* (New York, 1936), pp. 255-256.

15

specific clauses in the suffrage laws of every colony. The most stringent treatment was that afforded Maryland Catholics and Catholics resident in New York, where they were disfranchised by statute in 1701 if they would not take a special oath. The tendering of oaths to Catholics who, in the words of the New Jersey statute of 1722, would "intermeddle" in the voting procedures, undoubtedly rendered them a nullity wherever they lived and whenever they might wish to play a role in the government, a rare occurrence save in Maryland.[32] There were legal discriminations also against the non-Christian element of the population of the colonies, with particular reference to the Jews. Rhode Island, Maryland, New York, and South Carolina denied the vote to Jews, in one way or another. The assembly of New York deprived them of the franchise in 1737, alleging, as a reason, that they were not permitted to vote in Britain.[33]

The qualifications for voting in colony elections were seldom if ever the same as those for voting in local elections in town, borough, city, or county. In New England, the qualifications for voting in town meetings and for local officials varied considerably from colony to colony. Massachusetts permitted all inhabitants rated in the tax books for an estate, both real and personal, of at least 20 pounds in the provincial currency, rather than in sterling, to vote in these elections. Those living in towns where lists of assessable property were not made could qualify after 1736 by paying a tax equal to two-thirds of the poll tax.[34] New Hampshire also opened the vote in towns to those rated at 20 pounds, provincial currency. Con-

[32] Nevill, Samuel, *The Acts of the General Assembly of the Province of New Jersey* (n.p., 1752, 2 vols.), I, p. 92.

[33] *Journals of the General Assembly of New York, 1691-1743*, I, p. 712. See also Goodman, Abram V., *American Overture: Jewish Rights in America* (Philadelphia, 1947); Marcus, Jacob R., *Early American Jewry: The Jews of Pennsylvania and the South: 1655-1790* (Philadelphia, 1953); Olbrich, Emile, *The Development of Sentiment on Negro Suffrage to 1860* (Madison, 1912).

[34] See the fine analysis in Brown, R. E., *Middle Class Democracy and the Revolution in Massachusetts, 1691-1780*, pp. 78-99.

necticut permitted all freemen—that is, persons qualified to vote in colony-wide elections—to vote in town affairs and in the election of town representatives to the legislature. In theory, it was possible for a person who was not a freeman to qualify for voting in town affairs and for voting for the town representative, if he owned a freehold with an annual income of 50 shillings or if he possessed 40 pounds of personal property assessed for taxes. Alone among the New England colonies, Rhode Island did not draw any distinction between town and colony elections, making admission to the freemanship in towns the prerequisite for freemanship in the colony.

In the middle colonies the establishment of towns, boroughs, and cities resulted, more often than not, in the creation of lower qualifications for voting in local elections than in provincial elections. Local elections in New York and Delaware, unless otherwise provided for by city or borough charter, were confined to the freeholders, and in Pennsylvania to the freemen, that is, to those entitled to vote in colony elections. In New Jersey, tenants and householders were given the local suffrage. In Perth Amboy and Burlington, householders had the privilege of voting in provincial elections, even if not freeholders. The cities of New York and Albany extended the suffrage not only to 40-pound freeholders but also to all persons who had been made freemen of the cities. In this way, non-freeholders received voting rights in municipal and colony elections as well as the right to engage in certain mercantile and other pursuits. In the so-called close, as distinct from open, boroughs in which the principle of co-optation was the basis for filling vacancies in borough personnel, the vote in colony elections was given variously to freeholders or tenants. In the case of some Pennsylvania boroughs, the vote was extended to householders and inhabitants.[35]

[35] See the relevant statutes governing local elections which have been published by the various states. See also the analysis of them in the works cited above, in footnote 25.

The southern colonies were equally liberal in creating a broad franchise in local elections and, where they were authorized, in assembly elections. In Annapolis, Maryland, not only could all freeholders qualify but also all who had served a five-year apprenticeship, had held their freedom for three months, and were householders or inhabitants. Virginia's requirements were about as liberal for the population of its towns, boroughs, and cities, particularly with regard to the election of members of the House of Burgesses. Williamsburg and Norfolk, for example, had franchise qualifications similar to those of Annapolis. Furthermore, Virginia created a large number of towns in the eighteenth century which, although undemocratically controlled by the practice of co-optation, did permit all town freeholders to vote in county elections for the members of the House of Burgesses.[36] Perhaps the most remarkable of all voting qualifications were those of a number of boroughs created in North Carolina before the Revolution. In one of these, the borough of Campbelltown, all could vote who were within two miles of the borough on election day.[37]

Because of the relative absence of towns in the southern colonies, county and parish units of government were of greater significance there than elsewhere. Although county officials were appointive in all the southern colonies where they existed at all, elections at the level of local government were not totally absent. In Maryland, North Carolina, Georgia, and particularly South Carolina, vestrymen entrusted with many secular responsibilities were elected by the freeholders who, more often than not, had to be tax payers. Only in South Carolina did the law confine voting for vestrymen to members of the Church of England, if they were otherwise qualified.[38]

[36] Brown, R. E., *Charles Beard and the Constitution* (Princeton, 1957), pp. 65, 71.

[37] Smith, Mary P., "Borough Representation in North Carolina," *North Carolina Historical Review* (vii, April 1930), pp. 177-191; Griffith, *op.cit.*, p. 207.

[38] Bishop, *op.cit.*, pp. 214, 215; Howard, *op.cit.*, pp. 125-126, 128;

It is obvious from this description of colonial suffrage legislation that it was designed to confine the vote to desirable elements of the population. It was drafted in the conviction that efficiency, honesty, and harmony in government rested, in the last analysis, upon a salutary degree of homogeneity of interests, opinions, and fundamental loyalties—religious, ethnic, and class. Confining the vote in colony elections to those who were free, white, twenty-one, native-born Protestant males who were the owners of property, especially real property, appeared to be the best guarantee of the stability of the commonwealth. The drafters of colonial suffrage legislation, to whatever extent they attempted to formulate ideas, seem to have thought that undue disparities of interest, opinion, and loyalty among electors would weaken and distract government. It is in the light of their principles, rather than those of the present times, that the suffrage laws of colonial times can be understood.

History made plain, or so it was thought, how calamitous were the results of government unmixed, unbalanced, and democratic. John Adams only reflected these principles when he defined tyranny as the result of giving all power to the people and concentrating that power in a single chambered legislature. It was not a purely fortuitous circumstance that, when the crisis between Britain and colonials rose to its climax, the Continental Congress should appeal to the mother country in the language of the freeholder: "Why should not the freeholders of America," demanded the Congress, "enjoy the same rights enjoyed by the freeholders of Great Britain?"[39]

McKinley, *op.cit.*, pp. 159-162; Saye A. B., *A Constitutional History of Georgia* (Athens, 1948), p. 66; Ingle, Edward, *Parish Institutions of Maryland* (Baltimore, 1883), pp. 6-7.

[39] Quoted in Namier, Lewis B., *op.cit.*, I, p. 22.

CHAPTER 2

THE COLONIAL ELECTORATE

THE eighteenth century in Great Britain saw a notable rise of enthusiasm not only for the arts of husbandry and pastoralism but also for the freehold, family-sized farm. Paradoxically, however, this enthusiasm for the rural life was confined almost exclusively to kings, princes, lords, statesmen, scientists, philosophers, and poets. As one historian has said, "Some of the most famous expressions of this philosophy came from great lords who probably never touched a plow, spade, or pruning hook."[1]

Another and more fundamental paradox, one which has a bearing upon the bifurcation of political as well as economic developments in America and Britain, was the fact that the cult of the freeholder was most strong at the time when his future was by no means bright if he were, at the same time, a relatively self-sufficient, small-scale farmer, or, as he was called, a yeoman. The enclosure movements of the sixteenth century, designed to increase the wool clip, had been followed by the enclosure movement of the eighteenth century, designed to increase the efficiency and productivity of English agriculture by placing it on a scientific and thoroughly capitalist basis at a time when the decline of the death rate and greater urbanization made necessary a greater supply of food. Large-scale agriculture, whether under freehold or leasehold, increasingly characterized English rural life.[2]

[1] Johnstone, P. H., "Turnips and Romanticism," *Agricultural History* (XII, July 1938), pp. 224-255.

[2] For a balanced treatment, see Clapham, Sir James H., *An Economic History of Modern Britain* (2nd ed., Cambridge, 1950-1952, 3 vols.), I, pp. 100-111. For the older view, see Taylor, Henry C., *The Decline of the Landowning Farmers in England* (Madison, 1904) and Johnson, A. H., *The Disappearance of the Small Landowner* (Oxford, 1909).

Regardless of the causes—and historians differ greatly as to what they were—it would seem to be a fact that the free-holding element of the population was declining during the eighteenth century, although not so cataclysmically as has often been thought. Forces which had their major beginnings in the Age of the Tudors were coming to their logical conclusions. Historians dispute, however, whether or not there had been an increase in the gentry, that is, large-scale land-owners who worked or leased their lands, in the two previous centuries and they disagree as well as to the extent of the decline of the freeholding and non-freeholding yeomanry. According to one authority, R. H. Tawney, 20 percent of the rural population were freeholders in the sixteenth century. A pilot study of the small landowner, undertaken about thirty years ago and based on land-tax assessments, shows that by 1790 about 90 percent of the land was occupied by tenants-at-will or by tenants on short lease. Modern capitalist types of leases for a definite number of years had replaced the medieval type of lease for a life or lives.[3] As a result, fewer yeomen or others who rented land could qualify as freeholders. Henceforth, leases for an indefinite number of years were less characteristic of England than of Ireland, where, after the enfranchisement of the Irish Catholics in 1793, 40 shilling freeholds of this description were created in order to increase the power of English Protestant landlords in the Irish Parliament and, later, in the British Parliament after the Act of Union in 1800.[4]

The situation in the boroughs was almost equally restrictive by the beginning of the eighteenth century. Although 25 percent of the English boroughs had qualifications sufficiently

[3] Tawney, R. H., *The Agrarian Problem in the Sixteenth Century* (London, New York, 1912); Davies, E., "The Small Landowners 1780-1832, in the Light of the Land Tax Assessments," *The Economic History Review* (I, 1927), pp. 87-113.

[4] Pomfret, John E., *The Struggle for Land in Ireland, 1800-1923* (Princeton, 1930), p. 11.

liberal to meet the requirements of the first Reform Bill, the size of the electorate was surprisingly small. The reason for the small electorate was that the population of only a portion of the territory of a borough was given parliamentary representation. It has been estimated that, as a result, 40 percent of the English boroughs had less than 100 voters, 62 percent less than 500, and only one-eighth had 1,000 or more. Only three boroughs had an electorate of more than 4,000.[5]

If these figures are representative of England as a whole, it is quite clear that the freehold and borough qualifications left unenfranchised a numerous and possibly increasing proportion of the population. This situation, together with the underrepresentation of the new manufacturing areas, was a major cause of the modern movement for reform of suffrage and representation. Benjamin Disraeli's conception of a Venetian oligarchy in Britain during the eighteenth century had indeed a basis in fact.

Whether or not an identical or similar situation existed in the British North American colonies has been questioned not only by eighteenth-century commentators but also by historians, John Franklin Jameson of an earlier day and Charles S. Sydnor, Richard P. McCormick, Robert E. Brown, and Jack R. Pole of our own times.[6] If the conclusions of McCormick's study of the pre-Revolutionary situation in New Jersey, Sydnor's of Virginia, and Brown's of Massachusetts are applicable to all the colonies, it would seem that the diffusion of real and personal property was so great as to render the property tests for voting much less restrictive than they appear to be.

The proof of this contention would be almost beyond the resources, financial and otherwise, of one individual to determine in a wholly satisfactory way. In the first place, it would be necessary to assemble tax books for all the colonies for a distinct period so as to secure a representative cross section

[5] Walcott, *English Politics in the Early Eighteenth Century*, pp. 19-23.
[6] See Chapter 1, *supra*, footnote 25.

of urban and rural areas. Secondly, it would be necessary to exclude all those who, although listed as owners of real property, were not otherwise qualified to vote. This would require the exclusion of minors under guardianship and of free male polls, 16 to 21 years of age, widows, and most free Negroes. Almost impossible to determine would be the number of unnaturalized residents, particularly important in a colony like Pennsylvania. More significant would be the determination of the percentage of absentee landowners in boroughs, towns, cities, counties, and parishes. Because tax lists are not self-explanatory and must be interpreted, their study involves the possibility of error. They are, unfortunately, often the basis for more than one set of inferences. A correction would have to be made also for those who were permitted to vote, if otherwise qualified, because they held types of leaseholds to which the suffrage had been conceded. Lastly, it would be necessary to establish the size of the freeman, housekeeper, inhabitant, or freeholder electorates in towns, boroughs, and cities and to draw the distinction between the franchise in local elections and in colony elections, where such a distinction was made by statutory enactment. Only by such a procedure would it be possible to determine the extent to which adult white male residents could meet the property and other tests for voting in all kinds of elections.

Obviously, the procedure outlined above is a counsel of perfection for any but a large staff of researchers. Nevertheless, the more modest objective of collating a considerable part of the material now in the archives of the various seaboard states from New Hampshire on the north to Georgia on the south (with the exception of Delaware, whose geographical position made it not unlike Pennsylvania) might enable us to make an informed guess as to the size of the electorate in relation to the total adult male population. The reader should bear in mind that there is a certain danger in doing so, like that involved in the sampling work of R. H. Tawney and H.

R. Trevor-Roper[7] by which each came to quite different conclusions as to the status of the gentry in England during the seventeenth century. What is crucial for the success of such a technique is to know whether or not the material is genuinely representative. The British historian George Elton has summed up the Tawney-Roper controversy judiciously by saying that both are correct in the light of the material each used. A final disposal of the British controversy awaits a thorough analysis of all counties, an analysis which, it is perhaps safe to say, will never be completed.[8]

In American history, similarly, there is a difference of opinion between Robert E. Brown and Robert J. Taylor as to the size of the legal electorate in Massachusetts about the time of the Revolution. Taylor's figures for towns in the extreme western part of Massachusetts are far lower than any figures cited by Brown for any town whose pre-Revolutionary figures he has examined, and lower than one would anticipate from the slight upward revision of the Massachusetts property tests by the constitution of 1780.[9]

With these reservations in mind, one can proceed forewarned and forearmed to determine by the evidence available the likely proportion of the adult male population which were freeholders in the colonies at a time when the freeholders, either in law or by the nature of things, were the most important element in the electorate. We can accept as relatively correct the view that about 20 percent of the population at that time consisted of adult males, probably a conservative estimate for newer communities on the frontier or in western parts of the colonies.[10] Where an adult male landowner was neither

[7] See Tawney, *op.cit.*, and Trevor-Roper, H. R., *The Gentry: 1540-1650* (Cambridge, 1953).

[8] See Elton, George, *England under the Tudors* (New York, 1955), pp. 255-259.

[9] See Taylor, Robert J., *Western Massachusetts in the Revolution* (Providence, 1954), the Appendix; Brown, R. E., "Democracy in Colonial Massachusetts," *op.cit.*

[10] See Brown, R. E., "Democracy in Colonial Massachusetts," *op.cit.*;

polled nor listed for the kind of property which would indicate residence, he has been considered by this author to be a non-resident. For this reason, the percentages of adult male resident freeholders which are cited below may, in some cases, err on the conservative side.

The most easterly of all the colonies, and a colony with a freehold qualification exclusively, was New Hampshire. New Hampshire tax lists, called inventories, are available in microfilm in the State Library, covering the period from 1727 to 1812, the greater number originating in the late eighteenth century. The tax lists for 28 towns in various sections of the colony show that freeholding among adult males (excluding minors under guardianship, and minors 18 to 21 years of age) varied from 90 percent in Hollis in 1761 to 50 percent in Hopkinton in 1791 and in Bath in 1793. In Portsmouth, out of 495 males resident in 1732 no less than 307 owned their houses.[11] How many of these persons were worth 50 pounds cannot be determined because taxation of real property in colonial New Hampshire was based, not upon value, but upon income from various categories of land and tenements determined by legislative fiat.

With regard to Rhode Island, it has proved difficult to determine the proportion of adult males who were resident freeholders as well as the number of persons who voted as the eldest sons of freeholders. The tax lists examined by this author do not draw a distinction between taxes or assessments upon real and personal property, making it difficult to determine precisely the number of adult male residents who were freeholders in either Providence or any other town. Some clue,

---

American Statistical Association, *Collections* (Boston, 1897), I, pp. 121-216; Greene, E. B., and Harrington, V. D., *American Population Before the Federal Census of 1790* (New York, 1932). See "Note on Methods of Calculation," following p. xxii.

[11] The tax lists for the 28 towns are available on microfilm, New Hampshire State Library, Concord, New Hampshire, and were consulted there.

however, is provided by the tax lists for 1760 and the number of voters in 1763 in the town of Little Compton.[12] The tax list of 1760 for Little Compton lists 179 adult male residents, excluding the 111 listed only for real property and, as such, assumed to be absentee owners, and 91 ratable polls, males 16 years of age and over who were not listed for any property, real or personal. Three years later, 120 votes were cast in the colony elections. If all were legal votes—and there is good reason to suppose that not all were, as will be shown subsequently—about 66 percent of the adult male taxables were voting in that year. If we assume, perhaps correctly in this particular case, that the 111 freeholders not listed for personal property were residents of Little Compton, the percentage of freeholders among all males on the tax list rises to 75.

Similarly, of the 181 adult males who resided in West Greenwich in 1762, 81 percent or 160 voted in the election the following year. Possibly, this figure does not represent the percentage of freeholders among adult males. Eldest sons of freeholders were voting, as well as a number of persons totally unqualified to vote. In Providence as late as 1790, 50 percent of the adult males were qualified freemen, although 70 percent had so qualified earlier in the century.[13] In the colony election of 1762, 4,000 persons voted at a time when there were 8,285 ratable polls, 16 years of age or over. If 25 percent of those polled were 16 to 21 years of age, possibly the adult males totalled 6,213 in the colony. If so, 62 percent of adult males voted in 1762. Probably one can take at face value Cadwal-

---

[12] The Little Compton and West Greenwich tax lists are available in the Archive Room, State Capitol, Providence, R.I. See also the collection of legislative records known as *Deputies and Freemen*. Without disclosing his methods for determining the percentage of resident freeholders, David S. Lovejoy, in his *Rhode Island Politics and the American Revolution, 1760-1776* (Providence, 1958), pp. 16-18, states that 75 to 84 percent of adult males could qualify for the freemanship in 5 towns in 1757.

[13] Stokes, Howard K., *The Finances and Administration of Providence* (Baltimore, 1903), pp. 134-137; N.Y.P.L., *Bancroft Transcripts*, Colden Papers, II, pp. 132-133.

lader Colden's report that, according to a member of the Governor's Council of Rhode Island, all freemen could vote, rich or poor.

Fortunately, figures for Connecticut are more satisfactory than for Rhode Island because the sampling, although restricted, is really more representative of various parts of the colony. In East Guilford, situated on Long Island Sound east of New Haven and now the town of Madison, the extraordinarily large number of 102 adult males out of a total of 110 were freeholders in 1740. Of these, 79 percent could meet the 40-shilling freehold qualification and thus were eligible for admission to freemanship. In 1751 in Kent, in the extreme western part of the colony, 79 percent could qualify, although the percentage of men who took the trouble to become freemen was only 51. In East Haddam it would appear that, in 1742, 64 percent of adult male residents were freemen.[14]

Despite the undemocratic features of New York political life, particularly the great power of its landed aristocracy, the size of the electorate there does not seem to have been very different from that of its eastern neighbors. It has been estimated that assembly electors, that is, freeholders, were a little more than one-half of the adult males about 1771.[15] Sampling for the period of the Revolution shows figures even higher. A study of eleven tax districts and townships, widely scattered throughout the state, shows that among adult male residents, and in some cases among all male taxables, 50 to 80 percent were freeholders in 1779—a figure larger than the estimate for the state as a whole in 1771.[16]

One of the reasons for a larger electorate in New York than

[14] The East Guilford tax lists are in the New York Historical Society. For Kent, see Grant, *op.cit.*, pp. 204-241. For East Haddam, see *East Haddam Town Records* in the Connecticut Historical Society, Hartford.

[15] See Mark, Irving, *Agrarian Conflicts in Colonial New York, 1711-1775* (New York, 1940), pp. 95, 96, 96n.

[16] The tax lists are on deposit in the Manuscript Division of the New York State Library, Albany.

one might otherwise expect was the fact that there were more leaseholds which qualified as freeholds there than existed anywhere else, except perhaps in Virginia. The weight of historical opinion is distinctly favorable to the belief that, with the exception of the special situation in Westchester County, the overwhelming majority of leaseholds would qualify as freeholds. This was true of the lands leased by James Duane, Lieutenant-Governor George Clark, and the Phillips family. On the Beekman Patent, 111 leases for land have survived for the period 1742 to 1796. For these leases, a printed form was used. All were for terms of lives, and one was inscribed in ink with the phrase, "hold forever." On Philip Schuyler's Saratoga holdings, at least 201 adult males resided who were tenants right after the Revolution. Of these, 141 would be deemed freeholders, the remainder being holders of leases running from 2 to 21 years. On the Manor of Rensselaer, virtually all leases would qualify as freeholds. Of 326 males on one list for 1779, only 37 were not assessed for taxes on land. Among the leaseholders, totalling 289, only 48 were not assessed, that is, not valued, at 40 pounds. It is of some interest to note how large a proportion of male taxables on this manor, although tenant farmers, could have qualified as yeomen in the English sense of the word.[17]

Tenants at will, of course, were not deemed freeholders. They probably comprised the poorer element among the rural population. An act of 1724 described tenants of this description as "generally very poor Indigent and mean persons who are supplied with stock and all necessarys by lessors. . . ."[18] There were more tenants of this description in Westchester County than elsewhere, and many among the lessees of Peter Warren and the residents of Cosby's Manor in Herkimer County.

---

[17] New York Public Library, *Schuyler Land Papers*, Box xx, Beekman Patent Account Book, 1769-1805; Saratoga Rolls. New York State Library, *Tax Lists for Northwest Quarter of the Manor of Rensselaer, 1779.*

[18] *The Colonial Laws of New York* (Albany, 1894), II, pp. 206-207.

The large number of tenants at will, and for years, on the Manors of Cortlandt and Phillipsburg placed a heavy burden of jury duty upon freeholders. To ease it, John De Lancey tried to secure from the assembly in November of 1769 a bill to confer jury rights upon 60-pound holders of estates of less than freehold. Sensing that the creation of more jurors would mean the creation of more voters as well, persons not in the "De Lancey interest" blocked the passage of the bill.[19]

The colony directly to the south of New York, New Jersey, presents difficulties all its own. The suffrage laws of this colony were so numerous and often so conflicting that about all that can be said is that freeholders of any description were at least permitted to vote.[20] The election writs appear to confirm this, inasmuch as they merely mention the freeholders as the electors.[21] If all freeholders were indeed allowed to vote, it would be very interesting to have a really representative sampling of New Jersey freeholding. Fortunately, such a sampling is possible. Township tax lists, 12 in number, from 6 counties drawn from the northern, southern, eastern, and western parts of the colony for the years 1773-1778, show that among adult male residents 50 to 75 percent could meet a bare freehold qualification. This range may not be far from the mark, for voting statistics show that about this proportion of adult males was voting.[22]

For Virginia we have figures which are not out of line with the overall estimates for New York, or for most of the other colonies. According to a pioneer study of this subject, anywhere from one-third to one-half of the adult white males in

[19] *Journal of the General Assembly of the Province of New York, Nov. 21, 1769, to Jan. 27, 1770*, pp. 5, 6, 80-81.

[20] See McCormick, *op.cit.*, pp. 61-62.

[21] Election writs may be examined in the New Jersey Archives, the State Library, Trenton.

[22] These tax lists were examined in microfilm at the New Jersey State Library. Original tax lists may be examined also in the Monmouth County Historical Society, Freehold, and in the New Jersey Historical Society, Newark.

Virginia could vote before the Revolution, probably a conservative figure. The percentage of voters was actually even higher because this study did not include qualified leaseholders. Virginia landlords during the eighteenth century leased lands for life or for lives. In the Northern Neck, for example, about one-fourth of adult males were tenants. Tenantry was particularly characteristic of Loudon County, where, in 1782, one-third of the male residents were tenants for life or lives. In towns, freeholders, as well as tenants for life or lives, were permitted to vote for assemblymen. In Harrisonburg, 50 percent of all male taxables could vote under this qualification in 1798.[23] The importance of the freehold qualification in practice may be exaggerated, however. The *Richmond Enquirer* stated on December 4, 1824, that it was understood that non-freeholders "generally" had the vote before the Revolution.

Freeholding in North Carolina appears to have been more widespread than in Virginia. For example, in Caswell County in 1777 there were 846 adult white resident males. Of these, 281 were landless and about 62 percent, if the figures are correct, were 50-acre freeholders. In Randolph County in 1779, 81 percent were 50-acre freeholders. In 1784 in Johnston County, of 656 adult males only 116 were non-landowners, meaning that 83 percent were landowners, all of whom were qualified to vote under the 50-acre requirement. The tax records for parts of Pitt and Richmond counties about the same period indicate that the percentage of freeholders eligible to

[23] See Sydnor, *op.cit.*, pp. 32, 141-143. Independent examination of tax lists for the Revolutionary period, made possible by microfilming, suggest that these figures are conservative. On tenantry and leases for life or lives, see Main, J. T., "The Distribution of Property in Post-Revolutionary Virginia," *Mississippi Valley Historical Review* (XLI, Sept. 1954) and his "Sections and Politics in Virginia 1781-1787," *William and Mary Quarterly* (XII, Jan. 1955); Gray, L. C., *History of Agriculture in the Southern United States to 1860* (Washington, D.C., 1933-41, 2 vols.), I, p. 406; *Fauquier County, Deed Book*, no. 9, 1785-1787 (microfilm, Virginia State Library); Wayland, John W., *Historic Harrisonburg* (Staunton, 1949), p. 21.

vote was approximately the same. In a part of Pasquotank County, situated along the seaboard, only 52 freeholders can be identified among the 116 free white males. A study of landowning among taxable adult white males over 16, living in 10 counties about 1780, shows that the percentage of freeholding varied from 50 to 86 percent.[24]

The last colony with an exclusively freehold qualification was Georgia. A latecomer to the ranks of the royal colonies (1755), Georgia was still very much a frontier at the time of the Revolution, with the exception of the immediate region around Savannah. Tax lists for the pre-Revolutionary period are extremely scarce. One for the coastal county of Camden for 1794 shows that its freeholders comprised 51 percent of all male taxables. In Wilkes County, settled right after the Revolution, it would appear that in 1785 only 210 adult males out of 1813, or 10 percent, did not own at least 50 acres, meaning that about 78 percent were freeholders. In Montgomery County, there were 181 adult male landowners in 1797 and 67 non-landowners, indicating that about 73 percent owned land.[25] These figures are not surprising in the light of the favorable land policy in Georgia both before and after the Revolution. Between 1755 and 1758, 574 persons secured land grants, all for more than 50 acres. One Georgian said in 1757 that the people claimed as a right at least 50 acres of land for every person in a family, whether white or black. Governor Wright of Georgia was fully aware of the diffusion of land among the people and stated that, as a result, "by far the great number of voters, are the most Inferior Sort of People."[26]

[24] All the tax lists are available in the Department of Archives and History, Raleigh, North Carolina. See also Morris, F. G. and P. M., "Economic Conditions in North Carolina about 1780," *North Carolina Historical Review* (xvi, April 1939), pp. 107-133.

[25] Blair, Ruth, *Some Early Tax Digests of Georgia* (n.p., 1926), pp. 4-7; Davidson, Grace G., *Early Records of Georgia* (Macon, 1932, 2 vols.), ii, pp. 13-69; Georgia Archives, Atlanta, *Manuscript Tax Digest for Montgomery County,* 1797.

[26] Georgia Archives, *Manuscript Records*, xxviii, pp. 16, 682-683.

There are numerous difficulties in determining the size of the electorate in colonies with other than a freehold qualification for voting. In one of these colonies, Connecticut, the personal property qualification was almost meaningless in view of the fact that it was determined according to the amount of personal property assessed for taxes. As we have seen, personal property except livestock was not assessed for taxes until 1771. Therefore, this qualification was not applied until a few years before the Revolution.[27]

In the colonies where the personal property qualification was more effective, it has proved virtually impossible to determine with any degree of exactitude how this qualification was met. Only in Massachusetts can we be certain that the qualification for colony elections referred to 40 pounds of property (in sterling) at current values and without reference to tax books.[28] Regarding Pennsylvania, one cannot be so certain. In disputed elections, the tax books of real and personal property were used as an aid in determining the qualification, or the lack of it, of persons whose votes were challenged. Probably, in the counties, a freehold qualification was the usual basis for voting. The great exception in Pennsylvania was the city of Philadelphia, where, it is clear, the personal property qualification was the one under which most persons were voting. It is clear also that, if the tax books had been used to determine the 50-pound personal property qualification, a very much smaller electorate would have resulted. The use of tax books as the basis for determining the voting qualifications would have been severely limiting, because the assessment of both real and personal property was only a fraction of its real value and because colonial legislation, although subject to change without notice, more often than not failed to levy taxes on

[27] See *supra*, p. 14.
[28] Brown, R. E., *Middle Class Democracy and the Revolution in Massachusetts*, pp. 21-37.

those forms of personal property which even the poorest possessed: clothing, household utensils, and the like.

The property qualification of the colony of Massachusetts is of unusual interest because it is clear that this qualification bore no relationship to the tax books. Indeed, Lieutenant-Governor Hutchinson complained that all species of personal property qualified, with the result that "anything with the appearance of a man" was allowed to vote.[29] Under the Massachusetts system, anywhere from 50 percent to virtually the entire complement of adult male residents could vote, as they did in Stockbridge.[30] If Massachusetts had required a freehold qualification exclusively, the size of the electorate would have been narrowed considerably in many towns, although not necessarily in all. For example, in the town of Reading there were 271 male resident adults in 1755, of whom only 61 were not freeholders, indicating that 78 percent were. A similar situation existed in Topsfield in 1723, where 76 percent of the adult males were freeholders.[31]

In Pennsylvania, there was so much confusion as to exactly who could vote that, as in the case of New Jersey, one can say only that, with the exception of the city of Philadelphia, freeholders if otherwise qualified comprised the core of the electorate. For example, a poll of 1756 for the township of Kennett listed 97 persons. All were freeholders.[32]

In Philadelphia in 1774, 3,124 adult taxable males were on the list for the provincial tax. Of these, 1,701 were not taxed for land or for personal property. If the tax books were used to establish the property test for that year, only 46 percent

---

[29] New York Public Library, *Bancroft Transcripts*, Hutchinson Correspondence, ɪɪ, p. 87.

[30] Brown, R. E., "Democracy in Colonial Massachusetts," *op.cit.*, pp. 292-295.

[31] The New York Historical Society, *A True Copy of the Lists & Valuation of the Estates of the Inhabitants of Reading, 1755*; Essex Institute, *Collections* (xxx, 1897), Topsfield Bill of Estate, pp. 194-195.

[32] Historical Society of Pennsylvania, *Miscellaneous Manuscripts*, Chester County, 1684-1847, p. 33.

would have qualified. If tax lists were not used and the situation was analogous to that in Massachusetts, where all property, taxable or not, was used in determining the personal property qualification, the Philadelphia electorate would have been about 75 percent of all taxable males, if not slightly more. Actually in 1766, 50 percent of all taxables did vote, a sizable proportion indeed for actual voters as distinct from legal electors.[33]

In the counties of Pennsylvania, the size of the freehold electorate was not out of line with that of the other colonies. For example, before the Revolution 56 percent of resident and presumably adult males on the tax books were freeholders in Chester County and 60 percent in Lancaster County, exclusive of Lancaster Borough. In Bedford County in the extreme western part of the colony, 69 percent were freeholders, only 5 percent of whom were not assessed for 50 acres. In 29 townships in Berks County, 65 percent were freeholders, 79 percent of whom were listed for at least 50 acres. In 1769 in Philadelphia County, 48 percent were freeholders, 78 percent of whom were assessed for 50 acres.[34] It is highly probable that in practice the county electorate comprised the freeholders only. Quaker control, for example, was defended on the grounds that it "ever was and still is Agreeable to the General Mind of the Freeholders in the Country, who are and allways must be the legal Body of Electors."[35]

[33] *Pennsylvania Archives*, Third Series, xiv, pp. 221-303; *Votes of the Assembly*, v, p. 120; Thayer, T. G., *Pennsylvania Politics and the Growth of Democracy: 1740-1776* (Harrisburg, 1953), p. 102.

[34] For Chester County see *Pennsylvania Archives*, Third Series, xi, pp. 3-133; for Lancaster County, *ibid.*, xvii, pp. 3-165; for Bedford County, *ibid.*, xxii, pp. 159-201; for Berks and Philadelphia Counties, see Department of Public Records, Harrisburg, Pa. Most Pennsylvania tax lists are unique. They almost always include all persons owning taxable property as well as special categories designated variously as single men or inmates or freemen. They seem to refer to young adult males or to the superannuated, who were not owners of taxable property or were exempted from paying taxes.

[35] Historical Society of Pennsylvania, *Pemberton Papers*, iv, Richard Partridge to the Lords Committee of Trade, March 15, 1745.

In Maryland, where there was a 40-pound sterling property qualification in addition to the 50-acre freehold qualification, no precise information about the size of the electorate has come to light for the colonial period. A few tax lists available in the Maryland Historical Society throw some light on the subject. In 1782 there were in Ann Arundel County about 1583 male white adult residents taxed for property, of whom about 46 percent were landowners. A tax list for Upper Langford's Bay Hundred in Kent County for 1783 shows 45 landowners among 127 white male residents, or 36 percent. Lower Langford's Bay Hundred, in the same county, had about 55 percent landowners, of whom only 3 did not own 50 acres. In Chester and Western Hundreds, Kent County, 50 percent were landowners. In Longamore and Sugar Loaf Hundreds, situated in Montgomery County, 237 of 411 males on the list were landowners. These fragments are not much out of line, interestingly enough, with the figures for Pennsylvania or Virginia.[36]

South Carolina is of particular interest because the law admitted to the vote 20-shilling taxpayers, if of two years' residence, as well as the 50-acre freeholders. If the freehold qualification exclusively determined the electorate, and one contemporary account tells us that the assembly was elected by the freeholders of the parishes, a conservative estimate would be that a comfortable majority could vote. A Christ Church Parish tax list for 1784 shows that 82 percent of adult white male residents were owners of 50 acres. Similar tax lists for St. Bartholomew's Parish for 1783 and St. Paul's Parish for 1787, although incomplete, show an equally high proportion of landowners assessed for taxes.[37] In the 1768 election for the assembly of St. Philip and St. Michael parishes, approximately 66 percent of adult white males were voting.[38] There is much

[36] These tax lists are in the Maryland Historical Society, Baltimore.

[37] These lists are in the possession of the South Carolina Archives Department, Columbia, S.C.

[38] South Carolina Gazette, Oct. 10, 1768. The figures reported are correlated with population figures for 1768 in Sellers, Leila, Charleston Business on the Eve of the Revolution (Chapel Hill, 1934), p. 16.

evidence to show how easy it was to acquire a freehold in South Carolina. "Everyone," writes a chronicler, "upon his arrival obtained his grant of land and sat down upon his freehold. . . ."[39] If this is true, the taxpaying qualification was not the important factor in creating a broadly based electorate.

Material which would enable the historian to determine the size of the legal electorate in boroughs, towns, and cities is extremely hard to discover. In Massachusetts, the town meeting qualification of a 20-pound ratable estate was, except in periods of maximum depreciation of the provincial currency, higher than that for the provincial elections. For example, in Northampton in 1748, 85 percent were town voters, whereas 94.6 percent were colony voters.[40]

In Connecticut, where a 50-shilling freehold would qualify a person who was not a freeman to vote in town elections, 75 percent would have qualified to vote in town affairs in East Guilford in 1740, whereas 79 percent would have qualified to vote in colony elections.[41]

In New Hampshire the 20-pound ratable estate qualification, judging by contemporary accounts, does not seem to have been conscientiously enforced. Considering that 75 percent of adult males were householders in Portsmouth, it is difficult to believe that this qualification was very restrictive in the more prosperous towns. Yet an act of 1770 moved to liberalize the town suffrage by requiring that a person be rated for a 30-shilling estate, including the poll. Even this act was criticized as being unduly restrictive in the poorer towns. The sum, it was said, was "found too high and Excludes many Persons from the priviledge of Voting in Town and Parish affairs."[42]

[39] Carroll, B. R. (ed.), *Historical Collections of South Carolina . . .* (New York, 1836, 2 vols.), I, p. 381.

[40] I am indebted to Robert E. Brown for permission to read in manuscript a thorough treatment of this subject.

[41] New York Historical Society, *Tax Lists, East Guilford,* 1740.

[42] New Hampshire Historical Society, *Province Papers, XXI, 1770-1772,* p. 107.

The reduction in 1773 of the qualification to 18 shillings, ratable estate, including the poll, meant that henceforth all men who had paid a tax on their poll rated at 12 shillings and who were also rated at 6 shillings, at least, for their real or personal property could vote. A man with a couple of four-year-old cows or horses would have been able to vote under this qualification.

Elsewhere, the qualification for voting in local elections, with the exception of vestry elections in South Carolina and in Maryland, put the local franchise on as broad, if not a broader, basis than that for colony elections. Moreover, in boroughs and cities, those qualified to vote in local elections were allowed to vote in colony elections as well. With the vote in such elections given variously to all persons within two miles of the polling place on election day, to all inhabitant housekeepers, or freeholders, or freemen of borough or city corporations, it is highly probable that a higher proportion of adult males qualified in local elections than could qualify in colony elections outside New England. Samplings of participation of adult males in local elections west of Connecticut show that it was quite high. In Philadelphia City in 1764, 50 percent of taxables were voting. In New York City in 1767, slightly more than 50 percent turned out at the polls for provincial elections. In Annapolis in 1782, no less than 44 percent of adult white males on tax lists were lot owners and, as such, were voters. With a qualification broad enough to include ex-apprentices, the Annapolis electorate must have comprised a large proportion of the adult white males.[43]

The extent of popular participation in town elections aroused opposition. James Logan, the well-known Pennsylvanian, wrote to John Penn in 1728, "Populous towns with much Liberty and no sufficient Force to restrain disorder

[43] Pennsylvania, *Votes of the Assembly*, v, p. 120; Edwards, G. W., *New York an Eighteenth Century Municipality* (New York, 1917); Maryland Historical Society, *Tax Lists, Ann Arundel County 1782.*

stand in very precarious terms as to their Safety and Tranquillity." Campbelltown, North Carolina, quite willingly surrendered its extraordinary charter in 1772 because, under its terms, persons without property or permanent residence were voting. A new charter was adopted, enfranchising the freeholders of the borough. A major criticism, from a democratic viewpoint, was directed against the failure of many boroughs and cities to make all important offices elective or even to create a corporation, as in the case of Charleston, South Carolina.[44]

It has not been possible to obtain a sampling of the colonial electorate as representative as would be desirable to determine its size without question. Nevertheless, the evidence pointing toward a relatively large electorate under the property tests cannot be refuted by any empirical evidence to the contrary. Moreover, the conclusions which can be drawn from this sampling of the electorate are confirmed by contemporaries as well as by recent historians who have made studies of the subject for individual colonies. Of significance, also, is the fact that the proportion of freeholders varies as much within some colonies as it did from colony to colony and that fairly uniformly the electorate seems to have varied, on a freehold basis exclusively, from about 50 to 75 percent. Some communities exceeded, some fell below this range, but probably not as many as came within its limits.

That there should have been a more popular and widely based electorate in British America than in Britain itself was due largely to the fact that the Atlantic seaboard was a frontier in the sense in which F. J. Turner used the word in the last century, and W. P. Webb uses it in this. The spatial factor was much more favorable to the diffusion of real property in

[44] Historical Society of Pennsylvania, *Penn Official Correspondence*, II, James Logan to John Penn, p. 29 (Oct. 8, 1728); *North Carolina Records*, IX, pp. 270-271; Bridenbaugh, Carl, *Cities in Revolt, Urban Life in America, 1743-1776* (New York, 1955), pp. 218-219.

America than it was in Britain.[45] The difference between the size of a strip of land under the open-field system in Britain and a strip under a comparable system in the town of Fairfield, Connecticut, is an illustration.[46] An Irish immigrant resident in Pennsylvania wrote to friends back home, urging them to come to the colony, "it being the best Country for Working folk and tradesmen of any in the world." He added that he had at first been a tenant but had since bought good land, 500 acres for only 350 pounds.[47] When Joseph Trumbull of Connecticut visited Britain in 1764, he wrote his friends and relatives from Liverpool. "We in New England," he said, "know nothing of Poverty & want, we have no idea of the thing, how much better do our poor people live than 7/8 of the people of this much Famed Island."[48]

[45] Turner, Frederick J. *The Frontier in American History* (New York, 1920) and Webb, Walter P., *The Great Frontier* (Boston, 1952).

[46] Garvan, A. N. B., *Architecture and Town Planning in Colonial Connecticut* (New Haven, 1951), p. 57.

[47] Historical Society of Pennsylvania, *Miscellaneous Manuscripts*, Chester County, 1684-1847, Robert Parke to Mary Valentine, 1725.

[48] Connecticut Historical Society, *Jonathan Trumbull Papers, 1746-1784*, Trumbull to Colonels Trumbull and Fitch, June 17, 1764.

CHAPTER 3

THE COLONIAL VOTER
AT THE POLLS

AMERICAN colonial laws governing the conduct of elections were as indebted to British precedent as were colonial suffrage laws. The Maryland election law of 1717 expressed the prevailing aspiration in its requirement that elections in Maryland should be "held in the mode of English elections."[1] A Pennsylvania law sought the same end to the extent, it said, that circumstances should permit.

If there had been no modification of laws governing electoral procedures, elections would have been held by the method of viva voce, that is, an election by voice vote or, if called for, by poll. On the whole, the American colonies followed the English method with quite English results but with exceptions sufficiently numerous to be worthy of note. Even exceptions, however, were partly indebted to British ideas and practices. Colonial interest in the secret ballot, for example, was a reflection of the interest of seventeenth-century English thinkers, particularly James Harrington, in the use of the secret ballot in Venetian elections. Knowledge of the abuses of viva voce elections in the mother country heightened their interest. Colonials were pioneers in the reform of electoral procedures, some of which were not adopted in Britain until the nineteenth century.[2]

The secret ballot, or its approximation, was far from unknown during the colonial period. South Carolina, whose original constitution owed something to John Locke, employed

---

[1] Bisset, J., *Abridgment and Collection of the Acts of the Province of Maryland* (Philadelphia, 1759), p. 124.

[2] Fink, *The Classical Republicans*, p. 28.

secrecy in balloting in elections until 1766. North Carolina also conducted elections in this way from 1715 to 1760. Pennsylvania permitted secrecy in elections, as Connecticut was said to do, although secrecy was not expressly required by law. Massachusetts permitted the use of ballots but did not specify secrecy. Moreover, there is evidence that viva voce elections were held in this colony during the eighteenth century. In Rhode Island, ballots for colony elections were not accepted unless signed by the voter, although in town elections they could be cast secretly. In New Jersey, the law required lists of the voters and the candidates for whom they voted. Under certain circumstances these lists were made available to the public.[3]

In only one colony, New York, did the demand for secret elections become a major political issue. The issue arose largely because of coercion of voters in the city of New York and by manorial landlords in the countryside. The first effort to secure a secret ballot was underway as early as 1734, but not until the hotly contested elections of the 1760's, involving the rivalries of the De Lancey and Livingston factions, did the demand become great. Coercion and intimidation of voters by both factions created so great a scandal as to give rise to a campaign for a secret ballot modelled upon either the law or practice of Pennsylvania and Connecticut.

Nevertheless, prevailing electoral procedures had their defenders in some of the colonies. A "squinter" on public affairs in New York opposed electoral reform on the grounds that the use of a written or printed ballot was undesirable. He said that electors in Pennsylvania, particularly the Germans, were

[3] *Statutes at Large of South Carolina* (Columbia, 1836-1875, 13 vols.), III, pp. 135-141; *A Collection of all the Public Acts of the Assembly of the Province of North Carolina now in force and Use* (New Bern, 1752), p. 177; *The Statutes at Large of Pennsylvania* (Harrisburg, etc., 1896-1915, 18 vols.), VII, pp. 32-40; *Acts of the General Assembly of New Jersey* [1752], pp. 142-145; *Acts and Laws of the English Colony of Rhode Island* (Newport, 1767), p. 84; *Acts and Laws of Connecticut . . .* [1769], pp. 45-47.

handed prepared tickets and that they voted in sheer ignorance of what or whom they were supporting. Threats and outright coercion, he continued, were known not only in Pennsylvania but in Connecticut as well. Tavern and ale houses, he maintained, were as influential under secret as under viva voce elections. For these reasons, he appealed to the public to maintain the New York or British electoral procedures by which "every Elector is at Liberty to declare the Sentiments of his Heart publicly, which is the Glory of the British Constitution. . . ."[4] A secret ballot bill failed to pass the New York Assembly by a vote of 13 to 12 in the session of 1769-1770.[5]

The spirit in which the American colonial and the British voter went to the polls was as much alike as the electoral procedures under which they voted. In an age still pre-democratic in its conscious thought, although not in many of its practices and institutions, the voter generally was most concerned, as Sir Lewis Namier has written, with personal and local needs rather than with making and controlling the policies of the state. In Namier's opinion, the restricted franchise in eighteenth-century Britain was not responsible for the absence of real politics in elections. Corruption "was not a shower bath from above . . . but a water-spout springing from the rock of freedom, to meet the demands of the People. Political bullying starts usually from above, the demand for benefits from below; the two between them made eighteenth century elections."[6]

[4] Dillon, Dorothy, *The New York Triumvirate* (New York, 1949), pp. 82-123; Sydnor, C. S., Cunningham, N. E., "Voting in Early America," *American Heritage* (Fall 1952), pp. 6-8; McAnear, B., *Politics in Provincial New York* (Ph.D. thesis, Stanford University, 1935), pp. 414-415; New York Historical Society, *Broadsides*, "J. W., a Squinter on Public Affairs," Dec. 29, 1769; *New York Gazette and Weekly Mercury*, Jan. 9, 1769; *Connecticut Courant*, March 5, 1770.

[5] *Journal of the General Assembly of New York [1769-1770]* (Albany, 1820), p. 66.

[6] Namier, Sir Lewis B., *The Structure of British Politics at the Accession of George III* (London, 1929, 2 vols.), I, p. 128.

Probably an approximation of these conditions is characteristic of all pre-democratic societies with an electoral system. Sir Ivor Jennings tells us that the majority of Ceylonese voters at the present time have very little information about the world at large and as a result tend to be affected greatly by purely personal considerations, family pressures, religious and caste prejudices, ostentatious displays of wealth, and other "irrelevant" factors.[7] The New England divine, Samuel Stone, declared that political conditions were best when there was a speaking aristocracy, in his case the ministers, and a silent democracy, the mass of people.[8]

When and where colonial democracy was silent, or relatively so, it was often because of public apathy. Voter indifference was, in turn, often the result of the electors' living at an inconvenient distance from the polls. In New England, the basic unit for elections was, of course, the town. Because the total area of most towns was by modern standards relatively small, we are likely to conclude that they were a compact, closely knit unit. Such was not always the case. The size of the towns was sometimes so great as to give rise to the growth of several compact villages within their boundaries, one of these being the seat of elections and meetings.[9] It was often difficult for the electors living in the outlying villages to know what was going on, let alone to vote. In Kent, Connecticut, for example, the number of adult males who never became freemen, although qualified, varied inversely with the distance of their residences from the village of Kent, the seat of local government and elections.[10]

In the middle and southern colonies, save in South Carolina, where the parish was the unit, the county as the electoral unit

[7] Jennings, Sir Ivor, *The Commonwealth in Asia* (Oxford, 1951), p. 37.

[8] Quoted in Dorfman, Joseph, *The Economic Mind in American Civilization* (New York, 1946-1949, 3 vols.), I, p. 37.

[9] Wertenbaker, Thomas J., *The Puritan Oligarchy* (New York, 1947), pp. 183-207.

[10] Grant, *History of Kent*, pp. 204-241.

had great disadvantages from the voter's standpoint. In New Jersey, a voter might conceivably live twenty-five miles from the point where the elections were held. In South Carolina, the failure of the assembly to create additional parishes by subdividing existing ones forced some voters to travel one hundred and fifty miles or more. The parish proved too large also for a variety of other purposes. In 1742, St. Paul's Parish was rent by a struggle to remove the church to the center as more convenient for elections, meetings of road commissioners, and the like.[11] A suggestion made in New York that the voters of Suffolk County be favored by moving the poll from place to place within the county aroused strong opposition. "Publius," writing to the *New York Gazette and Weekly Mercury* on December 11, 1769, was convinced that this method would increase the "great Evil of Labourers, servants and Apprentices" who would gather more frequently for purposes of amusement. If freeholders would not travel, he said, they had no one to blame but themselves.

Even if the polling places had been easily accessible to all the electors, many would not have voted. They often stayed away from elections because of sheer lack of interest in a function which took time and effort from more pressing and immediate personal concerns. The "multitude," stated Ezra Stiles, the Connecticut minister, "will not leave the plow to have a governor of their taste."[12]

Often bad weather kept at home many who otherwise would have turned out at election time, a factor independent of time, place, or circumstance. A light vote in Edgcomb in the District of Maine, in 1778, was explained by the statement that it was "an Extream Rainey Day and very Difficult Travel-

---

[11] *Journals of the Commons House of Assembly, 1741-1742*, p. 508; "Publius" in *New York Gazette and Weekly Mercury*, Dec. 11, 1769.
[12] Dexter, F. B. (ed.), *Extracts from the Itineraries . . . of Ezra Stiles . . . 1755-1794* (n.p., 1916), p. 462.

ling as many had some distance to Travel."[13] A sudden change in weather conditions often brought out the voters in large numbers, as happened in Salem, New York, in January of 1793. Few attended the election at first, it was said, because of a January thaw. Then came more snow and "the next day [there was] Good Sleighing and away they went. . . ."[14]

Voters were indifferent also because there was often little choice in terms of personalities or issues, a situation deemed desirable rather than otherwise in a pre-democratic society. Staten Island voters in 1761 were so unanimously in favor of one candidate that no one raised any objection when election officials decided not to bother taking the poll, although one was required by law.[15] Studies of colonial political "élites" show the extent to which officials confidently expected that they would be returned again and again to the posts to which they had been elected, and which they filled partly for pleasure, excitement, prestige, or power or from a sense of *noblesse oblige*.[16] Upon the officeholding classes of Massachusetts and Connecticut, Cadwallader Colden made some interesting observations. "Seldom," he said, "are their officers changed while they strictly support the government and execute their laws, and the officers for the most part continue in the same families from father to son."[17] The same situation seems to have existed in New York, Maryland, Virginia, and South Carolina about the middle of the eighteenth century.

[13] Jameson, J. F., "Did the Fathers Vote?" *New England Magazine* (I, January 1890), p. 487.

[14] N.Y.S.L., Manuscript Division, *John Williams Papers*, III, p. 140.

[15] N.Y.H.S., *James Duane Papers*, Box 10, Contested Election. Henry Holland vs. Samuel Holmes.

[16] See Sydnor, *Gentlemen Freeholders*, pp. 60-93; Grant, *History of Kent*, pp. 266-306; Labaree, L. W., *Conservatism in Early American History* (New York, 1948), pp. 1-31; Brennan, Ellen E., *Plural Office Holding in Massachusetts, 1760-1780* (Chapel Hill, 1945), pp. 20-22; Rowland, Kate H., *Charles Carroll of Carrollton* (New York, 1892, 2 vols.), I, p. 103.

[17] N.Y.H.S., *Letters and Papers of Cadwallader Colden* (IX), p. 247.

In Connecticut, an exceptionally retarded notion of the role of the electorate was maintained into the nineteenth century. A law against blasphemy was invoked as a kind of anti-*lèse majesté* statute against Jeremiah Ripley, Jr., of Windham. He remarked as he went to vote on an election day in 1733, it was alleged, that the opportunity had come for the freemen to turn out "that knave Wolcott and that fool Talcott." For these partisan remarks, the assembly invoked the law against blasphemy and, in a high-handed and illegal manner, revoked his certificate of freemanship. It was restored to him in 1734 only upon his confessing that, while it would have been bad to talk about his equals in so un-Christian a manner, it was worse to have spoken so about his governor. As late as 1758, a Waterbury resident was officially rebuked for saying that only the devil himself could be worse than the current governor.[18]

When the colonial voter did turn out for elections, his reasons for voting were often as naïve as those which Sir Lewis Namier thinks influenced the English voter. A New York newspaper published in 1761 an analysis of those considerations which, in the writer's opinion, most influenced provincial voters in making their choice. When asked why they voted as they did, some said that the candidate was "affable without Singularity or Affectation, he . . . [was] unreserved and communicative whenever Information . . . [was] required of him." Another said, "He is my friend and often employs me in my Occupation, when perhaps others might have served him as well." One voter declared, "A Squeeze of the Hand of a great man, a few well timed compliments; . . . and Invitation to his Dining Room, . . . a glass of wine well applied, the Civility and good Humor of his Lady, the Drinking a health, inquiring kindly after the Welfare of a Family, a little facecious Chat in a strain of Freedom and Equality, have been sufficient to win the Heart of many a voter. . . ."[19]

[18] Connecticut State Library, Hartford, Archives Division, *Crimes and Misdemeanors*, III, pp. 176-184; v, pp. 107-117.
[19] *The New York Gazette*, Feb. 5, 1761.

It should not be assumed, however, that no real political issues ever aroused the interest of the colonial electorate or involved passionately held convictions. Occasions did arise, particularly from the late seventeenth century on, when matters of public policy or ethnic, religious, or economic considerations created strong feelings of partisanship, giving to certain pages of the political history of some of the colonies a surprisingly democratic, even modern cast. We cannot show, however, that any of these periods coincided with an effort to reduce or eliminate property qualifications for voting. Overt criticisms of the property tests, such as those in New Jersey in 1703 and 1704, were extremely rare until the crisis leading to the Revolution.

Certainly, "real politics" did arise with the struggle over paper money in Massachusetts, the merits of the Great Awakening in Connecticut, the sectional conflict in Rhode Island over the incidence of taxation, rivalry between the Presbyterian and Anglican factions in New York, the struggle between the Proprietary and the Quakers in Pennsylvania, and the drive of the dissenters in Virginia to secure religious liberty and church disestablishment.[20]

In these situations, voters often turned out in striking numbers. In Virginia, for example, voter interest was greater in the 1740's than it was for many decades after the Revolution. Figures of voting in Boston also reflect the serious interest of voters when the issues concerned them personally. One Pennsylvanian complained that annual elections helped to keep his colony in a ferment, and that those elected were so cowed by the voters as not to dare follow the dictates of their own reason or conscience. Another Pennsylvanian, Richard Peters, thought he knew enough about the complex nature of the

[20] See Brown, *Middle Class Democracy and the Revolution in Massachusetts*, pp. 120-149; Zeichner, O., *Connecticut's Years of Controversy* (Chapel Hill, 1949), pp. 20-43, 78-111; Dillon, *op.cit.*, pp. 31-123; Thayer, T. G., *Pennsylvania Politics and the Growth of Democracy: 1740-1776*, pp. 25-137; Sydnor, *op.cit.*, p. 137.

colony's politics to say that "merest trifles" caused disputes between rival sets of politicians. "It is not in ye. power of any man," he observed, "to prevent this it is ye natural & constant Consequence of republican principles. . . ."[21]

Occasionally, colonists were astonished by the intensity of interest in elections. "Our elections being over," wrote a Pennsylvanian, "the Borough [of Lancaster] is restored to its former Quiet, & the Inhabitants have again resumed their Senses."[22] Violations of laws often accompanied elections held in such an atmosphere. Americans unacquainted with this feature of colonial elections were sometimes appalled by corruption in British politics. "We that have been used to none but sober, regular, fair & righteous Elections," wrote a shocked William S. Johnson of Connecticut in 1768, "can hardly form any idea, without being on the spot, of those made here in [Britain]. . . . The whole depends upon Intrigue, Party, Interest and Money."[23] Connecticut people prided themselves upon being more virtuous than Britons and the inhabitants of other American colonies as well. The *Connecticut Courant* stated with smug satisfaction in 1770 that each Connecticut voter made up his mind independently, that none was swayed by alcohol or other forms of stimulant. There was no place in the British Empire, the writer observed, "in which Elections are conducted with so much Freedom and good Order as in this Colony."[24] There is, however, some evidence to the contrary. On occasion, liquor was dispensed in Connecticut elections, town meeting moderators and others employed every conceivable stratagem to control town meetings, and, when neces-

[21] H.S.P., *Penn Official Correspondence*, III, Colonel J. Thomas to Penn (?) March 15, 1739, p. 79. *Richard Peters Papers*, n.d., to Penn, 1737-1750.
[22] H.S.P., *Shippen Papers*, VII, J. Yeates to Colonel Burd, Oct. 6, 1773.
[23] Quoted in Sachse, William L., *The Colonial American in Great Britain* (Madison, 1956), p. 207.
[24] *Connecticut Courant*, March 5, 1770.

sary, votes were actually bought at 5 pounds a head, as in 1767 in the election of a governor.[25]

Elsewhere hypocrisy could not conceal nor ignorance excuse the seamy side of colonial elections. Most of the illegal, unethical, or questionable means by which elections were often conducted in Britain appeared on this side of the Atlantic.[26] Unqualified persons could vote if they would vote as election officials or other partisans told them to, a practice for which legal remedies existed. These remedies were rarely applied because it was apparently customary in some, if not all, colonies to allow all adult males, when known to the community and to any degree respected or liked, to vote. In such relatively homogeneous communities as those in Connecticut one wonders if the property tests were totally ignored more often than not.

Governor Oliver Wolcott prepared in 1821 for Rufus King of New York an illuminating analysis of the situation in Connecticut during the previous century. Wolcott wrote King that the freehold qualification had been much easier to meet than the personal property qualification and was the more usual means of meeting the suffrage requirements. But, he went on to say, property qualifications of any kind had for the last one hundred years been "essentially nugatory." "Few men of decent character have failed at some time," he continued, "to acquire the qualification when desired." Even town paupers had been permitted to vote, he said, from his "earliest recollections." Only during periods of political excitement had there been much in the way of attention to qualifications and

[25] *Ibid.*, April 16, 1767.

[26] See Douglas, Sylvester, *The History of Controverted Elections* . . . . (London, 1775-1777, 4 vols.); Beloff, Max, *Public Order and Popular Disturbances, 1660-1714* (London 1938); Albery, William, *A Parliamentary History of the Ancient Borough of Horsham, 1295-1885* (London, 1927); Perkins, Clarence, "Electioneering in Eighteenth Century England," *Quarterly Journal of the University of North Dakota* (XII, Jan. 1923), pp. 103-124. Neale, J. E., *The Elizabethan House of Commons* (New Haven, 1950), treats the earlier period comprehensively.

to the manufacture of voters.[27] One suspects that the same or a similar situation existed in most, if not all, of the other colonies, to say nothing of Britain itself. Colonials were often ignorant of or indifferent to the suffrage laws. Nevertheless, there were times when voting by unqualified individuals caused trouble. In New York, for example, John De Lancey alleged that five voters in a Westchester Borough election in 1769 were not freeholders. He was able to demonstrate that four were not, and there was a lively difference of opinion over the fifth, the value of his real property being disputed. One witness testified that it was worth 50 pounds and another that it was worth only 17 pounds.[28]

The practice of creating freeholds at the time of a crucial election was fairly widespread in the American colonies. When an office seeker and his friends thought an additional number of votes was necessary to win an election, it was not unusual for them to create small freeholds for the express purpose of manufacturing votes. The practice of giving deeds to freeholds in land, which were returned to the prior owner after election, was prevalent in England, especially in counties and in boroughs with burgage tenure. Although the creation of fagot votes, as they were called, was prohibited by Parliamentary statute in 1696, the practice continued undiminished to the last days of the unreformed House of Commons.[29] Colonials found it useful, and fagot votes were a factor in elections in Virginia, New Jersey, New York, Connecticut, and Rhode Island at various times and under various circumstances. Small lots were created in Amboy, New Jersey, to manufacture votes, according to Governor Burnet's statement

[27] N.Y.H.S., *Rufus King Papers*, Box 26, Wolcott to King, Oct. 4, 1821. There is also a copy in the Wolcott Papers, Connecticut Historical Society.

[28] N.Y.S.L., Manuscript Division, *General Assembly Journal*, III, 1766-1776, pp. 67-78.

[29] Dodd, A. H., "An Electioneering Lease of 1585," *English Historical Review* (LXV, April 1950), pp. 221-222.

of 1722. In the disputed Westchester Borough election in New York, already referred to, one man declared innocently that he had given his son a deed to make him a freeholder in the county, "that he might have the same privileges of other free-holders."[30] In the Queen's County election of 1761, a number of voters were challenged on the suspicion that their deeds were not passed three months before election, as required by provincial law. In Rhode Island during the 1760's at the height of the Ward-Hopkins controversy which involved per-sonalities, the incidence of taxation, patronage, and other im-portant issues, the creation of voters and illegal voting on an exceptionally broad scale caused Rhode Islanders to commend the new policy of the assembly after 1760.[31] In order to exclude persons who were voting on fagot freeholds, the as-sembly thereafter scrutinized the names of those admitted to the freemanship by the towns. The power of the assembly to reject, said one Rhode Islander of the next century, was neces-sary irrespective of a man's wealth, because he might still be useless and vicious. This power was asserted to be a very valuable privilege under Rhode Island's royal charter, and the means of preventing a person's voting illegally.[32]

In Pennsylvania, naturalization of aliens rather than fagot voting was the important means of increasing the number of votes for the Quaker party. The Quakers successfully in-gratiated themselves with the German voters of the eastern counties of the colony. About the middle of the eighteenth century, a significant experiment was under way in acclimating the Germans to electoral practices unheard of in the Germanies

[30] N.Y.S.L., *General Assembly Journal*, III, p. 73.
[31] Lovejoy, David S., *op.cit.*, pp. 21-29. Archive Room, State Capitol, see *Petitions to the General Assembly, Journals of the House of Deputies, Votes and Deputies*, particularly for 1761 and 1762; Rhode Island Historical Society, *Moses Brown Papers*, I, p. 104, James Wanton to Moses Brown.
[32] Rhode Island Historical Society, *Private Papers of Samuel Eddy*, no. 43.

of the time, and incorporating them as a significant factor in the government of the colony. The price which the Germans paid for their support of the anti-proprietary forces was a heightened degree of prejudice against them, on political as well as cultural and religious grounds. The anti-proprietary forces in Pennsylvania emerged as among the first in colonial politics with a distinct nativist element.[33]

The German population evidently voted and held local office, with or without benefit of either private acts of naturalization or the special provincial statute passed in 1742, two years after the imperial Parliament provided for naturalization in the empire as a whole. The local act was partly in response to a petition in 1734 which asked for all Germans the privileges which some already enjoyed by private bill. The petitioners said that they had held office, purchased lands, and now wanted to be naturalized so that they might hold "estates to us and our heirs and be qualified to enjoy the privileges of freemen of Pennsylvania."[34] It is perhaps no accident that before the elections of 1754 and 1765, a flood of naturalization papers was forthcoming, even though an increase in legal rights to land may have been the major cause.

Anti-German feeling in Lancaster was so great that one of its residents opposed the incorporation of the town as a borough in 1749 because "the Body of the People Consists of ye Lowest set of Germans unacquainted with our Constitution & Laws. . . ."[35] Another scouted the possibility of gerry-

[33] See Thayer, *Israel Pemberton, King of the Quakers* (Philadelphia, 1943), p. 113; *Pennsylvania Politics and the Growth of Democracy*, p. 120; Wood, Ralph (ed.), *The Pennsylvania Germans* (Princeton, 1942), pp. 10, 12; Johnson, W. T., "Some Aspects of the Relations of the Government and German Settlers in Colonial Pennsylvania," *Pennsylvania History* (xi, April 1944), pp. 81-102.

[34] H.S.P., *Bucks County Papers*, Miscellaneous, 1682-1745, p. 147. Henry J. Young in his *The Treatment of the Loyalists in Pennsylvania* (unpub. Ph.D. thesis, the Johns Hopkins University, 1955), p. 38, says the rush for naturalization was due to desire to clear land titles.

[35] H.S.P., *Lancaster County, Miscellaneous Papers*, 1724-1772, Thomas Cookson [?] to Thomas Penn, Dec. 4, 1749.

mandering the colony to reduce the German influence in the assembly. In 1755, William Allen, partisan of the proprietary interest, wrote a friend that it was his wish that the British Parliament prohibit Quakers and Germans from sitting in the assembly and that the Germans be forbidden to vote "till they know our Language, & are better acquainted with our Constitution."[36] An anonymous correspondent of Richard Peters advocated, probably in 1757, that free English schools be established, that further immigration be discouraged, and that English be used exclusively in all deeds and other legal documents. He confessed that it would be too harsh to suppress all German printing houses and importation of German books. In his opinion, there was no need to forbid intermarriage between the Germans and the English because the German women, being "thick & strong," would have little appeal for Englishmen.[37]

A similar situation had developed much earlier in the Carolinas, to which numbers of Huguenots had migrated in the latter part of the seventeenth century. The result was a quarrel between the minority and the majority, in which suffrage issues loomed very large. Many Huguenots, claiming that they had gained the right to vote because of prior naturalization in England, threatened to support the Protestant dissenters against the interests and the adherents of the Church of England in the colony. The electoral law had been so loosely drawn, it was said, that with only a property qualification every pirate of the Red Sea operating from a Carolina base could vote if he wanted to. One sheriff refused to allow French Huguenots to vote even when they were freeholders because they had not been naturalized.[38]

In the history of colonial suffrage and elections, contests

[36] H.S.P., *Penn Official Correspondence*, VII, p. 135, Nov. 25, 1755.
[37] H.S.P., *Richard Peters Papers*, VIII, p. 287.
[38] Carroll, B. R., *op.cit*, II, pp. 440-442; Hirsch, Arthur H., *The Huguenots of Colonial South Carolina* (Durham, 1928), pp. 1-125.

arose more frequently than might be expected from matters involving religion, ethnic, and national origins rather than from the issue of property per se. With property so widely diffused, differences and distinctions of other kinds appeared more significant. In 1747, Cadwallader Colden expressed the point of view of those with a British background or origin when he wrote that, while the populace was educated in republican principles, it also contained a number of "foreigners who know nothing of the English Constitution, and can have no esteem of it."[39]

A more popular method of increasing the number of voters than that of naturalizing foreigners was the simple though sinister method of purchasing them. Rhode Island was the leading example of this practice during the Ward-Hopkins fight. Ezra Stiles of Connecticut denounced the electoral practices of the little colony, including the buying of votes, as a sign of "Rhode Islandism" and branded it a "licentious Republic." During the controversy, individuals were paid to vote and also a number of persons were paid *not* to vote. The Browns of Providence apparently underwrote the election expenses of the Hopkins faction.[40]

New York was not exempt from this vice, nor were other colonies. What the situation must have been like in New York is indicated by the virtuous assertion of one candidate for public office in 1768, James Jauncey, that he had refused the offers of forty men in New York City to sell their votes to him.[41] Some voters were eager to sell their votes to the highest bidder, and many candidates for office used every means at their disposal to secure votes for themselves. In Virginia, a defeated candidate in the assembly elections of 1736 retaliated against those who had not supported him by

[39] N.Y.P.L., Manuscript Division, *Bancroft Transcripts*, Colden Papers, I, p. 479.
[40] See the analysis in Lovejoy, *op.cit.*, pp. 92-98.
[41] N.Y.H.S., *James Duane Papers*, Box I, "Brief of Mr. Jauncey's defense against bribery, charged by Mr. Scott.

foreclosing on thirty-three men who owed him money. All were said to have lost their property and some ended in debtors' gaol.[42]

There is abundant evidence of such practices in the records of the assembly election in New York City in 1768, involving the aspirations of James Jauncey and John Morin Scott, the latter being better known as a leading Son of Liberty. Each accused the other after the election of illegal and unethical practices. Scott was accused of having threatened to sue one man if he would not vote for him, of promising another that his vote would secure his admission as a freeman of the city, and of contributing to welfare funds of the journeymen and carpenters just before the election. Mr. Jauncey was similarly accused by the Scott forces. They asserted that he had loaned money before the election in such a way as to create voters in his interest, that he had persuaded his electoral agent, Nicholas Stokes, to abandon his suit against one Isaac van Hook if the latter would vote for him. Jauncey denied that he had dispensed his usual charities just before the election in order to influence voters, a denial which, like his others, his opponents failed to take seriously.[43] These practices often caused the voter to approach an election with mixed feelings and with considerable anxiety, not knowing whether the candidate would entertain or intimidate him, an anxiety often felt by his British counterpart. Use of troops, the arming of partisans with clubs, and other forms of voter intimidation make a long and undistinguished page in English political history.

Nevertheless, it is true also that an English election was often a social occasion of a kind experienced only several times in one's life. The famous mercantile house of Lascelles reported in 1768 that there had been an increase in the price of rum "occasioned by a great many Rums being bought up in

[42] Campbell, T. E., *Colonial Carolina: a History of Carolina County* (Richmond, 1954), pp. 86-87.

[43] N.Y.H.S., *James Duane Papers*, Box I. See James Jauncey's brief against the charge of bribery.

hopes of a large consumption this year as it is the General Election year."[44] In the southern colonies, election time was an occasion for eating, drinking, and being merry at the expense of the candidates, who acted the role of genial hosts of county or parish freeholders. It was as much a social as a political occasion, at least for the voter. James Madison failed of election to the Virginia House of Burgesses at one time because of his neglect of the voter in a social capacity.[45] In Annapolis, Maryland, a drunken spree before, during, and after an election resulted in the death of one man, who left a widow and orphans.[46]

On occasion, a quite different reception was prepared for those who turned out to vote, as records of New York and Pennsylvania show. In New York, Peter R. Livingston wrote Philip Schuyler in 1769, just previous to a very intense election, that if the other side dared to rob them of votes, there would be bloodshed "as we have by far the best part of the Brusers [sic] on our side who are determined to use force if they use foul play."[47] In Philadelphia, success at the polls for a number of years after 1738 depended upon control of the staircase of the building in which the poll was taken. Sailors from the harbor would reply, when challenged, that they "had as much right to be there as the damned Dutchmen." One Pennsylvanian advised that rumors be spread that violence would be employed at forthcoming elections. It was hoped that this, with other timely measures, would keep great numbers of Mennonites at home.[48]

[44] Pares, Richard, "A London West-India House," in A. J. P. Taylor (ed.), *Essays Presented to Sir Lewis Namier* (London, 1956), pp. 75-107.
[45] Sydnor, *op.cit.*   [46] *Maryland Gazette*, January 25, 1749.
[47] N.Y.P.L., Manuscript Division, *Philip Schuyler Papers*, Box 23, Peter R. Livingston to Schuyler, Jan. 16, 1769.
[48] Thayer, *Israel Pemberton, King of the Quakers*, p. 49; N.Y.H.S., *Joseph Reed Papers*, I, Charles Pettit to Reed, Nov. 3, 1764; H.S.P., *Peters Papers*, Peters to Penn, Nov. 17, 1742; *Shippen Papers*, VI, p. 127, Samuel Purviance [?] to Shippen [?].

In such situations, it was extremely important to have officials in control who could be trusted to ensure a fair return. Some lived up to their responsibilities, others did not. Whether justified or not, loud were the complaints against sheriffs in Virginia, church wardens in South Carolina, town moderators in New England, and inspectors of elections in such colonies as Pennsylvania, where they supervised the polls in company with the sheriffs. Officials everywhere were variously accused of admitting illegal voters to the polls, denying qualified persons the right to vote, suppressing legal votes in the count, stuffing ballot boxes (as in Pennsylvania), winking at intimidation of electors, opening and closing the polls capriciously, and dropping legal votes to the floor which later were burned with the genuine debris of electoral activities.[49] In New Jersey, a sheriff closed the polls in Trenton although he knew that forty voters were on their way to cast their ballots. In Maryland, one sheriff was accused of being "absent and intoxicated with liquor the greatest Part of the time, from the Opening to the Closing of the Polls."[50] The use of alcohol became so notorious a factor in New York that, in 1759, a group of New Yorkers, headed by Oliver De Lancey, John Cruger, Philip Livingston, and Leonard Lispenard, declared that they would dispense with the use of liquor in elections as "an old exploded custom," making a contribution to the poor of the city and county instead.[51]

Colonial assemblies tried to curb these electoral abuses by a spate of laws against bribery and corruption, against the treating of electors, and against intimidation of election officials at the polls. They took their cue from English statutes bearing upon the same subjects from the reign of Queen Anne forward.[52] Pennsylvania was particularly alert to electoral re-

---

[49] New Jersey Archives, *Item AM 1860.*
[50] *Maryland Archives,* LV, p. xxxiv.
[51] *Maryland Gazette,* January 25, 1759.
[52] McCormick, *op.cit.,* pp. 50, 50n.

form in Britain in the eighteenth century. The statutes in force just before the Revolution provided for check lists of voters and for township poll booths in county elections. They appear to be an effort to adapt to Pennsylvania the Statute of 18 George II, Cap. 18, providing for an optional method of polling which could be employed if the candidates so desired. Some colonials had little faith in the effectiveness of any efforts to control the elections in the interest of fair play. "They will never prevent bribery and corruption at the polls," wrote one person to Sir William Johnson. "If they can they can do more than their Mother Country ever could."[53]

Part of the difficulty arose from ignorance as to exactly who was qualified to vote. In Pennsylvania, there was confusion as to whether freemen who were not freeholders in the counties could vote; in Maryland, freeholders alone seem to have been the voters despite a personal property qualification. If an individual's right to vote were challenged, sometimes the only proof of qualification would be his taking an oath that he was a legal voter. If he refused, he would not be permitted to vote. In such circumstances, tax lists would be of help to a sheriff or other election official. Indeed, Pennsylvania required township tax officials to prepare lists of taxables to guide county officials in elections. On the other hand, there is good evidence that in Rhode Island the precise freehold qualification for voting was ignored. The law required the ownership of a freehold of 40 pounds value or one worth 40 shillings a year. Nevertheless, it is clear that towns were admitting to freemanship persons who qualified by possession of freeholds solely in terms of acreage, or by ownership of small town lots, or even by the holding of leases, as in Providence. Five of these leaseholders were not admitted by the assembly to colony freemanship.[54] In Delaware, as late as 1770, there was still

[53] *Sir William Johnson Papers* (Albany, 1921-57, 12 vols.), VII, pp. 333-334.

[54] Archive Room, Providence. See Lists of Freemen in *Votes and Deputies*, 1761, 1762.

considerable doubt over the meaning of the freehold qualification for voting in that colony. Charles Ridgely, a Delaware lawyer, complained that the casting of the freehold qualification in terms of monied estate led to uncertainty and, it might be added, to deception, confusion, and fraud.[55]

The British and hence the colonial concept of government as primarily a public service corporation, or an agency of administration pure and simple, became increasingly less tenable as primitive forms of political organization developed in the colonies. Officeholders were finding that good administration was not enough. Henceforth, they were engaged, whether willingly or not, in political as well as government business. The philosophy that the end justifies the means characterized a growing number of elections in which the rewards of office, material and otherwise, and the ability of the assemblies to advance the interests of some and retard the interests of others became more obvious. In varying degrees, the new perspective on government seems to have characterized all the colonies with the exception of Georgia, South Carolina, and perhaps Connecticut. Accompanying this change in emphasis were unmistakable signs of the growth of more modern political institutions and practices, operating more and more in a distinctly democratic atmosphere. In the late colonial politics of Rhode Island, New York, and Pennsylvania, one finds the employment of printed ballots in elections and the creation of county machines under the aegis of men who sought not only election to the assembly but also their own appointment to county office, or the control of the county patronage on behalf of their electoral agents. One sees also the employment of runners on a colony-wide basis, as in Rhode Island, to stimulate voter interest and keep "central headquarters" advised upon the state of opinion in the hinterland. One finds well-to-do men, like the Browns of Rhode Island, paying election ex-

[55] Ryden, George H. (ed.), *Letters to and from Caesar Rodney, 1756-1784* (Philadelphia, 1933), pp. 34-35.

penses; broadsides and skilled polemics addressed to news-papers designed as propaganda; the creation of ethnically balanced county tickets, as in Pennsylvania; and attempts to win favor of minority ethnic groups by the preparation of electoral material in a foreign language, as High Dutch was used in Pennsylvania before 1742.[56] Conrad Weiser, a leading Pennsylvania German, urged his people to vote because, he said, without the right kind of assembly, "we never would have obtain'd our Lands and Farms upon such easy terms & so many Privedges [sic] we can now boast of."[57] Politicians appealed even to fear. Quakers were accused in 1755 of trying to frighten Germans by threatening that, if the proprietary interest should win the election, "Germans would perhaps be obliged sometime to plough the Lord Proprietors Manors, as in Germany. . . ."[58]

Obviously a new era in politics had commenced in some of the colonies. Seekers after office were bringing about a more sophisticated education of the people in politics. They were learning, whether consciously or not, that they had a stake in government, that it existed for them as much as they existed for it. One result in the colony of New York was the incorporation in the government of a massive safeguard for the people, although that government was not democratic in the modern sense. As Rufus King remarked in 1789, the uneasy balance between the De Lancey and Livingston factions before the Revolution had forced each to keep watch of the other, and "neither dared any measure injurious to the mass of the people."[59] It was his opinion that the Revolution had swept

[56] Highly suggestive is the analysis of New York in McAnear, *op.cit.*, pp. 510-511.

[57] *Pennsylvania Magazine of History and Biography* (xxiii, no. 4, 1899), p. 518.

[58] H.S.P., *Penn Official Correspondence*, vii, William Smith to Penn, ca. 1755, p. 211.

[59] N.Y.H.S., *Rufus King Papers*, "Substance of a Conversation with Governor Clinton," June 1789.

away the people's bulwark in the form in which it had existed previously. King's statement, although exaggerated, cannot be lightly dismissed.

Some British observers were taken aback by what they saw or learned of political conditions in the colonies, and some were puzzled, even alarmed. In Britain the landed classes were identified in the popular mind with an aristocracy. In the colonies the same classes, with some exceptions, were identified with the small landed proprietor. Well might Lord Cornbury complain, as he did in 1705, "The Landed men are not the men of the greatest substance in this part of the world. . . ."[60] Furthermore, the democratic element in colonial government in its classic meaning was becoming increasingly strong in the royal colonies, at the expense of the council and of the governor. Governor Colden found food for thought in the fact that, although the government of New York was designed to imitate the "mixed" form of British government, the "democratical or popular part" was in his opinion too strong. With an eye to the future, he remarked, "In time it may swallow them both up."[61]

[60] *New Jersey Archives*, 1st Series, III, p. 72.
[61] N.Y.P.L., *Bancroft Transcripts*, Colden Papers, II, pp. 24-33, possibly written in 1760 or 1761.

CHAPTER 4

THE GENESIS OF DEMOCRATIC SUFFRAGE THOUGHT

WHEN Sir William Blackstone penned his comments upon the outer limits of safe suffrage concessions, he felt obliged to state that, as a matter of right, all adult males should be allowed to vote and only the unfortunately dependent status of tenants and workers made even these dangerous to the state as voters. That Blackstone should have acknowledged the franchise as a right was a tribute to the great prestige and sanctions of the eighteenth-century doctrine of natural rights, the impact and influence of which was never greater in Britain and the colonies than at about this time. Both Blackstone's suffrage principles and the natural rights philosophy of the Enlightenment were reflected henceforth in the history of suffrage in America no less than in Britain. This is understandable because the religious and intellectual currents of the times were not confined to any one country. Because of the colonial connection, the intellectual debt of Americans to Britain was greater than that to any other country. The same political thought which influenced British history influenced the seaboard colonies, although the manifestations were uniquely American.

Two of the most celebrated expressions of the philosophy of the Enlightenment in Britain were Adam Smith's *Wealth of Nations* and Major John Cartwright's *Take Your Choice*, both published in 1776. As we can see from the vantage point of today, Cartwright, advocating reform of suffrage and representation, defined the issues which lay at the heart of the political history of Britain during the nineteenth century.[1] While he

---

[1] Brebner J. B., "Laissez-faire and State Intervention in Nineteenth

anticipated the future, he also reflected the past. His program contained a number of ideas associated at the time of the Puritan Revolution with Parliament men, Levellers and members of the Cromwellian Army. These ideas, expressed in the Putney Debates of 1647, are the classic illustration of the opinions on suffrage matters held by English Puritans whose theology was derived from John Calvin. Soldiers who were also Levellers had at these debates an admirable spokesman, Thomas Rainsborough, whose words are often quoted. "Has not the meanest He," queried Rainsborough, "as much a life to live as the greatest He?"[2] Nevertheless, not all Levellers agreed with Rainsborough in his advocacy of adult male suffrage. John Lilburne, for example, wanted to broaden the suffrage but exclude all foreigners, servants, and persons who did not pay taxes. John Milton, no Leveller and not even a democrat, favored confining the vote to the "better part" of the people and to this extent was in partial agreement with some men who called themselves Levellers.[3] It is undoubtedly true that the seventeenth century had as much trouble defining "the people" as have had succeeding centuries. Suffice it to say that the army sought to reform the suffrage in such a way as to approximate universal manhood suffrage. Some of the more conservatively minded Parliament men sought merely the abandonment of the freehold as the only qualification in county elections.

Demands for suffrage reform in Cromwell's army came by and large from the core of young men, and their sympathizers, who had not as yet been able to qualify for the franchise either in the boroughs or in the counties. Men who had fought against royal tyranny to restore the ancient liberties of Eng-

---

Century Britain," in Schuyler, R. L., and Ausubel, H. (eds.), *The Making of British History* (New York, 1952), pp. 501-510.

[2] Wodehouse, A. S. P., *Puritanism and Liberty* (Chicago, 1950, 2nd ed.), p. 53.

[3] *Ibid.*, p. 357; Fink, *Classical Republicans*, pp. 118-119.

lishmen could surely be trusted, their spokesmen said, with the right to vote. That suffrage reform would bring in its train an attack upon property was stoutly denied. Rights of property stood upon the same grounds as rights to liberty and the suffrage reform which figured later in the American Revolu- conservatives that the army had fought to recover old rights and so had gained the right to vote, even if propertyless. "If we had not a right to the kingdom," he said, "we were mere mercenary soldiers."[4] He was anticipating an argument for suffrage reform which figured later in the American Revolution, and culminated in that wedding of universal suffrage and universal military service in France at the time of the Great Revolution.

On the other hand, the Puritan Revolution was the occasion for the revival of the Aristotelian argument against manhood suffrage. It became a standard answer to demands for suffrage reform on even a moderate scale. Henry Ireton, a conservative spokesman during the Putney Debates, argued that persons who did not have a fixed, permanent interest in the country should not be allowed to vote. "He that is here today, and gone tomorrow," said Ireton, "I do not see that he hath such a permanent interest." To admit such persons to the vote, he warned, would in time endanger property rights.[5]

Because much of the argument of the Levellers sounds so familiar to the democratically minded of this century, historians and others have concluded that the Putney and other debates of this period represent the debut of modern democratic thought in Britain. In the same way, the origins of American democracy have been attributed to Roger Williams.[6] Nevertheless, it appears that a mistake has been made in both instances, that an identity of words has been taken for an

[4] Wodehouse, op.cit., p. 69.   [5] Ibid., p. 58.

[6] Bernstein, E., Cromwell and Communism (London, 1930); Parrington, V. L., The Colonial Mind (New York, 1927); Brockunier, R. S., The Irrepressible Democrat, Roger Williams (New York, 1940).

identity of spirit. The religious conviction of left-wing Puritanism that men without grace were nevertheless endowed by nature with the attributes of human reason was not the same as the modern democratic theory with its secular assumptions of the equality and innate goodness of man. All the same, their faith in men's natural reason, regardless of whether or not they were at the same time in a state of grace, made for equality between men in this world if not in the next. The Levellers' theory of human nature, when divorced from its fundamental religious orientation, helped to place emphasis upon the concepts of human reason and equality which became so important a part of eighteenth-century thought.

The conception of man as a being naturally endowed with reason was bound to conflict with the environmentalist conception of man implied in the freehold qualification, to wit, that in politics at least it was the physical and external attributes of a freehold agriculture which showed a man's fitness to vote and to participate in government. An attack upon the freehold qualification for voting was an understandable consequence of this conflict, as were other demands for various forms of political equality. When carried to their logical conclusions, and Calvinists were prone to carry matters in that direction, abstract notions of human reason and equality inevitably led to the assumption that government should exist for the people, instead of the reverse. With these questions and criticisms, the essentially medieval structure of English political thought began to crumble.

Some Calvinists, as might be expected, attempted to reconcile their religious beliefs with the older, conventional ideas about the suffrage and even mixed government. They found themselves challenged by co-religionists opposed to freehold tests and critical of mixed government, even of the institution of Parliament itself. Others, like Gerald Winstanley, entertained notions that true Christian equality or true Levelling implied greater equality, not only of political rights but also of material goods, than existed under prevailing property arrangements.

Although unwittingly preparing the way for the Enlightenment, these theorists did not display much faith in the idea of worldly progress, or undue optimism about the future of the human race. As Roger Williams wryly observed, Pharisees made good citizens, but this was scarcely a philosophy to serve as a basis for the democratic thought of Tom Paine and others like him.[7] Eighteenth-century thought repudiated revelation and exalted reason in a way which would have horrified all Calvinists of the preceding century. Nevertheless, eighteenth-century British reformers used the language of those of the seventeenth, if only in the manner of the lawyer who seeks precedents in past events without consideration of the historical circumstances which give them their full meaning.[8] What the modern historian must not overlook is the difference in the basic ideologies of the Age of Faith and the Age of Reason.

Perhaps it would be most accurate to say that Puritan thought in Britain and in the colonies did make a positive contribution to democratic thought by providing a bridge between the late Middle Ages and the Enlightenment. As Ralph Barton Perry has written, democracy is not only a revolution against Puritanism; it is also an evolution from it.[9] This may be seen in the changing content of New England election sermons. A study has shown that, although New England divines freely

[7] Narragansett Club, *Publications* (Providence, 1867), ii, pp. 124-125. See also Miller, Perry, *Roger Williams* (New York, Indianapolis, 1953); Calamandrei, Mauro, "Neglected Aspects of Roger Williams' Thought," *Church History* (xxi, Sept. 1952), pp. 239-258.

[8] Schuyler, R. L., "The Historical Spirit Incarnate," *American Historical Review* (lvii, Jan. 1952), pp. 303-322.

[9] Brown, B. Katherine, "A Note on the Puritan Concept of Aristocracy," *Mississippi Valley Historical Review* (xli, June 1954), pp. 105-112. See also Perry, Ralph B., *Puritanism and Democracy* (New York, 1944), pp. 190-204.

acknowledged a place for a democratic part in government, they circumscribed it in a way which recalls Talleyrand's jibe against Alexander I of Russia. The Tsar, said Talleyrand, wants everyone to be free on condition that everyone obeys him absolutely. In this spirit, election sermons into the eighteenth century encouraged the people to be submissive to their rulers. "Men," one of them wrote, "have liberty to serve God according to the ways outlined by ruling magistrates."[10]

So long as ministers believed that this was mete and just, matters of who could and who could not vote, and what the voters could do, were often academic questions. The location of moral authority was not the same as the location of the ultimate political power in a formal sense. So long as this remained so, the political theory of American Calvinism was pre-democratic, rather than specifically anti-democratic. Ministerial sanctions may have been less compelling as one moved south of Connecticut, but this difference did not mean that the spirit and pattern of government were any more democratic, as that word is understood today.

With Jonathan Mayhew, famous Massachusetts minister, the election sermons of that colony show a distinct change. Partly under the influence of John Locke and his theories, Mayhew acknowledged the right of revolution and in other ways showed that a new era had commenced even in ministerial thought. By 1776, ministers claimed that the people had a right to judge if they were oppressed, a duty to complain, and the right to rebel if necessary.[11] These ideas, however, were given almost exclusively an anti-British, rather than a domestic, application.

While a considerable gulf separated seventeenth- from eighteenth-century thinkers on suffrage matters, there was one particular in which their ideas were the same. British reform-

[10] Quoted in Counts, Mary L., *The Political Views of the Eighteenth Century Clergy as Expressed in Election Sermons* (unpub. Ph.D. thesis, Columbia University, 1956), p. 53.

[11] *Ibid.*, pp. 250-253.

ers of both centuries sought to bring prestige to their cause by appealing to their own interpretation of English constitutional developments since Anglo-Saxon times. In their history they found what they were looking for: support for their conviction that, far from being innovators, they were actually restorers because they worked to recapture the political institutions of Anglo-Saxon times. They believed that a representative and much more democratic form of government had existed in England under the institution of the monarchy before the Norman Conquest. Legislative power had been vested in a single-chambered legislature, the Witan; all adult male tax-payers could vote; and a large degree of local self-government had existed. These quite democratic institutions had continued until modified, overthrown, or corrupted subsequent to the Conquest. In one form or another the cult of the Anglo-Saxon, or more correctly, the cult of the Goths, figured in European, British, and American history from the times of Otto of Freising through those of Pelloutier, Molesworth, Vartot, Kames, and Blackstone to those of J. Toulmin Smith and Herbert Baxter Adams.[12]

Historians have been prone to smile at this view that English history since the Conquest was a kind of fall from initial grace to which a return was within the realm of feasibility. Nevertheless, George L. Haskins is not ready to dismiss the significance of the continued influence of pre-Conquest political institutions upon post-Conquest developments.[13] In Britain, it was deemed the responsibility of the descendants of the Goths to overthrow the hated Norman yoke and restore to themselves and their posterity the blessings of Anglo-Saxon institutions.

[12] See Kliger, Samuel, *The Goths in England: a Study in Seventeenth and Eighteenth Century Thought* (Cambridge, 1952); Hill, Christopher, "The Norman Yoke," in Saville, John (ed.), *Democracy and the Labour Movement: Essays in Honor of Dona Torr* (London, 1954), pp. 11-66.
[13] Haskins, *The Growth of English Representative Government*, pp. 25-26.

For a time after the Stuart Restoration of 1660, the Gothic cult was in eclipse and it was not revived until after the midpoint of the eighteenth century. Even Whig interest in Gothic architecture, as in the case of Horace Walpole, seems related to this revival which can perhaps be dated from the publication by Samuel Squire in 1753 of a work on Anglo-Saxon government. From this time forward, works of a similar kind, often in several volumes, were published and gained considerable audiences.

Perhaps the most representative and at the same time the best written of these was published anonymously in London, in 1771, with the compendious title: *An Historical Essay on the English Constitution: or, an impartial Inquiry into the Elective Power of the People, from the first Establishment of the Saxons in this Kingdom, wherein the Right of Parliament, to tax our distant Province is explained, and justified, upon such constitutional Principles as will afford an equal Security to the Colonists, as to their Brethren at Home.*[14] In swift-flowing prose, the author explained how the northern peoples, the Saxons in particular, had improved upon the political institutions of the Greek and Roman commonwealths. They were able in England to establish effective government for local and central affairs in such a way as to be compatible with the liberty of the individual. The preservation and the protection of the freedom of the individual lay largely in granting the right

[14] This work has been ascribed by the *Catalogues of the British Museum*, Sabin's *A Dictionary of Books Relating to America*, and the *Dictionary of National Biography* to the Scots portrait painter, Allan Ramsay. Ramsay's biographer, Alastair Smart, *The Life and Art of Allan Ramsay* (London, 1952), states a convincing case, however, that there has been a mistake in identity. The authorities on which this author relied for his identification of Ramsay as the writer of a work which was a very important link between English and Pennsylvania radicalism are in error, although the writer cannot now be determined with any certainty. See Williamson, C., "The Artist in Politics: Allan Ramsay and the Revolution in Pennsylvania," *Pennsylvania Magazine of History and Biography* (LXXVII, Oct. 1953), pp. 452-456.

to vote for a representative to the "Wittenagemot" or the single chambered legislature to each householder who paid scot and lot. Unfortunately, this and other splendid institutions were overthrown at the time of the Norman Conquest by William the Bastard, in close collaboration with the Roman Catholic clergy. The conquest greatly increased the power of the crown, established taxation without representation, destroyed democratic local self-government, intruded an hereditary aristocracy between king and people, and established a legislature upon the bi-cameral principle. The English Civil War might have been the occasion for attempts to return to indigenous political principles and institutions but lamentably never was. The Glorious Revolution similarly brought disappointment because it failed to return to the primitive Anglo-Saxon principles. Instead, property tests for members of the House of Commons were instituted in 1710 and bills for annual parliaments failed of passage. The author advocated a return, where feasible, to the pre-Norman state of affairs, and concluded his work with proposals to restore scot-and-lot suffrage in the boroughs, to employ the secret ballot in elections, to repeal property tests for officeholding, and to institute the practice of instruction of representatives in order to make them responsive to the will of the people. The author, however, did not wish to change the suffrage qualifications for voting in the counties, advocating the retention of the 40-shilling freehold qualification.

Like others of its kind, this essay indicates the extent to which the institutions of oligarchic Britain were undergoing stiff criticism not long before the colonial crisis with America broke in full fury.[15] Furthermore, the Wilkes Affair in London made the British populace more critical of the abuses of suffrage and representation and of the entire governmental system of George III.[16] Partly to defend Wilkes' right to sit

[15] Butterfield, Herbert, *George III, Lord North and the People* (London, 1949).

[16] Pares, R., and Taylor, A. J. P. (eds.), *Essays Presented to Sir Lewis*

in Commons after having been duly elected, partly to create a vehicle to spread reformist propaganda, a group of men, among whom John Horne Tooke was prominent, founded the Society of the Supporters of the Bill of Rights in 1769.[17] In time, this organization enjoyed a national reputation and extended its influence across the Atlantic to the American colonies. Its considerable influence was due to the character of its leadership. It was able to attract the attention and excite the enthusiasm of a number of talented and dedicated men. They popularized their ideas in a way which foreshadowed the methods used by modern voluntary organizations to take their case to the public.

Although reformers, such as Richard Price, Granville Sharp, and Joseph Priestley, were in considerable agreement as to the specific evils of the time, they were by no means in agreement as to the extent and desirability of necessary reforms. As we have seen, the author of *An Historical Essay* was happy to continue with a freehold qualification in the English counties. On the other hand, Major Cartwright stood forth unequivocally for manhood suffrage in the tradition of extreme Levellers. John Horne Tooke was opposed to manhood suffrage, as was Joseph Priestley, despite his resounding phrases on behalf of liberty and reform. "POLITICAL LIBERTY," wrote Priestley, "consists in the power which the members of the State reserve to themselves, of arriving at the public offices, or, at least, of having votes in the nomination of those who fill them. . . ." But, he went on to say, "those who are extremely dependent should not be allowed to have votes in the nomination of the Chief Magistrates; because this might, in some instances, be only throwing more votes into the hands of those persons on

---

Namier (London and New York, 1956); Postgate, Raymond, *That Devil Wilkes* (New York, 1929).

[17] See Veitch, G. S., *The Genesis of Parliamentary Reform* (London, 1913); Hall, Walter P., *British Radicalism* (New York, 1912); Kent, C. B. R., *The English Radicals* (London, 1899).

whom they depend."[18] To obviate this danger, he advocated confining the lowly to voting for the less important elective offices and indeed confining their right to hold office to these alone. Some Parliamentary reformers, like James Burgh, were so little interested in suffrage reform as to devote most of their attention to abuses of the rotten borough system of representation.[19]

Nonetheless, a critical spirit was abroad in Britain after the end of the Seven Years' War. When agitation and occasionally riot resulted, defenders of the status quo developed a reactionary frame of mind as they did to a much greater extent many years later at the time of the French Revolution. The British people had begun to intervene in a modern way, if only for a time, in an arena of politics hitherto reserved almost wholly for monarch, placeman, and aristocrat.

The excitement attending the various efforts of John Wilkes to take his seat in Parliament had echoes and repercussions in the American colonies. The colonials followed his career with interest and sympathy.[20] One American, long after the event, recalled the tremendous impression which the Wilkes affair had made upon him. Reminiscing in 1806, Ezra Sampson of Massachusetts recalled how, at the time of the Stamp Act troubles, he saw a small boy standing near the Liberty Pole. The boy saw him, pulled off his hat, and shouted, "Wilkes and Liberty!"[21] Sampson confessed that he himself had idolized Wilkes until he became convinced from reading David Hume that Wilkes was primarily a demagogue and a precursor of Marat and Robespierre. At one time, however, he had thought

[18] Priestley, J., *An Essay on the First Principles of Government* (2nd ed., London, 1771), p. 13.

[19] Burgh, James, *Political Disquisitions* (London, 1770), 3 vols., II, pp. 269-270.

[20] Ritcheson, C. R., *British Politics and the American Revolution* (Norman, 1954), pp. 114-119.

[21] Sampson, Ezra, *Who Shall Be Governor, Strong or Sullivan? or the Sham-Patriot Unmasked* (n.p., 1806), p. 5.

Wilkes' cause to be the cause of political reform, the right of the people to send whom they chose to represent them in the act of legislation. When, just before 1772, Robert R. Livingston of New York was refused a seat in the colonial assembly of that province over a technicality in the election laws, the cry was "Livingston and Liberty."[22] The South Carolina assembly voted to contribute to Wilkes' defense with a grant of 1,200 pounds.[23] Today his memory is preserved by the combination of his name with that of Colonel Isaac Barré to form the name of the Pennsylvania city of Wilkes-Barre. Georgia still has a Wilkes County.

The activities of the Bill of Rights Society attracted the attention of Americans. They were quite fully covered in as important a newspaper as the *Pennsylvania Gazette*, and in other newspapers as well. While in Britain, Arthur Lee wrote a letter to Samuel Adams in 1771, describing his own efforts to secure the election of reform candidates to the House of Commons and outlining a plan to "unite the cause" of Britain with that of America. Adams, himself an overseas member of the Society, appeared interested in Lee's plan, writing him that he hoped to see the creation in America of similar societies affiliated with the parent organization in London. A London paper saw the logic of such a connection, declaring in 1775 that the Empire could be preserved by repealing all obnoxious colonial laws and by reform in Britain of suffrage and representation. Thomas Hutchinson of Massachusetts Bay also saw the connection, although in a different light, saying that John Wilkes and Samuel Adams were "one and the same thing."[24]

Lastly, the American press began to show that editors and correspondents were assimilating rapidly the reformers' con-

[22] N.Y.H.S., *Livingston Papers*, "Livingston and Liberty."
[23] *Pennsylvania Journal*, Aug. 26, 1769.
[24] N.Y.P.L., *Samuel Adams Papers*, Box 1, June 14, 1771. *Virginia Gazette* (Dixon & Hunter), Dec. 2, 1775; N.Y.P.L., *Bancroft Transcripts*, Hutchinson Correspondence, III, p. 25.

demnation of oligarchical Britain. One writer in *Rivington's Gazette* of New York said in 1774, "North Briton and the Junius Letters are the standard of some mens politicks in this city."[25] As early as 1766, the revival of seventeenth-century political thought in Britain was reflected in the *Connecticut Gazette* when it printed on February 14 an item which identified the phrase, "all men are born equal," as of Saxon origin. On the very eve of the Revolution, the anonymous *Historical Essay* was identified as the model from which Pennsylvania was drawing its first constitution. Attention was given in newspapers also to the works of James Burgh, Granville Sharp, and Richard Price.

Some Americans, overlooking the seamy side of their own electoral practices, tended to moralize when discussing the electoral abuses of the mother country. Algernon Sydney's seventeenth-century attack upon the English government as arbitrary and resting upon bribery was reprinted with relish in Virginia. Henry Laurens of South Carolina wrote his son from London in 1774 that he was shocked by the methods used to carry British elections, how different he found them from those prevailing in the Carolinian parish of St. Philip, and how, in his opinion, only frequent elections held under a secret ballot could cure the dreadful disease. In New York, in 1774, William Livingston penned some remarks upon the British constitution proving to at least his own satisfaction that Britain's future was indeed dark and that corruption and other evils showed that Britons enjoyed no more freedom than the Turks.[26]

While many colonials believed that the decline of Britain's government was due to the corrupting influence of crown, aristocracy, and wealth, there were some who believed that

[25] Dec. 15, 1774.

[26] *Virginia Gazette* (Rind), Sept. 8, 1774; *South Carolina Historical and Genealogical Magazine* (III, Jan. 1902), pp. 141-149; *Livingston Papers*, "Some Thoughts on the British Constitution," 1774; *Pennsylvania Gazette*, March 13, 1776.

the shameful state of British elections was due to the fact that the electorate was willing, even eager, to be corrupted. If this were so, how valid was eighteenth-century radical theory which assumed that the people, on the whole, were the repository of virtue and that the rich, not the poor, were the real source of electoral scandal? What indeed could be done if the root of the evil was the seeking of favors from below? The logical answer might even lead to a stand, in the name of electoral purity, against suffrage reform. There was one American colonial who took this position in 1775 and refused to abandon it during the remainder of his career as a Federalist statesman of Maryland. Samuel Chase, the distinguished opponent of manhood suffrage, wrote his friend James Duane of New York, on February 5, 1775, that when he reflected upon the enormous influence of the crown and other abuses in Britain he could not help but conclude that the venality of the electors was the source of every other evil which oppressed the British people.[27]

Chase's skepticism about suffrage reform and the virtue of the people was probably a minority opinion. Generally speaking, the colonists thought they would escape, as they believed they had in the past, those malevolent influences which had corrupted Britain and which led them to sympathize with British reformers. Although their institutions were not free from criticism, most Americans were convinced that they were basically sound. "Remember," exhorted the *Pennsylvania Gazette* on March 13, 1776, "the corrupt, putrified state of that Nation, and the Virtuous, sound, healthy state of your own young Constitution."[28]

[27] N.Y.H.S., *James Duane Papers*, Samuel Chase to Duane, Feb. 5, 1775.
[28] *Pennsylvania Gazette*, March 13, 1776.

CHAPTER 5

A FAMILY QUARREL

COLONIAL rethinking of suffrage and related matters was stimulated and affected by British suffrage reformers, it is true, but
it was furthered by British government measures designed to
reorganize the machinery of imperial government and finance
along more systematic lines. According to the conventional
interpretation, widely accepted until recently, colonial reaction
to these measures and counter measures between 1765 and
1776 forced not only the issue of independence but also the
issue of independence under more consciously democratic institutions than had hitherto prevailed. Recent scholarship has
shown the many exceptions to this interpretation, how limited
was the number of genuinely internal revolutions, and how
much the Revolution was made in a spirit of conservation or
restoration rather than of innovation. It is clear that inequities
in representation of backcountry areas, upon which the older
school of historians relied for evidence, have been greatly
exaggerated.

With regard to the suffrage, however, the older point of view
is still valid, within limits. The period leading up to the Revolution, as well as the Revolution itself, was the turning point
in the conscious democratization of ideas about the suffrage
and in the actual liberalization of colonial suffrage laws. These
repercussions of the Revolutionary crisis were logical outcomes
of a movement resting upon a philosophy of natural rights.
As a New York newspaper which later became Tory explained, the majority of the people had neither the need nor
the inclination to figure much in public life. There was, however, a latent spark in their breasts capable of being "kindled
into a flame; to do this has always been the employment of the

disaffected. They begin by reminding the people of the elevated rank they hold in the universe, as men; that all men by nature are equal."[1]

The doctrine that all men are created equal was the philosophical basis for the program upon which American democrats embarked at this time and which reached its climax with Jacksonian Democracy. For example, suffrage reformers of the Revolutionary period emphasized the necessity of having representatives guided by whatever instructions the voters should choose to give them; they raised the issue of rotation in office; they discussed the merits of a secret ballot; they advocated publicity for the votes of assembly members; they emphasized the right of the public to listen to the legislative proceedings by encouraging the erection of public galleries in the quarters of the New Hampshire and Massachusetts assemblies; and they sought to secure more equitable representation in some colonies, as in South Carolina and New Hampshire. They were, in short, groping in the direction of the Jacksonian program of vindicating the right of the people to rule.

The elected, not the electors, were henceforth the subject of intimidation and coercion. Political power was changing sides. As a group of Philadelphia men said in 1774, "The people . . . should be consulted in the most particular manner that can be imagined."[2] In the same year, a meeting was held in Virginia expressly, as was explained, to "feel how the pulse of the common people beat."[3] In 1774 the electors of Williamsburg agreed to renounce the prevailing practice of the candidates' treating electors, telling Peyton Randolph that because merit alone entitled a person to the votes of a free people, they would entertain him instead. Certainly there was considerable logic and significance in the fact that a meeting held in New York City to protest the abuses of open voting and to advocate

---

[1] *Rivington's New York Gazette*, Jan. 12, 1775.
[2] *American Archives*, 4th Series, I, p. 442.
[3] *Virginia Gazette*, July 7, 1774.

the secret ballot should have been held under the shadow of the Liberty Pole.[4]

The opponents of British policy realized fully that they faced a condition as well as a theory. First, it was very important to have as large a proportion of the population behind them as possible if they were to succeed in holding the British at arm's length. Second, their slogan, "no taxation without representation," was capable, as has often been remarked, of cutting both ways. It could be used to combat parliamentary taxation, but it also could be the grounds for criticizing any situation in the colonies where so much as one taxpayer was either denied the right to vote or was inadequately represented. Even men who had no quarrel with established institutions gave away the show when they asserted that the essence of the British constitution was that none should be taxed without his consent. It was, therefore, virtually inevitable that colonial reaction to British acts should lead to an effort, largely successful, to make the people a formidable factor in anti-British politics.

British officials and their sympathizers in America saw clearly what was happening. "It is incredible," wrote Thomas Gage on November 8, 1765, "the great pains that have been taken to raise people of all ranks against the Stamp; which many begin to repent of, though too late."[5] Governor Bernard of Massachusetts was equally impressed by what had happened during the Stamp Act troubles. "The popular leaders," he wrote in 1766, "have labored so successfully, that the very principles of the common people are changed, and they now form to themselves pretensions and expectations which had never entered into their heads a year or two ago."[6] One correspondent of Gage wrote in 1775 that, although deference to authority had been carried to an extreme in Massachusetts

[4] N.Y.H.S., *Broadside*, Dec. 28, 1769.
[5] N.Y.P.L., *Bancroft Transcripts*, America, 1765-1766, p. 151.
[6] *Bancroft Transcripts*, America, 1766-1767, p. 268.

during the previous century, the opposite extreme was now apparent by which "all distinction and subordination to government are set at defiance."[7] Taking a more objective and broader view of the situation, Governor William Bull of South Carolina considered the crisis as the outcome of the great religious and civil indulgences that the crown had granted to its colonials to encourage rapid settlement.[8]

There can be no doubt that the machinery of American elections and American propaganda was used with telling effect against Britain. The colonials should have realized that rejection of theories of virtual representation, in relation to the British Parliament, logically required rejection of the same theory in America and consequent support of domestic reform of suffrage and representation. Some such consideration helped to change Benjamin Franklin's mind on suffrage matters. He had at one time deemed it improper to allow any but freeholders to vote. By 1770 he had changed his mind. His papers include a printed item of British origin which advocated a democratic suffrage, among other reforms. Franklin appended to it his own comment that these were "Good Whig Principles." Shortly afterward, he wrote that "the franchise is the common right of freemen."[9]

Another force operating in the same direction, and of the utmost importance, was unleashed by the events at Lexington and Concord. The war of words threatened to become a full-fledged shooting war. If Americans were to take up arms against Britain, it was clear that men were going to be needed to fight in the militia, in other state levies, or in a continental army. Those most affected would be young men in the prime

[7] Quoted from *Boston Gazette*, in *Rivington's New York Gazette*, Jan. 5, 1775.
[8] N.Y.P.L., *Chalmers Collection*, Papers Relating to South Carolina, I, p. 165.
[9] Bigelow, J. (ed.), *The Complete Works of Benjamin Franklin* (New York and London, 1887-1888, 10 vols.), IV, pp. 435-437; Smyth, A. H., *The Writings of Benjamin Franklin* (New York and London, 1905-1907, 10 vols.), IX, p. 342.

of life, either on a voluntary or conscript basis. On their shoulders would rest the greater burden of combat. It so happened that a larger proportion of these men was unable to meet the property or freehold tests than any other age group. As Cromwell's men had demanded the right to vote if they were deemed fit to fight for their country and its liberties, colonials of military age demanded the same right for the same reason. By the end of the Revolution, civilians had long since become bored with the claims of the army men. Elbridge Gerry of Massachusetts complained in 1784, "It is very extraordinary, that the military gentlemen should be so vain as to suppose they have all the merit for effecting a Revolution."[10] War or rumors of war spoke as loudly as words. Together they gave rise to a situation which led Governor Martin of South Carolina to say that, in New York, people saw a "Monster of their own creation, become formidable to themselves, usurping dominion and giving law, instead of submitting to be the instrument of their will and continuing subject to their direction."[11]

The extent and significance of complaints against the suffrage laws do not support any such extreme view of the situation in any colony. Nevertheless, criticism of the suffrage laws was out in the open. Here and there along the seaboard, letters, newspapers, and resolutions of public meetings show the current of public opinion running in the direction of suffrage reform. "A Friend of Liberty" in Pennsylvania asked if those who had come to the province against their wills should be "taxed without their consent, and without being represented."[12] In New Jersey, a correspondent declared that the equivocal attitude of the colony regarding suffrage might even give the British an opportunity to fish in troubled waters. One Jerseyman suggested that all who paid taxes but could not vote

[10] N.Y.P.L., *Samuel Adams Papers*, Box 1781-1785, March 4, 1784.
[11] N.Y.P.L., *Bancroft Transcripts*, America, 1774, II, p. 248.
[12] *Pennsylvania Gazette* (supplement), June 7, 1770.

should, in fairness, either be given the vote or exempted from paying taxes.[13] Others thought that military service was its own reward, and an effort was made to convince the soldiers that their service was a stimulating and rewarding one which civilians regrettably were missing. It was the civilian who "must toil more hours in proportion to the scarcity of labor, pay heavy taxes to support you in the field, endure all that anxiety which the Patriot feels for his suffering country" and had not the "privilege of shining in the HEROIC page."[14]

The hope of military honors, however, was not sufficient reason to go to war if only to maintain the suffrage status quo. A most revealing episode took place at the meeting of the militia of Frederick County, Maryland, on February 26, 1776. Robert Gassaway stepped out of rank and declared "that it was better for the poor people to lay down their arms, and pay the duties and taxes laid upon them by the King and Parliament, than to be brought into slavery, and to be commanded and ordered about as they were." He went on to say, when questioned as to who particularly wished to enslave him, that it was "a parcel of great men" who, not knowing how to save themselves after the Boston Tea Party, ordered all the colonies to "be brought under arms, and say, Now, my brave boys, fight away (clapping his hands to his neck), for fear their necks would be stretched. . . ." A Jerseyman, in a comparable frame of mind, said, "What have we in present state of affairs to induce us to shed our blood?" One Yorker, when nominated by militia men for an officer's post, was criticized because he was not a property owner. He answered that if this were ground for refusing him an officership he hoped it would excuse him also from bearing arms.[15]

[13] *New York Journal*, Sept. 28, 1775; *American Archives*, 4th Series, IV, p. 1498.
[14] *Continental Journal*, Jan. 9, 1777.
[15] *American Archives*, 4th Series, v, p. 1555; New Jersey Archives,

The conviction grew that injustices could be eliminated and the suffrage made more democratic by admitting to the vote either all taxpayers or those who served in the militia or fought in the army, if qualified by age. A Committee of Privates of Philadelphia stated that even those not naturalized, as in the case of some of the Germans, should be allowed to vote if they were to bear arms because "Good Policy, as well as Gratitude suggest the Propriety of granting every Indulgence which can attach them to this country, and animate them in its defense."[16]

Whigs sought to commit the future soldiers to the defense of the American cause by allowing them to elect all or some of their officers. Judging from the record, the lack of popular election of militia officers had been an issue in previous colonial wars. About one hundred years before the Revolution, one John Young of Southold, Long Island, had been heard to say that he was "unsatisfied" because he "had not had his vote in chusing military officers."[17] Some of the colonies, like Massachusetts, had for a time allowed militia men to choose their lesser officers, but had long since rescinded this indulgence. With the approach of the Revolution, the demand for democratic election of militia officers became as important an issue as that of the future electoral privileges of civilians.

The rivalry between Whigs and Tories was quite naturally evident at election time. Complaints that, in times of stress, sheriffs and other election officials made their own election and suffrage laws were again current. Those who supported the American cause, but whose opinions on suffrage were those of Blackstone and Montesquieu, flooded newspapers, assem-

---

Loose Manuscripts, Box 16, Remonstrance of Freemen of Salem . . . (n.d.); N.Y.H.S., *Tryon County Papers*, Abner French to Tryon County Committee, Aug. 23, 1775.

[16] *Pennsylvania Archives*, 8th Series, VIII, p. 7,406.

[17] *New Haven Colonial Records, 1653-1665*, p. 61.

blies, and provincial and local committees with complaints that persons who were not freeholders, or were otherwise unqualified to vote, were appearing at the polls to cast their ballots. In New York, for example, tenants unqualified to vote, as well as a number of under-age males, turned up at the White Plains Court House for the elections of 1775. At a meeting in New York, unqualified voters were said to have been admitted merely "to make a show of numbers."[18] *Rivington's Gazette* criticized this kind of meeting on the grounds that freeholders and freemen, who alone were entitled to vote, were thereby exposed to insult. In Boston, Governor Hutchinson declared in 1770 that "bells [were] set a ringing in the afternoon for a general Meeting of Tom, Dick and Harry." In 1771, he complained that men of "best character & estates" seldom went to town meeting, where they were sure to be outvoted, "all being admitted, and it being very rare that any scrutiny is made into the qualification of the voters."[19]

Unlike previous occasions when complaints of illegal voting were common, the Revolutionary period was a time when opinion on the suffrage was changing quite rapidly under the pressure of new ideas and circumstances. Whig creation of extra-legal machinery of election after the passage of the Intolerable Acts in 1774 was an acknowledgment of this situation. Nothing hitherto had given so great a shock to public opinion, nor heightened anti-British sentiment so much as these evidences of the violence of British reaction to the Boston Tea Party of the previous year. There sprang into existence a system of provincial congresses and, for the colonies as a whole, the first and second Continental Congresses. Although sentiment seemed to favor the election of the members

---

[18] *New York Gazette and Weekly Mercury*, April 17, 1775. Becker, Carl, *A History of Political Parties in the Province of New York, 1760-1776* (Madison, 1909), pp. 180-181.

[19] *Bancroft Transcripts*, Hutchinson Correspondence, II, to Bernard, May 20, 1770; to Lord Hillsborough, II, April 19, 1771; see also II, p. 87.

of the Continental Congress by the various provincial congresses, there were some demands to allow the people to elect the representatives to that body. In 1774, pressure in Pennsylvania and in New York was exerted in this direction. As late as the spring of 1776, conservative Connecticut was supporting Tom Paine's advice in *Common Sense* that qualified voters, district by district, select their representatives to the Congress.[20]

Much greater pressure was exerted in certain colonies to broaden the electorate for the provincial congress elections, with the emphasis upon permitting taxpaying adult males to vote. New Hampshire, having endeavored to preserve the freehold qualification, abandoned it forever on November 10, 1775, when it admitted all taxpayers to the franchise. Georgia took the same step during the same year. At this time, the Continental Congress did not advocate the abandonment of the prevailing qualifications for voting in elections held under its sponsorship. Indeed, the first Congress recommended that the Committees of Inspection be selected by legally qualified voters in the various colonies.

In New York City, suffrage reform was sponsored in part by that successor of the Sons of Liberty, the Committee of Mechanics, an organization in which Alexander McDougall and Isaac Sears were prominent. Under the leadership of Henry Remsen, it was possible to secure in 1774 the abandonment in the city of the freehold and freeman qualifications for voting. It proved more difficult to preserve this reform than it had been to secure it. In the following year, electors to the provincial congress were confined to freeholders, freemen, and tenants of land or tenements worth 80 pounds. For the remaining congresses, all freemen, freeholders, and persons worth 40 shillings were allowed to vote.[21]

[20] Van Der Weyde, W. M., *The Life and Works of Thomas Paine* (New Rochelle, 1925, 10 vols.), ii, pp. 144-145.

[21] Becker, *op.cit.*, pp. 72-192, 252; *New York Gazette and Weekly*

In New Jersey, similar pressure was exerted by residents of a number of counties and townships in favor of a taxpaying or household taxpaying qualification. One proposal to permit all single men with an estate worth 50 pounds failed to secure a sympathetic hearing in the provincial congress of 1775. In 1776, the congress capitulated to reform sentiment by issuing instructions that all inhabitants worth 50 pounds, proclamation money, should be allowed to vote. With these instructions, the congress brought to an end the freehold qualification in New Jersey.[22]

In South Carolina, suffrage grievances were, as far as available records show, non-existent. Christopher Gadsden, a leading figure in anti-British politics in Charleston, and others like him were excoriated during the height of the agitation against the Stamp Act for not supporting demands for reform of representation. "Lo such are the Men who bounce, and make such Noise about Liberty! Liberty! Freedom! Rights! Privileges! and what not, and at the same time keep half their fellow Subjects in a State of Slavery. . . ."[23] William Bull, the royal governor, defended the backcountry settlers against the charges made against them. "They are not," he said, "Vagabonds, the Canaille, the meer Dregs of Mankind, they are mostly tenants of His Majesty, Landholders though poor. They are in general an industrious hardy race of men. . . ."[24] In Charleston, voting at times seems to have been open to any who approached the polls, regardless of whether or not he was

---

Mercury, Aug. 1, 1774, Nov. 6, 1775; *American Archives*, 4th Series, III, pp. 1,305, 1,341, 1,413.

[22] Pole, J. R., "Suffrage Reform and the American Revolution in New Jersey," *Proceedings of the New Jersey Historical Society* (LXXIV, July 1954), pp. 173-194. See also *Minutes of the Provincial Congress and the Committee of Safety of the State of New Jersey* (Trenton, 1879), pp. 231, 365, 373.

[23] Hooker, Richard J. (ed.), *The South Carolina Backcountry on the Eve of the Revolution: the Journal . . . of Charles Woodmason* (Chapel Hill, 1953), p. 262, quoting *South Carolina Gazette*, March 28, 1769.

[24] N.Y.P.L., *Chalmers Collection*, Papers Relating to South Carolina, I, p. 171.

qualified. In 1775, all persons who contributed to the general tax were permitted to vote for the membership of the local committees to enforce the Non-Importation agreement.[25]

In North Carolina, there was some criticism of the freehold qualification but none at the time of the Regulators' movement, save the advocating of a return to the use of ballots in elections. With the development of a revolutionary machinery in the colony, however, demands for suffrage reform grew apace. In 1775, the provincial congress enfranchised settlers on the Granville Tract who had found it impossible to secure title to their lands, but it refused in the same year to entertain proposals to abandon the freehold qualification for voting generally and for officeholding. Nevertheless, the resolutions of Mecklenburg County of May 30, 1775, recommended that authority in each county be given to eighteen "selectmen," to be elected by manhood suffrage.[26]

Like New York City, Philadelphia was an important center of agitation against existing suffrage qualifications. Unlike New Yorkers, however, Philadelphians were unable to secure any relaxation in the provincial suffrage laws, although their city was the center of a vocal mechanic and tradesman movement which sought to exert more power and influence in the political life of city and province. As early as 1770, they had protested that a mechanic had no more opportunity to be elected than "a Jew or a Turk" and that they would no longer tamely submit to a situation in which persons who were not mechanics represented them. If mechanics had represented them, they asserted, the act providing for the easy eviction of tenants would not have been passed. London mechanics were standing up for their rights, they said; why should not those of Philadelphia do the same?[27] In response to these demands, the

[25] *New York Gazette and Weekly Mercury,* April 10, 1775.
[26] Sikes, Enoch W., *The Transition in North Carolina from Colony to Commonwealth* (Baltimore, 1898), p. 50.
[27] *Pennsylvania Gazette,* Sept. 27, 1770.

Patriotic Society was founded in 1772 to advance the interests of mechanics and tradesmen. This organization became the Mechanic Association in 1774.

The press of the city did an excellent job of keeping the public informed of what was happening in suffrage reform in other colonies. On December 28, 1774, the *Pennsylvania Gazette* informed its readers of the liberalization of the rules for electing military officers in Georgia, and of a concession in that colony of a taxpaying qualification for provincial congress elections. Some Philadelphians waited impatiently for change in their own colony. In 1776, the *Pennsylvania Packet* published a letter which declared that if mechanics and farmers, who comprised nine-tenths of the population of the colony, were not to elect their own kind to represent them, it would then be best to acknowledge the jurisdiction of the British Parliament, which was composed entirely of gentlemen.[28]

The association, as such, does not appear to have been identified with demands to lower the voting qualification in the province. Those elements of the population which were allegedly oppressed by the freehold or 50-pound qualification in Philadelphia were the Germans, who were not naturalized, and young, native-born Pennsylvanians who joined the military associations which were formed after the affrays at Lexington and Concord. It is difficult to believe that the non-naturalized had a legitimate grievance in view of the relative ease with which naturalization could be achieved. With regard to the young natives, a difference of opinion as to the legitimacy of their grievance has been expressed. At least one contemporary derided their assertions of the injustice of the personal-property qualification on the grounds that almost everyone possessed 50 pounds property, but others claimed that only one-fifth of the Military Associators over twenty-one years of age could meet such a qualification. Regardless of whether or not there was a deliberate exaggeration of suffrage grievances for

[28] *Pennsylvania Packet*, March 18, 1776.

political purposes, the personal property qualification was contrary to the principles upon which Pennsylvanians took their stand against the British. The failure of the pre-Revolutionary government of the colony to meet this grievance, and others, both real and fancied, contributed greatly to its overthrow in 1776.[29]

While the force of events was bringing the abandonment of the freehold qualification in some of the colonies and questioning of property tests in others, criticism was virtually universal of the undemocratic way in which militia men and military associations were being selected and maintained. Potential soldiers considered themselves in a special category, deserving of privilege. In Pennsylvania and elsewhere, proposals were made to ensure payment for them, to care for their dependents in case of war, and to provide a system of public works upon which they could be engaged until they were needed for specific military purposes.[30] The proposal most widely and frequently made was to place ultimate authority over the inferior and superior officers in the hands of the common soldier. Wherever this issue became important, calculated concessions were made to the spirit of the times, although the Continental Congress delayed a consideration of the problem until July 18, 1775. On that date, it recommended that all able-bodied males between sixteen years of age and sixty be enrolled in the militia and that officers below the rank of field-officer be selected by them. In Suffolk County, New York, some inhabitants wanted to confine the right to vote in provincial congress elections to those who, whether or not they had enrolled in the militia, had sworn to uphold the boycott against Britain.[31]

Partly by accident and partly by design, the anti-British

[29] *Pennsylvania Evening Post*, Oct. 24, 1776.
[30] See, for example, *Pennsylvania Gazette*, Feb. 14, 1776.
[31] *American Archives*, 4th Series II, p. 1776; 4th Series V, p. 275; 4th Series III, pp. 109, 519, 42-43, 397; 4th Series I, pp. 1,022, 1,032, 1,146.

elements found themselves allied with the democratic sentiments of the times. It was natural, therefore, that they should view the advancement of democracy with great favor. The same cannot be said of their opponents, to say nothing of British officialdom here or in Britain. At home, officials were alarmed by colonial reform sentiment and were naturally opposed to the means by which colonial resistance to the mother country had been made effective and widespread. Without publicity, the British government moved to prevent any enlargement of the colonial electorate by an addition to the royal instructions, prohibiting in 1767 any further assent by the governors in royal colonies to any bill to increase or diminish the number of assemblymen or "change the qualifications of electors." Six years later, assent to any law for the naturalization of aliens was likewise forbidden to royal governors.[32] The effect of these efforts to prevent further democratization of the suffrage was not always what the British government had anticipated. In Georgia, for example, the effort of pro-British elements in Savannah to increase their strength by admitting to the franchise those who owned town lots equal in value to a 50-acre freehold and allowing non-freeholders to sit in the assembly, was balked by the governor's conscientious desire to obey the royal instructions. He obeyed them, although he was alarmed by the growing strength in the colony of Anglophobe Yankees who were accused of being "of the Puritan Independent Sect" and still retaining "a strong tincture of republican or Oliverian principle. . . ."[33]

Other royal governors acted as if the extent of popular participation and control over the governments of their colonies was incompatible with the preservation of the British connec-

[32] O'Callaghan, E. B. (ed.), *Documents Relating to the Colonial History of the State of New York* (Albany, 1853-87, 15 vols.), VII, p. 946; *Collections of the New Jersey Historical Society* (Newark, 1858), V, p. 434.

[33] Georgia Archives, *Miscellaneous Colonial Records of Georgia*, Part IIB, XXVIII, 1757-1763, p. 730; *Bancroft Transcripts*, America, I, p. 391.

tion. Acting on the assumption that the system of government was wrong because it was working better for their opponents than for themselves, some royal officials and their American sympathizers decried as undemocratic the methods by which their opponents had endeavored to have their way. Joseph Galloway, the famous Pennsylvania loyalist, when examined before a committee of the House of Commons, declared that the whole congressional system had rested on undemocratic practices. Governor James Wright stated, in 1775, that in one parish in Georgia only 36 persons out of 700 "effective men" had voted to send a delegate to the provincial congress. To his knowledge, he said, the same situation existed in at least one other parish. "And in this way all these things are carried in this province."[34] In Pennsylvania a similar situation was alleged to exist, in which in some counties committees were chosen by a mere handful of voters. "Can you, my countrymen," exclaimed Cato, "acquiesce in such a horrible doctrine?"[35] In New York, *Rivington's Gazette* made much of the distortion of popular government implicit in some of the arbitrary, undemocratic acts of the defenders of American liberty. The Continental Congress, declared the *Gazette* on December 1, 1774, in an address to the people of New Jersey, "have tickled you by increasing the number of your committees, that you may appear to have a greater share in this new government."[36]

Nevertheless, wherever pro-British elements thought they could gain by manipulating the machinery of government to their advantage they did not hesitate to do so. In South Carolina, for example, Governor Bull called the assembly to meet at Beaufort, at some distance from Charleston. By this move he hoped to transfer the government from the scene of the triumphs of those tribunes of the people, Thomas Lynch and

[34] *Miscellaneous Colonial Records of Georgia*, Part I, xxxviii, p. 372.
[35] *American Archives*, 4th Series v, p. 444.
[36] *Rivington's New York Gazette*, Dec. 1, 1774.

Christopher Gadsden, and keep it there permanently.[37] In Massachusetts, Governor Bernard hoped in 1769 to remove the capital to Cambridge "to put the Govt. out of the reach of the Seditious spirit which prevails in Boston."[38] Thomas Hutchinson had another cure for the ills which beset government by town meeting in Boston. He wanted to create a municipal corporation modelled upon that of New York, in which only freeholders and freemen of the corporation could vote for offices made elective under its charter.[39] The anti-Hutchinson element sensed that the cause of more popular forms of government was theirs. The *Boston Gazette* said, on May 9, 1774, that friends of the American cause voted for them because the Hutchinson element agreed fundamentally with what was said "publicly in England," that the people of Massachusetts elect "too many Representatives."[40]

Some true friends of American liberty and independence were concerned almost as much as Thomas Hutchinson that the future might bring an undesirable increase in popular government. A correspondent of Samuel Adams wrote him on May 24, 1776, that it was doubtful if there were enough virtue in Massachusetts or in other colonies to set up and maintain that "Democracy they almost universally desire." He feared that opinion was so averse to monarchy as not to see the dangers of democracy.[41] There was more than one "Spirit of 1776," as Carl Becker demonstrated many years ago.

[37] N.Y.P.L., *Chalmers Collection*, Documents Relating to Maryland, I, p. 42.
[38] *Bancroft Transcripts*, Bernard Correspondence, pp. 194-195.
[39] *Ibid.*, Hutchinson Correspondence, II, p. 188.
[40] *Boston Gazette*, May 9, 1774.
[41] N.Y.P.L., *Samuel Adams Papers*, Box 1775-1776.

CHAPTER 6

AMERICAN WHIGS AND
THE SUFFRAGE

THE exigencies of practical politics, the imminence of war, and the sanctions of revolutionary sentiments did not assure the incorporation of suffrage reform in all of the new constitutions of the Revolutionary era. Suffrage reform was advanced in a clearcut fashion in only six states: Pennsylvania, New Hampshire, Vermont, New Jersey, Georgia, and Maryland. In Massachusetts, suffrage change was in a reactionary direction; in New York and North Carolina, balanced forms of government were instituted, with different qualifications for electors of the upper and lower houses of the legislature. In these three states, a demand for balance in government and a democratic electorate was successful. The remaining states either did not have to face the issue or resisted efforts to raise or lower the old colonial property tests. Obviously, American Whigs were divided on the subject of suffrage reform, some in favor, some against, and many indifferent. Because less than a majority of the states liberalized their voting qualifications, much unfinished business remained for future generations.

The most striking, if not the most democratic, advance was made in Pennsylvania, where in 1776 Whigs, particularly of Philadelphia and the Scotch Irish interior, with the full support of the second Continental Congress overthrew the government of the old charter and wrote the most widely publicized, praised, and condemned of all the constitutions of the Revolution. In view of the not illiberal suffrage law of the colonial period, the plan of representation which only near the time of the Revolution was becoming genuinely inequitable, and the form of government placing great power in a single-chambered legislature, recent historians have questioned the older interpretation that the colony was fundamentally undemocratic and that an internal revolution was long overdue.[1]

Nevertheless, a considerable upheaval did take place, due largely to the failure of the old assembly to take the leadership of the anti-British movement soon enough. Largely for this reason, the Continental Congress, meeting in Philadelphia, turned against the provincial government and encouraged rebellion by those Pennsylvanians who were discontented and who had indicted the old assembly for conservatism, timidity, and lack of enthusiasm for the cause of American liberty. During the summer of 1776, it was forced to give way to the patriotic and democratic pressures exerted by a number of reformers. Led by famous figures—Benjamin Franklin, Thomas Paine, Dr. Thomas Young of Dutchess County, ex-member of the Committees of Correspondence of Massachusetts, and Timothy Matlack, a representative of the mechanic interests—the rebels and democrats of Pennsylvania made astonishing progress in achieving their aims. It was their determination to make Pennsylvania and the other colonies independent of Britain and to reform suffrage and representation in such a way as to guarantee their ascendancy in the politics of the colony. Of the two, representation was the more important. As Paine wrote in *Common Sense*, "both a small number of electors and representatives are dangerous but if the number of representatives be small and unequal the danger and evil are greater."[2]

Defenders of the old proprietary assembly failed to see the injustices in Pennsylvania which reformers decried. They declared their intention of defending all the charter rights of the colony, including the existing suffrage laws. To do otherwise

[1] See Young, *The Treatment of the Loyalists in Pennsylvania*; Thayer, *Pennsylvania Politics and the Growth of Democracy*. The older point of view is best stated by Lincoln, Charles H., in *The Revolutionary Movement in Pennsylvania 1760-1776* (Philadelphia, 1901).

[2] Lincoln, *op.cit.*, p. 243.

93

"would be giving a fatal stab to our liberties. . . ." The subversive activities of the reformers demonstrated "what we are to expect should we suffer men professing such principles to get the direction of our affairs."[3] One conservative claimed that many Military Associators who complained that they could not vote did not have a legitimate grievance on this score because many were apprentices, minors, or men only recently arrived in the province. He declared also that the people of New Jersey were considering following the example which Pennsylvania had set for many years of allowing nonfreeholders to vote. The only people, he said, who were denied the vote in Pennsylvania were the poor and necessitous, those who were easily bribed or coerced. For these reasons, he felt safe in asserting that the real motive for the agitation of the suffrage issue was the desire to make political capital, increase the unpopularity of the existing government, and secure the allegiance of those unenfranchised to the cause of independence and revolution.[4]

While it was true that suffrage reform was something to get in on, it was also something to stand on. More perhaps than those of other colonies, Pennsylvania reformers, organized in the Whig Club of 1775, were children of the British reform movements rooted in the school of natural rights and in the school which advocated a return to the institutions of Anglo-Saxon times. Whatever its antecedents, this school stressed the right of revolution and the compact theory of government. As to specific details, it advocated the unicameral form of legislature, the right of local self-government, and the extension of the suffrage to all adult male taxpayers and to those who contributed to the defense of their country.

Pennsylvania reformers were convinced that their government needed purification in the fires of revolution before they would be able to restore the rights which their ancestors in

[3] *American Archives*, 4th Series v, pp. 1,144-1,146.
[4] *Ibid.*, pp. 1,140-1,143.

England had enjoyed before the Norman Conquest. It was in this light that William Penn's charter was judged and found wanting in some particulars. When the Revolution got under-way and reached its climax with the writing of the constitution of 1776, writers in the Philadelphia press referred to the anony-mous *Historical Essay* on more than one occasion, and to other works in the same vein. They disclaimed any desire to attack property rights or to exclude men of property, if they were of the right spirit, from a share in government, and as-serted that their only aim was an Anglo-Saxon restoration. "Eudoxus," on April 22, 1776, advocated a return to the "*beau-tiful fabric,* first contrived in the *German* woods," and lauded the original English constitution before it had been "mangled and adulterated by the feudal system."[5] "An Elector" declared on May 15, 1776, that to return to scot and lot, that is, a tax-paying franchise, would be merely a reversion to the "Simple Saxon establishment," a goal advocated by at least one other newspaper writer.[6] One reformer advocated abandoning the word "county" as a Norman one and hence a "badge of slavery."[7]

The provincial conference met on June 18, 1776. It moved on the twentieth to permit all Military Associators who had paid a tax, or who had been assessed, to vote in the ensuing elections to create a new machinery of revolutionary govern-ment. Seeking to make political capital of this reform, the conference admonished the military men five days later to support the new state of affairs. "We need not remind you," it said, "that you are now furnished with new motives to animate and support your courage. You are not about to contend against the power of Great Britain in order to displace one set of villains, to make room for another."[8]

The delegates wrote a constitution which showed the wide

[5] *Pennsylvania Packet*, April 22, 1776.
[6] *Pennsylvania Gazette*, May 15, 1776.
[7] *Pennsylvania Packet*, Sept. 17, 1776.
[8] *Ibid.*, July 1, 1776.

variety of influences stemming from the Anglo-Saxon cult and from indigenous institutions and traditions. It established a unicameral legislature, denied both the executive and the judiciary any genuine independent power, and, by so doing, established the supremacy of the legislature. The vote was granted to adult male freemen who were taxpayers. Elections by ballot were promised, and counties were divided into election districts to encourage voting.[9]

Pennsylvania Whigs were sincerely convinced that their constitution was a break with the immediate past and a great step forward in a democratic direction. However, it would seem that they exaggerated the difference between the new constitution and the old. For example, the increase in the size of the legal electorate was probably small, because about half of the freemen in the state were freeholders and a shift from a property to a taxpaying qualification enfranchised only the younger men. The real significance of the suffrage clauses of the new constitution lay in the theory, rather than in the result, of reform.

In assessing the role of the new constitution in the evolution of democracy in Pennsylvania, no one can afford to overlook the fact that it was criticized, and still is, as undemocratic because it over-represented the backcountry, gave the vote to the eldest sons of freeholders, and confined to the freeholders the nomination of two men as justices of the peace, one of whom would then be selected to serve by the executive council.[10] Most open to criticism were the acts of the new government of 1776 and 1778 by which electors were forced to take a test oath, which was so worded as to make virtually impossible any criticism of the new regime. The act of 1778, for example,

[9] Thorpe, F. N., *The Federal and State Constitutions, Colonial Charters, and Other Organic Laws* (Washington, 1908-1909, 7 vols.), v, pp. 3,081-3,082.

[10] The constitution is printed as an appendix in Thayer, *Pennsylvania Politics and the Growth of Democracy, 1740-1776*. The standard reference for all constitutions is Thorpe, F. N., *op.cit.*

required all males over eighteen to take the oath, on pain of disfranchisement and double taxation. The act was defended, however, by Tom Paine and other Whigs as a measure of self-defense in time of war against the enemy within.[11] It was now the turn of the defenders of the new status quo to deprecate illegal voting on the grounds that taxes had not been paid nor the oath subscribed. To the Quakers, and to the Germans as well, the new state of affairs was an unhappy retrogression from the pre-Revolutionary regime. A Quaker memorial of 1781 lamented the loss of that "mildness & liberal temper" of government for which Pennsylvania was once celebrated.[12] Pennsylvania's troubles stemmed in part from the times, for periods of war and revolution hinder as well as favor the development of democratic practices.

With all its faults, however, the Pennsylvania constitution of 1776 became a beacon for like-minded patriots in America. Its clearest influence was upon the government of that product of a revolution within a revolution, the state of Vermont. Rebellion against New York, as distinct from rebellion against the British, resulted from a variety of causes, including dislike of Yorkers, the conservative character of New York Whiggery, and, last but not least, resentment against New York for not having accepted as valid unsettled lands granted under New Hampshire between 1749 and 1764. It so happened that on all these grounds Ethan Allen and his brothers wished to repudiate the New York as well as the British connection. They and their allies were sufficiently astute to ingratiate themselves with the actual settlers who were not necessarily engaged in speculation in New Hampshire titles, in order to gain their support for erecting a state independent of both the British Empire and New York. They sought to create a government

---

[11] *Statutes at Large of Pennsylvania,* IX, pp. 110-114, 303-308.
[12] Department of Public Records, Harrisburg, *Revolutionary Papers,* Memorial from the People called Quakers, Nov. 22, 1781. Participation in elections declined rather than rose with the "growth of Pennsylvania democracy." See Young, *op.cit.,* pp. 380-382.

which would vindicate the old New Hampshire land titles and, in the process, gain for themselves and their posterity a more congenial and democratic polity than that afforded even by the new state of New York.[13]

The Allens were men of many skills, but they were not skilled in making constitutions. However, their friend from the days when they moved about western Connecticut and Dutchess County, New York, Dr. Thomas Young, was in Philadelphia at the time and was therefore able to provide them with a copy of the Pennsylvania constitution. When, in 1777, the time had arrived for the New Hampshire Grants to create a government independent of New York, they seized upon this document so fundamentally congenial to their political tastes, made a few changes where they thought necessary and desirable, and adopted it as their own. The most significant difference between the Pennsylvania and Vermont constitutions was abandonment by the latter of the taxpaying qualification in favor of one giving the vote to all adult males who would take the Freeman's Oath. This suffrage clause established Vermont as the first American state formally to divorce property or taxpaying from the electoral right. Actually, the dropping of the taxpaying qualification was perhaps not exclusively the result of democratic convictions. It must be borne in mind that without a state tax-collecting machinery, a taxpaying qualification would have disfranchised every inhabitant. Moreover, if Vermont were to adopt the New England system of levying poll taxes on males, as it in time did, even a taxpaying qualification would have established universal manhood suffrage, if the voters did not evade the payment of this compulsory tax which was levied on them and non-voters alike.[14] It should be remarked, also, that the Vermont constitution, like

[13] Williamson, C., *Vermont in Quandary* (Montpelier, 1949), pp. 35-67.

[14] Williamson, C., "Suffrage, Property and Democracy in Windham," *Vermont History* (xxv, April 1957), pp. 135-141.

that of Pennsylvania, was open to criticism as being undemocratic. The Freeman's Oath, the religious qualification for holding office, and the clause anticipating the creation of established churches in the towns were scarcely reconcilable with advanced democratic views. Yorkers took considerable pleasure in denouncing the Freeman's Oath as disqualifying all persons who wanted to return the New Hampshire Grants to New York.[15]

For many conservative Whigs, the Pennsylvania constitution was a prophet without honor at home and abroad. Benjamin Rush wrote that his friend, John Minton, had such hatred for it and concern for the evils which it would bring in its train that it brought on "political hypochondriases which put an end to his life" a year or two after the Declaration of Independence.[16] Of all Americans, John Adams could most appreciate John Minton's attitude. In Adams' opinion, the Pennsylvania constitution set a bad example for other colonies because it exemplified his definition of tyranny, a government with all power in the people, and all that power concentrated in the legislature. Adams, more than any other member of his generation, showed a comprehensive understanding of the distinction between a separation of the *power to govern* and a separation of the *powers of government*. By the first, he meant the classical separation of monarchy, aristocracy, and democracy, or mixed or balanced government. By the second, he referred to the separation of powers between an executive, a legislature, and a judiciary. In his opinion, both were the chief bulwarks against attacks on liberty and property from whatever quarter. He treats of these ideas in his *Thoughts on Government*, which he prepared at the suggestion of George Wythe of Virginia in 1776. There was little or nothing in this work

[15] N.Y.H.S., *James Duane Papers*, III, Micah Townshend and Israel Smith to George Clinton, May 27, 1778.
[16] Warner, George W. (ed.), *The Autobiography of Benjamin Rush* (Princeton, 1948), p. 149.

to which a loyalist like Thomas Hutchinson would have taken exception.[17]

Translating these ideas into the American idiom, Adams advocated annual elections and the creation of a bicameral legislature which should represent the "aristocratic" and the "democratic" elements of society. He acknowledged to a friend that there was not any free government "without a democratical branch in the constitution," but he did not advocate universal manhood suffrage for elections for this branch, partly because he was acquainted with something approximating it in Massachusetts, partly because he had been deeply impressed by the Blackstonian argument against it. Although critical of Aristotle's reservations about allowing tradesmen and mechanics to vote in aristocratic societies, because he saw that from them sprang "the most splendid geniuses," he wanted to preserve existing property tests for voting because they represented in his opinion the outer reaches of safety for state and society. He wrote James Sullivan on May 26, 1776, that the moral foundation of government rested upon the consent of the people but that there was a perplexing problem of how far to extend the principle in practice, inasmuch as it would be dangerous to allow those who did not have a will of their own—children and the poor—to vote. He recognized that in Massachusetts the "multitude" possessed estates and that officials had never been "rigid" in scrutinizing the qualifications of voters. For these reasons, he was strenuously opposed to a change in the suffrage qualifications at that time. "Depend upon it, Sir," he wrote, "it is dangerous to open so fruitful a source of controversy, and altercation as would be opened by attempting to alter the qualification; there will be no end of it." He feared that new claims would arise among women, lads less than twenty-one, and "men without a farthing," the result

[17] Adams, C. F. (ed.), *Works*, IV, pp. 193-202. See also Haraszti, Zoltán, *John Adams and the Prophets of Progress* (Cambridge, 1952).

being to destroy all distinctions and "prostrate all ranks to one common level."[18]

Adams was not very sanguine that his fellows would agree with him, recognizing that his ideas were not "popular" enough.[19] At the time he wrote, such would seem to have been the case. Although the leading Whigs in Massachusetts were opposed to allowing the poor and those who were not white to vote in elections under the constitution, they were nevertheless eager that the constitution itself should be ratified by a broader electorate. They allowed all adult male inhabitants to vote in elections for calling constitutional conventions, selecting delegates to them, and approving their handiwork, thus making explicit the conviction that the form of government should rest upon all the people, i.e., adult males. In 1776, all free male inhabitants of Massachusetts, twenty-one years and older, were authorized to vote on the question of whether or not the legislature should write a constitution. Nevertheless, the first draft, when completed in 1777, was very much in keeping with Adams' ideas. It established a balanced form of government, permitting free white males, if taxpayers, to vote for the members of the house of representatives and governor, but only those worth 60 pounds to vote for the members of the senate.[20]

Among the criticisms of this constitution, which was never ratified, were those of the Reverend William Gordon, who aired his objections in the pages of Boston's *Independent Chronicle* in 1778. He complained of the absence of a secret ballot, the failure to provide for rotation in office, the religious tests for officeholders, and the maintenance of a multiple church establishment. The exclusion of Negroes, Indians, and mulattoes, he said, showed the world that the white people

[18] Adams, *Works*, IX, pp. 375-378.
[19] Massachusetts Historical Society, *Collections*, Warren-Adams Letters, LXXII, p. 242.
[20] Taylor, R. J., *Western Massachusetts in the Revolution*, pp. 142-143.

meant "their own rights only, and not those of mankind, in their cry for liberty." Such selfish aims elsewhere, he said, had produced deplorable results. He mentioned specifically the situation in Jamaica, where, in 1733, mulattoes had not lifted a finger to help the whites suppress the great slave rebellion of that year. He criticized also as unjust and unnecessary the violation of the natural rights of men by the clause establishing different property qualifications for voters for the bicameral legislature.[21]

The constitution which finally went into effect in 1780 was not an improvement over the first from a democratic point of view. Its suffrage provision, for example, established a 60-pound property qualification for all state elections. The abandonment of the use of the word "sterling" meant that the stiffening of the property qualification represented only a 17 percent increase, and was probably intended as a means of making the new qualification approximate the old in value. Possibly popular vote was not the determining factor in the ratification of this constitution. Frauds in the official reporting of the returns of the town voters alone made it possible for the government to proclaim the new constitution in force.[22]

As might be expected, the suffrage provisions excited considerable comment. Attacking the constitution from the standpoint of the natural rights school, the town of Stoughton declared: "Ye right of election is not a civil; but it is a natural right, which ought to be considered as a principle cornerstone in ye foundation for ye frame of Government. . . ." Northampton agreed that property should be entitled to protection in the senate, but asserted that the lower house should represent persons, as distinct from property, and should be

---

[21] *Independent Chronicle* (Boston), April 9, 1778. See also *Continental Journal*, June 4, 1778.

[22] Douglass, Elisha, *Rebels and Democrats* (Chapel Hill, 1955), pp. 210-213; Morison, S. E., "The Struggle over the Adoption of the Constitution of Massachusetts, 1780," Massachusetts Historical Society *Proceedings*, L, pp. 353-411.

elected as a matter of right by all ratable male polls, twenty-one years and older; and that, furthermore, the admission to the suffrage of all men who were willing to lay down their lives for their country was a matter of simple justice.[23] This latter criticism was taken seriously elsewhere, as is shown by the violent reaction of Captain Samuel Talbot and Lemuel Gay, officers of the Sixth Company of Militia in the Third Regiment of Suffolk County. They wrote Governor Hancock that they were angered that the document did not permit all taxpayers to vote for governor and for the members of the lower house. No longer, they said, could they encourage their fellow soldiers "who are so poor as to be thus deprived of their fundamental Rights, that they are fighting for their own freedom." The claims that one part of society made upon another, they said, were comparable to those Britain made upon Americans which was the cause for "a deluge of blood." So strongly did these officers feel that they tendered their resignations. Joseph Hawley, leading citizen of Northampton, sympathized with these men. He advocated adult male suffrage.[24] What was patently undemocratic in principle, however, may not have been so in practice. A strong possibility exists that the constitution did not change a situation in which adult male taxpayers were voting in both town and colony elections with the support of opinion at large.

A qualification, relating to town elections, of possibly greater significance than those under the constitution was established by an act of 1782 which built upon a statute of 1735-1736. The earlier statute had allowed persons who had not filed a list of assessments to vote if, in addition to paying the poll tax, they had paid a tax equal to two-thirds of a poll

[23] Clune, M. C. (ed.), "Major James Hawley's Criticism of the Constitution of Massachusetts," *Smith College Studies*, III, no. 1, pp. 18-19.

[24] Massachusetts Historical Society, *John Hancock Papers*, Samuel Talbot and Lemuel Gay to Hancock, Nov. 16, 1780; *Pickering Papers*, V, p. 76; *Smith College Studies*, III, p. 50.

tax. The act of 1782 applied this qualification to all towns regardless of whether or not lists of assessments were available. With all but transients and paupers subject to poll taxes, voting in towns was by law placed upon a quite democratic basis. Probably all legal distinctions between town and colony voter had no more effect than previously, although they could always be invoked and used in a partisan way.[25]

The corpus of ideas which produced the Pennsylvania and the contrasting Massachusetts constitutions forms the framework within which most of the other constitutions can be understood, either as copies or as hybrids. The first constitution of New Jersey, for example, shows its plural origins. It established a bicameral legislature and, in recognition of popular pressures which had already forced the abandonment of the freehold qualification for provincial congress elections, conceded the vote to all inhabitants worth 50 pounds' proclamation money, a qualification which in time gave widows owning this amount of property the justification for voting in Jersey elections. Influenced probably by the struggle for the secret ballot in nearby New York, the election law of 1777 provided for its use in elections in seven New Jersey counties.[26]

Another state to abandon the freehold qualification was Georgia. Impelled by a number of merchants and mechanics resident in Savannah and by a number of Yankees who lived for the most part in St. John Parish and were eager to help their hard-pressed brethren in Massachusetts, Georgia was swept into the Revolution in 1775. The taxpaying qualification for provincial congress elections was abandoned when Georgians wrote a constitution in 1776-1777. They tried, in theory if not in practice, to return to more conservative suffrage principles. The constitution confined the electorate to

[25] Pole, J. R., "Suffrage and Representation in Massachusetts: A Statistical Note," *William and Mary Quarterly* (xiv, Oct. 1957), pp. 560-592.
[26] McCormick, *op.cit.*, pp. 68-73.

10-pound property owners liable to taxes, or to mechanics by trade.

In general, Georgia's efforts to create a satisfactory government reflected strong Pennsylvania influences. One Savannah merchant declared that the constitution of 1777 was "very Democratical & has thrown power into such Hands as must ruin the country, if not timely prevented by some alteration in it." Another Georgian complained that in practice the government was the antithesis of democracy, being controlled by daily meetings at a tavern and by another "nockturnal Society called the Liberty Society." He said, "They bellow Liberty but take every method in their power to deprive the best part of the community of even the Shadow of it." Although criticized for lack of democratic procedures, the structure of Georgia's government had become more democratic with the abandonment of the freehold qualification.[27]

New Hampshire was unwilling to move so rapidly in abandoning the freehold qualification. But the successful attack upon the restrictive town meeting qualification in 1773 was followed by the relinquishment by the provincial congress of the freehold qualification for voting under its authority, and its replacement on November 14, 1775, by a taxpaying qualification.[28] The state had as much trouble as any developing a congenial constitutional framework, not so much because of any significant differences over the suffrage as because of the issues of indirect versus direct election of the legislators, the justice and expediency of property tests for officeholders, and, most important, the plan of representation. The latter would

[27] Thorpe, II, p. 779 (Georgia); Coleman, Kenneth R., *The American Revolution in Georgia* (unpub. Ph.D. thesis, University of Wisconsin, 1952); *The Revolutionary Records of the State of Georgia* (Atlanta, 1908), I, pp. 254-255; Georgia Historical Society, *Manuscripts*, John Wereat to George Walton, August 30, 1777.

[28] Upton, R. F., *Revolutionary New Hampshire* (Hanover, 1936); *New Hampshire State Papers*, VII, p. 657; Turner, Lynn W., *William Plumer, Statesman of New Hampshire, 1780-1820* (unpub. Ph.D. thesis, Harvard University, 1944).

determine where in the state would lie the balance of sectional power. Fourteen different sessions of conventions were necessary before any degree of success was attained.[29]

Nevertheless, suffrage matters also were of some concern in New Hampshire as an examination of the various constitutional drafts indicates. The draft of 1779 perpetuated the taxpaying qualification of the revision of 1775. It was criticized in the press as making possible the outvoting of property owners by those with no property, so that a number of transients, some Scotch, some Irish, and "even French peddlers" would be able to vote away the assets of the well-to-do.[30] The proposed constitution of 1781 met this criticism by confining the election of senators to those who were freeholders or who owned 100 pounds of property, and by creating an indirect system of election by taxpayers for the members of the lower house. This effort to create a better balance in the legislature for the protection of the well-to-do against the marginal power of the poor produced in turn a reaction in favor of a more democratically oriented constitution. Reflecting this influence, the draft of 1782 permitted all poll taxpayers to vote, if they were otherwise qualified. Subsequent constitutional change did not reopen the suffrage issue, which, like most of the other issues, did not greatly interest the New Hampshire voter. During 1785, a "Sailor" wrote the *New Hampshire Mercury* that he was pleased to see the "worthy lower-class of people" participate in town meeting.[31] Generally, however, the people of the state were apathetic and what interest there was in constitution making lay elsewhere than in the suffrage.

Critics of the various drafts of the New Hampshire constitution were concentrated in the Connecticut Valley. They considered themselves under-represented, although all the drafts would have permitted small towns to combine forces to

[29] Turner, *op.cit.*, p. 139.
[30] *New Hampshire Gazette*, Aug. 17, 1779.
[31] *New Hampshire Mercury*, March 15, 1785.

send a representative to the legislature. Quite understandably, the seaboard was reluctant to increase the power of the western sections of the state as well as to create an overly large and unwieldy legislative body. Here as elsewhere, critics, overlooking the religious qualification for officeholders, deprecated the property tests required of them. To this criticism, Meseach Weare, a leading statesman, replied that common safety required that all persons entrusted with the disposal of property should have some property themselves.[32] The instability of New Hampshire politics and the secessionist movement in the Connecticut Valley during 1778, and again in 1781, did not involve the suffrage issue, but was caused by sectional jealousies, the desire to avoid paying taxes, and to share some of the fruits of the truce with the British which Vermonters enjoyed at this time.[33]

The New York constitution of 1777 was the result of the control of the Revolution in that state by conservative Whigs. Although there were demands in the press for more democracy in New York's institutions, including suffrage, the convention chose by and large to ignore them. Typical of convention opinion, which was decisive, was that of Robert R. Livingston, who said in 1799 that he still favored not only the bicameral principle but also a balanced form of government. He approved of this form, he said, because it recognized different orders in society "as necessary to a steady government."[34]

New York's constitution established a dual qualification for voting, intended to assure a balanced government. The election of the senators and the governor was confined to those who owned 100-pound freeholds. The assembly was to be elected by those who owned 20-pound freeholds or were 40-

[32] New Hampshire Historical Society, *Meseach Weare Papers*, XII, p. 107.
[33] Williamson, C., *Vermont in Quandary*, pp. 79-82, 100-101, 111-113.
[34] *Bancroft Transcripts*, R. R. Livingston Papers, 1777-1799, to General Jonathan Armstrong, Jan. 2, 1799.

shilling tenants at will or for years.[35] The suffrage clauses cut in half the freehold qualification for the lower branch of the legislature and enfranchised tenants where, as in Westchester County, they had not hitherto been permitted to vote. Under the proddings of John Jay, the convention agreed to require the use of the secret ballot in state elections after the Revolution.[36] The most backward suffrage provision of the constitution denied the vote in the future to men made free of the corporations of Albany and New York.

The state in which considerable public pressure was exerted for suffrage reform and which was able with considerable success to fight it off was Maryland. The origin of this situation lay partly in the involvement of all freemen in the signing of the Continental Association and other exciting political activities before the outbreak of the Revolution. Here also, young men liable to bear arms felt with especial keenness the fact that under the provincial statutes many of them were unenfranchised. This situation led to a considerable crisis in the late spring and summer of 1776 over demands to lower the voting qualifications for the convention elections in order to include all adult male taxables who bore arms.

Proposals made by the inhabitants of Ann Arundel County in July 1776 show what some reformers had in mind.[37] They envisaged a bicameral legislature elected by "the people," annual elections, a thoroughly elective local government, and the democratic selection of militia officers. When elections were held in August for delegates to the constitutional convention, the depositions taken afterward show that the crisis in Ann Arundel County rose to a head. A group of men who were drilling on the outskirts of Annapolis agreed to go to the polls in small groups on the understanding that everyone who

[35] Thorpe, op.cit., v, pp. 2,623-2,638.
[36] Bernheim, A. C., "The Ballot in New York," Political Science Quarterly (IV, March 1889), pp. 130-152; Journal of the Provincial Congress (Albany, 1842), I, p. 867.
[37] Maryland Gazette, July 18, 1776.

bore arms should be allowed to vote, although they were aware that the "whole company was not worth 40 pounds sterling." When their qualifications for voting were challenged, they left in anger and some of their leaders were heard to say, according to one deposition, that the men should lay down their arms.[38] Similar trouble involving illegal voting and protests against the suffrage laws arose in Frederick County, in Prince George's County, and in Kent County.[39] Part of the trouble came from fear of men under arms and the influence they might have in elections under the orders of their officers.[40] "Watchman" in the *Maryland Gazette* claimed that one-half of the freemen could not meet the voting qualifications and were denied the "inherent right" to vote, despite the fact that they had as much to defend as the rich.[41]

After the convention began, a group of freemen of Ann Arundel County drafted a letter to their representatives, Charles Carroll, Samuel Chase, and F. B. Worthington, instructing them to secure the vote for all native-born freemen, "if well-affected" and resident in the colony one year, and for all foreign-born residents worth 30 pounds currency visible estate or the owners of 50-acre freeholds. These and other demands their representatives found totally unacceptable. The three men, declaring that the instructions were incompatible with "good government" and the "public peace," resigned their seats. In a new election held in the following September, only Chase was returned.

The answer of the drafters of the first Maryland constitution to the adverse criticism of their contemporaries was to insert into the Maryland Declaration of Rights the Blackstonian

[38] Maryland Archives, *Calendar of Maryland State Papers*, The Red Books, pp. 80, 84.

[39] Crowl, Philip A., *Maryland During and After the Revolution* (Baltimore, 1943), pp. 29-30; *Proceedings of the Conventions of the Province of Maryland* (Baltimore, 1836), pp. 211, 215, 217-218.

[40] See *American Archives*, 4th Series, v, p. 1,021.

[41] *Maryland Gazette*, August 15, 1776.

statement that "every man having property in, a common interest with, and an attachment to the community ought to have a right of suffrage."[42] Actually, the suggestion of the Ann Arundel County dissidents that none of the foreign-born should vote except those who owned a freehold of 50 acres or were worth 30 pounds visible estate became the basis for the electoral qualification for state elections for the lower house and for other elections, direct and indirect, which were established under the constitution. The prejudice of reformers had been directed against the foreigners while men like Samuel Chase extended their prejudices to all the poor, whether foreign- or native-born.

Willing to go much further in the way of suffrage reform than Marylanders were those who framed the North Carolina document. The result of their deliberations was the establishment of a form of balanced government as notable in its own way as New York's. So far as can be determined, there was little demand among North Carolinians for thoroughgoing suffrage reform. Inhabitants of Orange County, in the interior, supported a plan to allow householders to vote for the lower house, and freeholders for the senate. Conservatives, such as Thomas Jones, were unwilling, however, to abandon a freehold qualification. Undoubtedly because balanced forms of government had their own checks against undue democratic power, the people of North Carolina could accept with equanimity the compromise finally adopted—a taxpaying qualification for the lower house and a 50-acre freehold for the upper house and for the election of the governor. Efforts made during the Revolution to make electoral qualifications and procedures more democratic failed of passage. A bill to require the use of the secret ballot in elections was rejected on

[42] *Ibid.*, Aug. 22, 1776. See also Delaplaine, Edward S., *The Life of Thomas Johnson* (New York, 1927) as well as Thorpe, *op.cit.*, III, pp. 1,686-1,701.

May 4, 1777, as was a bill to allow all householders in certain counties to vote on December 13, 1777.[43]

With a much stiffer qualification for officeholding, South Carolina did not feel the need to draw a distinction between the voters for the upper and lower houses of the legislature. The constitution of 1778 allowed all free white males owning 50 acres or having paid a tax equal to a tax on 50 acres to vote. This qualification was about as liberal as that established earlier by the act of 1721, which had been the legal basis of the suffrage until the Revolution.[44]

The effect of suffrage change upon the size of the electorate during and after the Revolution perhaps will never be determined. Nevertheless, estimates have been or can be made of the percentages of potential or actual voters in some of the states. In Pennsylvania, where a taxpaying qualification was effected in 1776, taxables comprised about 90 percent of the adult males. Possibly, the electorate outside Philadelphia was increased anywhere from 10 to 40 percent by the abandonment of the freehold test, depending upon conditions in the counties, if one totally ignores the effect of other forms of proscription which the Whigs substituted for the old ones. In New York, on the other hand, possibly 65 to 70 percent of all adult males could vote about 1790 for assemblymen, a figure representing little if any increase, while only about 33 percent of all electors could vote for senators and governor. While it was a step forward to increase the number of elective offices in New York, the qualifications for these new offices were the highest in the history of New York.

The Revolution probably operated to increase the size of that majority of adult males which had, generally speaking, been able to meet the old property and freehold tests before

---

[43] Ketcham, E. J., "The Sources of the North Carolina Constitution of 1776," *North Carolina Historical Review* (vi, July 1929), pp. 215-236; *North Carolina Colonial Records*, x, p. 870, and xii, pp. 68-69, 196-197.

[44] Thorpe, *op.cit.*, vi, pp. 3,248-3,257.

1776.[45] Of course, this analysis ignores the role of any but the property element in the suffrage clauses of the state constitutions. The increase in the number of voters was probably not so significant as the fact that the Revolution had made explicit the basic idea that voting had little or nothing to do with real property and that this idea should be reflected accurately in the law. Minorities in America with democratic ideas had already shown a tendency to become majorities, in time. For this reason, if for no other, the future of suffrage reform looked bright.

The remaining states, Connecticut, Rhode Island, Virginia, and Delaware, did not at this time change the suffrage qualifications which they had inherited from colonial times. Rhode Island, for example, continued to exist under its royal charter, with a few changes, until the Dorr War forced the writing of a constitution as the fundamental law of the state. Neither the background nor the events of the American Revolution involved the issue of a more democratic suffrage for Rhode Island, perhaps because of the disillusionment of the colony with the corrupt, popular elections of colonial times. A group in Newport had actually considered trying to make Rhode Island a royal colony in order to curb its licentious ways.[46] Delaware similarly remained untouched by the democratic forces which surrounded it on all sides. The Revolutionary constitution merely stated that the suffrage should "remain as at present," thus perpetuating the old freehold and personal property qualification.[47]

[45] See Pole, J. R., *The Reform of Suffrage and Representation in New Jersey, 1744-1844* (unpub. Ph.D. thesis, Princeton University, 1953), p. 125; Luetscher, G. D., *Early Political Machinery in the United States* (Philadelphia, 1903), p. 18. For Pennsylvania taxables, see Coxe, Tench, *A View of the United States* (Philadelphia, 1794), p. 413. See also Luetscher, *op.cit.*, p. 12.

[46] *Bancroft Transcripts*, Colden II, pp. 132-133; Bridenbaugh, Carl, *Peter Harrison: First American Architect* (Chapel Hill, 1949), p. 125.

[47] Thorpe, *op.cit.*, I, pp. 563-565.

The state of Connecticut did not lower the property qualification for voting or otherwise change the nature of the government under which it had existed for over a hundred years.
The Committee of Inspection of Hartford County declared in
1775 that the people were happy with their government. About
a year later, a Friend of Liberty exhorted his countrymen,
"Let us be firm and steady and not join with those who are
given to change."[48] Among those given to change, however,
there were a number who claimed Connecticut as their home.
Silas Deane wanted every freeman to be given the vote. A
militia man addressed the General Court on October 14, 1776,
saying that most of the 140 men recently sent to New York
to defend American liberty were of little property, while those
who stayed at home were "all men of interest, and pray what
have they done to defend it?"[49]

Connecticut had already moved to conciliate militia men by
exempting them from paying the poll tax. It refused, however,
to entertain a bill introduced into the assembly in June of
1779 which proposed enfranchising steady inhabitants, twenty-
one years of age and over, who paid taxes, on the grounds
that the existing freeman qualification kept many worthy inhabitants from voting. The bill was briefly debated and left
over for the next year, when it was forgotten, either by accident or by design.[50]

Virginia reformed neither its plan of representation nor its
colonial suffrage laws, although both were just being recognized as grievances in the colony and outside. Samuel Ward of
Rhode Island twitted a Virginia delegate at the first Continental Congress for advocating representation by population
in that body while he came from a state in which representation was far from equitable. There were adherents in Virginia

[48] *Connecticut Courant*, April 1776.   [49] *Ibid.*, Oct. 14, 1776.
[50] Connecticut State Library, Archives, *Miscellaneous*, Series I, III,
p. 314. For a full treatment of the background of the Revolution, see
Zeichner, Oscar, *Connecticut's Years of Controversy*.

of the Anglo-Saxon school of political thought, however, as is shown by a copious quotation from the *Pennsylvania Ledger* which appeared in the *Virginia Gazette* on May 25, 1776. A rebuttal followed on June 8 and June 15, derived from Montesquieu and attacking the pure democratic form of government. No advocate of this form of government, Patrick Henry expressed approval of John Adams' *Thoughts on Government* instead. Jefferson, an adherent of the Anglo-Saxon school, drafted at this time various sketches for a constitution, all of which abandoned the freehold as the only qualification for voting.[51] George Mason wanted to enfranchise all householders with families and holders of non-freehold kinds of leases with 7 years to run, but to exclude from officeholding all whose freeholds were not worth a considerable amount.[52]

Unwilling to tamper with the old qualification, Virginians voted that it should remain "as at present" and that, at all events, the right to vote belonged only to those who had a common interest in and a permanent attachment to the community. Edmund Randolph was probably correct when he stated that confining the suffrage to the freeholders was understandable after one hundred years or more of the practice. "It was not recollected," he said, "that a hint was uttered in contravention of this principle. There can be no doubt that, if it had been, it would have perished under discussion."[53] Long after the war, a correspondent who had fought in it commented in a letter to the *Richmond Enquirer* upon the passivity of Virginia troops when, in 1781, they witnessed without interest, or desire to participate, an election in which they were not qualified to vote.[54]

[51] Boyd, Julian P. (ed.), *The Papers of Thomas Jefferson* (Princeton, 1950), I, pp. 341-358; Malone, Dumas, *Jefferson, the Virginian* (Boston, 1948), pp. 238, 341, 348, 358.

[52] Boyd, Julian P. (ed.), *The Papers of Thomas Jefferson*, I, p. 366.

[53] Rowland, Kate M., *The Life of George Mason* (New York, 1892, 2 vols.), I, p. 260.

[54] *Richmond Enquirer*, April 28, 1829.

Although suffrage distinctions based upon property were the center of discussion in the various states, other bases for discrimination figured in the constitution making of the times. Prejudice against the vote for the foreign-born, if not naturalized, was clearly present, as the use of the word "citizen" in the constitutions shows. If the word "freeman" is taken as a synonym, Pennsylvania and Maryland were unusual in confining the vote to him. All the states, save New Jersey, confined the vote to persons over twenty-one, and to males. Residency (or inhabitancy) was specifically required by only four constitutions or statutes in force at the end of the Revolution. Georgia, South Carolina, and Virginia continued to deny the vote to Negroes. All the states, as a war measure, either specifically disfranchised or required oaths of Loyalists in a way recalling the loyalty oaths imposed by Parliament during the English Civil War. One step forward was the abolition of religious tests for voting which discriminated against non-Christians. The last religious test for voting was that of South Carolina requiring that voters acknowledge the existence of God.[55]

It is evident that much remained to be done before the electoral institutions and suffrage qualifications of the states could be said to be thoroughly democratic. Equally undemocratic were property tests for officeholding, the failure to make elective all or most institutions of local government, particularly in the south, and the perpetuation in most New England states of established churches. The apportionment of seats in the legislatures of some of the states was undemocratic, and becoming more so, because of understandable failure to foresee the extent to which great changes in distribution of population would render it inequitable.

Nonetheless, the changes in suffrage made during the Revo-

[55] These statements rest upon a collation of relevant clauses drawn from Thorpe, *op.cit.*

lution were the most important in the entire history of American suffrage reform. In retrospect, it is clear that they committed the country to a democratic suffrage. Those opposed to this commitment fought a series of delaying actions almost down to the Civil War, all of which failed.

THE REVOLUTIONARY AFTERMATH

ALTHOUGH the Continental Congress abetted the revolutionary and democratic movement which resulted in the Pennsylvania upheaval, it never again played a positive role in the history of American suffrage reform. On the contrary, its role in terms of democratic suffrage theory was negative, even retrogressive. This is evidenced by the efforts it made to create a new colonial system to solve the problem of admitting portions of the national domain to statehood after 1781.

Thomas Jefferson, who prepared a draft of the Northwest Ordinance of 1784, envisaged a more democratic form of government for the territories than the congressional committee was willing to accept. He proposed to create a legislature very early in the territorial stage and an electorate consisting of all adult males without reference to property or even to taxpaying.[1] The committee refused to accept the Jefferson draft and, among other changes, incorporated a 50-acre freehold qualification for voters, to become effective at the time designated for erecting a legislature.[2] Although this ordinance was repealed in 1787, the celebrated Northwest Ordinance of that year also incorporated the 50-acre freehold qualification.

This was a stiffer qualification than existed anywhere along the seaboard, with the exception of the North Carolina 50-acre freehold qualification for voting for members of the state senate. It was similar to that in the provinces of Upper and Lower Canada into which the old Province of Quebec had been divided under powers granted by the Constitutional Act

[1] Ford, P. L. (ed.), *The Works of Thomas Jefferson* (New York, 1904-1905, 12 vols.), IV, pp. 274-281.
[2] *Journals of the Continental Congress, 1774-1789* (Washington, D.C., 1904-1937, 34 vols.), XXXI, p. 671; XXXII, pp. 317, 334, 337-338.

of 1791. Many important provisions of this act showed how much the British government believed that democratic sentiment and unbalanced government had been important factors in causing the American Revolution.[3] Despite great differences of opinion on many matters, the British Parliament and the Continental Congress were in tacit agreement on the wisdom of a freehold qualification. "Cato" in the *New York Packet* expressed the democratic view when he denounced the Northwest Ordinance of 1787, declaring that the governments erected under it would be arbitrary and despotic, controlled by Congress and not "by magistrates elected from out of and by the people."[4]

The Congress was not responsible, however, for the acts passed by the states during the Revolution which specifically disfranchised loyalists or other persons who, for any reason, refused to take the loyalty oaths. As late as 1784, New York passed an act which denied the vote to those who had left the state or served the enemy, an act repealed in 1786.[5] New Jersey pressed the attack until 1788. Loyalists and others considered this legislation a prime example of their contention that the patriots were not democratic unless it was in their interest to be so. They overlooked the fact that proscription of loyalists and others suspected of loyalism, or even indifference, was a normal accompaniment of war and revolution. A Delaware captain of militia expressed the sentiment of many when he told the sheriff of Lewes County that, if the latter did not tender the state oath to all Tories, he would "make Lewes Town Too Hot for every Tory in it."[6]

[3] Manning, Helen Taft, *British Colonial Government after the American Revolution, 1782-1820* (New Haven, 1933), pp. 327-338.

[4] *New York Packet*, Nov. 24, 1786.

[5] Spaulding, E. Wilder, *New York in the Critical Period, 1783-1789* (New York, 1932), pp. 124, 130. The subject is treated generally in Flick, A. C., *The Loyalists of the American Revolution* (New York, 1902).

[6] Ryden (ed.), *Letters to and from Caesar Rodney*, pp. 238-239.

Particularly stringent were the loyalty oaths passed by South Carolina in 1777 and 1779. When the war was carried into the south, many Carolinians sought the protection of the British, some bearing the names of Pinckney, Lowndes, Middleton, and Rawlins. In 1782, the assembly tried to solve the embarrassing problem of how to deal with these men by an act permitting all who had accepted British protection to vote in assembly elections if they would seek pardon within thirty days and serve six months in the militia. If the last were not possible, they might offer substitutes to serve in their places. All those, however, who had borne arms or furnished substitutes on or before September 27, 1782, would be permitted to vote without further question.

Almost immediately, critics asserted that these complicated arrangements were made for the purpose of assisting those who had accepted the protection of the British and lived near the seat of government to qualify easily and thus control the state. Upcountry folk, it was said, who had compromised themselves would find it difficult to meet the terms of the act and become legal voters. In 1782, "Cassius," possibly Aedanus Burke, the well-known North Carolinian statesman, wrote a vitriolic critique of the legislation as contrary to the suffrage provisions of the constitution of 1778. He said that the right to vote was an inherent right for which men had fought against the British for many years. The real reason for the act, he said, was to throw the state government into the hands of a few leading families who were united in the belief that the people were incapable of governing themselves. "Does not this let the Cat out of the bag," queried Cassius, "and account for some late proceedings?"[7]

Partisan advantage as well as patriotic objectives were

---

[7] *Statutes at Large of South Carolina* (Columbia, 1838), IV, pp. 510-511; Singer, Charles G., *South Carolina in the Confederation* (Philadelphia, 1941), pp. 107, 107n; Cassius (pseud.), *Rights of Suffrage* (Philadelphia, 1783).

charged against the Pennsylvania Whigs for their efforts to enforce a harsh system of loyalty oaths, so harsh indeed as to be incompatible with their professed regard for democratic practices. By the act of 1777, non-jurors (those who had not taken the oath) were disarmed, disfranchised, and deprived of many legal rights. The act of 1778 withdrew many penalties of the earlier legislation, but subjected non-jurors to double taxation and required that, in the future, jurors must swear that they had never done anything to help the British. Probably 56,000 persons took the oath, with perhaps 9,000 to 17,000 refusing.[8] Reasons for not taking the oath were often understandable but not always creditable. One German refused, he said, because when he was naturalized he had taken an oath of allegiance to George III and was afraid he might be deemed guilty of perjury; "moreover it is very uncertain upon which side the victory will fall therefore I can't do it for the present time." For this and other "indiscreet utterances," the man was jailed.[9] Others attacked the oath on the high ground that it was "Tiranical" and "intended for naught, but to hinder substantial good disposed People to illicit and be illicted, depriving them of the Rights of Freemen."[10]

The confusion and turmoil of wartime and the outright contempt of many Pennsylvanians for the government account for the apathy of voters in wartime elections. The opponents of the oath, who were, generally speaking, opponents of the constitution, doubtless exaggerated when they said that it disfranchised one-half of the adult males. Nevertheless, Pennsylvania Whigs found themselves in the unenviable position of upholding restraints upon the right to vote which made Pennsylvania suffrage less democratic than it had been before the Revolution, although property tests had been abandoned.

[8] Young, *Treatment of the Loyalists in Pennsylvania*, p. 284.
[9] Department of Public Records, Harrisburg, *Revolutionary Papers*, June 16, July 24, 1777, p. 74.
[10] *Ibid.*, John Hubley to President Wharton, July 1777, p. 66.

Despite the undemocratic features of many of the loyalty oaths, there was an advance in democratic practices of voting and suffrage in most of the states during this period. In several instances, the advance was the unforeseen result of depreciation of state paper money issues. Depreciation of paper money must have disconcerted conscientious election officials who wanted to enforce suffrage requirements when they were expressed in terms of market value and not in terms of tax-book assessments, or of real property expressed in terms of acreage. The issues of the "critical period" often had the same effect. While the paper money of South Carolina, Pennsylvania, and New York did not depreciate in the manner so often ascribed to that of, say, Rhode Island, the paper money of Georgia, Maryland, and New Jersey did.[11] Where the suffrage qualification was expressed in terms of local currency, a decline in its value would lower, perhaps even sweep away, the property test. Paper money depreciation nullified the 10-pound qualification in Georgia, the 30-pound qualification in Maryland, and the 50-pound qualification in New Jersey. By 1798, one Jerseyman was saying that the qualification was not enforced "from a conviction of its repugnance to the principles of republicanism, and from the impracticability of its observance."[12]

The general drift toward more popular government was the result also of deliberate planning in some of the states. During this period, New York honored its constitutional obligation to institute the secret ballot by authorizing its use in most of the elections of state officials in 1788. In the same year, it established the township as the basis for elections, thus making the polls more accessible to all voters and alleviating a grievance which had caused inhabitants of a portion of Rensselaerwyck to complain as late as 1780 that, being situated forty miles from the place of voting in Greenbush, they found it impossible to

[11] Jensen, Merrill, *The New Nation* (New York, 1950), pp. 302, 312.
[12] *The Federalist: The New Jersey Gazette*, Dec. 24, 1798.

121

"enjoy those Liberties and priviledges which as free people they were entitled to enjoy."[13]

New Jersey moved along similar lines in response to complaints over the abandonment of the secret ballot in 1782, an action taken to intimidate the Tory vote. Its restoration in 1783, however, affected only those counties where the ballot had been authorized by an earlier election law. There were demands for a wider use of the ballot in subsequent years. A petition from Cumberland County of 1786 stated that public voting made it possible for "men of large estates or who have many debtors" to "influence a great many Voters in an undue manner contrary to the spirit of the Constitution."[14] As in New York, there was a demand for more accessible polling places. Monmouth County freeholders requested in 1787 that the county poll be moved from township to township because "we are well convinced that the Voters of the Different Townships have not an Opportunity of giving their Votes on account of living so far from the place of Election. . . ."[15] Hunterdon County voters proposed that New Jersey follow the custom of "a sister state" by holding one-day elections in each township as the present mode was "burthensome, expensive and wasteful of time and money."[16]

Responding to criticism of its electoral procedures, New Jersey enacted legislation in 1788 which increased the number of counties employing the ballot and provided for the moving of the poll from place to place within each county. This practice itself was so abused during the first congressional elections that Madison referred critically to the "singular manner" in which they were conducted.[17] The bringing of the poll closer

[13] N.Y.S.L., *Legislative Papers*, Petition of East District of Rensselaerwyck, Jan. 14, 1780.

[14] New Jersey State Library, *Manuscripts*, AM 1,135.

[15] *Ibid.*, AM 1,132.   [16] *Ibid.*, AM 1,134.

[17] McCormick, R. P., *Experiment in Independence* (New Brunswick, 1950), pp. 297-298; Pole, J. R., *The Reform of Suffrage and Representation in New Jersey, 1774-1844*, pp. 98-106.

to the voters was, possibly, as important an event as the prior abandonment of the freehold qualification for voting.

Popular control over government was increased in other ways during this period, at the level of local as well as state government. The logic of the Revolution favored not only an increase in the scope of representative government at the local level but the development of a more democratic suffrage as well. When the city of Charleston, South Carolina, was incorporated in 1783, the vote in municipal elections was extended to all persons who were resident freeholders for one year, or who were free white citizens who had paid a tax of 3 shillings, sterling, the preceding year.[18] Similarly, Savannah allowed all proprietors of houses or lots to vote in 1789. Richmond, when incorporated in 1782, allowed all freeholders to vote in state elections and 100-pound property owners to vote in local elections, thus opening the way for non-freeholders to vote.[19] Connecticut moved in 1784 to incorporate New Haven and Hartford (the latter favored incorporation to get better roads, lighting, and the like) and at that time non-freeholders in those towns were permitted to vote.[20] About 56 percent of the adult males of New Haven could meet the requirement that the voter be either the owner of a freehold which would rent for 2 pounds a year or the possessor of a 40-pound personal estate.[21]

As towns grew and became less homogeneous, the inhabitants of the rural areas often desired to be set off from the commercial sections as separate towns. The people living in the northern part of Stonington, Connecticut, for example, petitioned that the town be divided in such a way that they would

[18] *Statutes at Large of South Carolina* (Columbia, 1840), vii, pp. 97-101.

[19] Hening, *op.cit.*, xi, p. 45.

[20] Connecticut Archives, 1st Series, *Towns and Lands*, x, pp. 10-18.

[21] Library of Congress, *Force Transcripts*, Ezra Stiles Diary, iii, pp. 58-65; Osterweis, O., *Three Centuries of New Haven, 1638-1938* (New Haven, 1953), pp. 164-165.

not have to travel twelve or thirteen miles to vote, or concern themselves with the problems of those engaged in the commercial activities of the little port.[22]

New York followed the trend to lower qualifications for voting in local elections. In 1787 the legislature passed an act permitting all freeholders, regardless of the value of their freeholds, to vote in elections of New York City officials. In the same year it conceded the franchise in town meetings to male residents who were citizens and either freeholders or 40 shilling leaseholders.[23]

In Pennsylvania, the greatest change was in the form of government for the city of Philadelphia. Hitherto it had rested upon the principle of co-optation but, by the charter of 1789, a balanced form of government was instituted for the city. Under the terms of the charter, all freeholders, if otherwise qualified, could vote for aldermen but only state electors could vote for members of the common council. The English type of close borough government was thus brought to an end.[24] In 1790, New Jersey gave the vote in town elections to taxpayers. In the following year, New Hampshire brought to a successful conclusion the movement for reform of local suffrage, underway since 1770, with an act conceding the vote in town affairs to male residents who had paid their poll tax.[25] With few exceptions, the state legislators confined officeholding to freeholders in an effort to maintain high standards of administration.

The creation of the federal government by the Constitution of 1787 made the suffrage a nationwide concern. No tyroes in either political theory or practical politics, the fathers had the

[22] Connecticut Archives, 2nd Series, *Towns and Lands*, III, pp. 134-137.

[23] *Laws of the State of New York* (Albany, 1886), II, pp. 431-433, 384.

[24] Tinkcom, H. M., *The Republicans and Federalists in Pennsylvania, 1790-1801* (Harrisburg, 1950), pp. 48-49.

[25] Pole, *op.cit.*, p. 120; *The Laws of New Hampshire* (Portsmouth, 1797), p. 179.

good sense, even on second thought, not to tamper with the existing suffrage regulations of the states. They rejected proposals to require a freehold qualification for voting for the members of the House of Representatives for the reason that that body directly represented the American people. At the time, however, a small but often important number of leading political figures were hostile to the wide extent of popular participation in state government. Some opposed a broad suffrage as a matter of principle, others on the grounds that the people had not voted wisely during the postwar period, and still others because Shays' Rebellion of 1786 showed a nasty distemper among the common people. For these reasons, a few political leaders hoped to revive the freehold concept of voting.

The most conspicuous was Charles Carroll of Carrollton, who drafted a plan in 1787 to solve the domestic problems of the times. In his opinion, a uniform plan of government should be established for the states, each to be provided with a bicameral legislature, the upper house of which would be elected indirectly and the lower house by the suffrages of the "yeomanry, middling class, and landholders" having 150 acres of land.[26]

Other members of the Federal Convention felt as keenly as Carroll about the defects of existing state governments. Edmund Randolph's statement that "our chief danger arises from the democratic parts of constitutions" and his belief that none of the states had sufficient checks against democratic government were endorsed by Gouverneur Morris, who made the convention a sounding board for the Blackstonian suffrage dicta. "The time is not distant," he said, "when this Country will abound with mechanics & manufacturers who will receive their bread from their employers."[27] In such circumstances, he

[26] Crowl, Philip A., "Charles Carroll's Plan of Government," *American Historical Review* (XLVI, April 1941), pp. 588-595.
[27] Farrand, Max (ed.), *Records of the Federal Convention of 1787* (New Haven, 1911-1937, 4 vols.), II, pp. 202-203.

asserted, democratic voting qualifications would make the House of Representatives the truly aristocratic branch of the legislature, because the poor would vote at the behest of their masters, the great and the rich. James Madison, having no illusions whatever that any class was inherently the repository of all virtue, sympathized nonetheless with the Morris critique, declaring his conviction that freeholders alone should vote because they would be the bulwark against the demagoguery and venality he saw in boroughs and cities, and against combinations dangerous to liberty and property in future.

Members of the convention rose to attack these principles. Their rejection demonstrates how deep and widespread was loyalty to the democratic suffrage philosophy to which the Revolutionary crisis had first given conscious expression. Oliver Ellsworth made a pointed reference to the Revolutionary slogan of "no taxation without representation." Pierce Butler declared that the right of election was the only security for the rights of the people. Franklin betrayed his artisan background and his devotion to democratic principles in his opposition to the Morris argument. The love of country flourished, he said, where the common people had the vote, and withered, as in England, where they were denied it; the military strength of modern states, in short, might depend upon enlightened ideas about the suffrage.[28]

Arguments of expediency supported those of principle. Franklin declared that the constitution would be much read and attended in Europe and if it should prove partial to the rich it would "not only hurt us in the esteem of the most liberal and enlightened men there, but discourage the common people from removing to this country." Oliver Ellsworth argued that the people would "not readily subscribe" to the document "if it should subject them to be disfranchised," an idea which seemed justified by the fact that Revolutionary changes had

[28] *Ibid.*, ii, pp. 204-205, 208.

almost eliminated the freehold qualification.[29] The committee had considered the possibility of writing a uniform suffrage clause, but James Madison declared that it would be difficult to establish a distinction between state and federal electors, or to write one which would please all the states in view of the considerable diversity already existing.[30]

Other members, agreeing in theory with the correctness of the Morris position, questioned, however, the relevance of a philosophy originating in and suited basically to a European, and particularly British, type of society. One took the position that the great mass of Americans were freeholders, and Charles Pinckney added that they were a "singular" people with more equality and liberty than prevailed elsewhere and that the abundance of land would prevent an increase in the number of poor and discontented. He warned his colleagues against ideas "applicable to a state full of people and manufacturing and credit."[31] Madison saw the truth of Pinckney's remarks insofar as the eighteenth century was concerned, but argued that in future there might be an increase in manufacturing and poverty. The poor, nursing ambitions to despoil property, might someday outnumber the well-to-do. "According to the equal laws of suffrage," he concluded, "the power will slide into the hands of the former." He declared that already there were signs and portents of a "levelling spirit."[32]

Madison thus touched on the fear of many members of his generation for the future of the country. Benjamin Rush's famous and oft-quoted remark that the war was over but not the Revolution shows that Tocqueville's trepidations in the 1830's were by no means new. The American people were free, and the majority would eventually control their governments. If government *for* the people was becoming more and more government *by* the people, the urgent problem was that of providing guidance and leadership for them and of maintain-

[29] *Ibid.*, ii, pp. 249, 201.　　[30] *Ibid.*, ii, pp. 204, 204n.
[31] *Ibid.*, i, pp. 397, 397n, 398.　　[32] *Ibid.*, i, pp. 422-423.

ing a social milieu favorable to liberty and equality. As a Pennsylvania newspaper had said, in an utterance betraying loyalist sentiment, "Numbers can never sanctify error . . . a majority is sometimes in the wrong."[33]

One could have reservations about the future of the United States and at the same time agree with the Virginian, St. George Tucker, that those who drew a parallel between the fate of the ancient republics of Athens and Rome and the American state must "either be totally ignorant, or guilty of wilful misrepresentation."[34] Jefferson hoped that in time the nation would disprove European and American prophets of gloom by timely measures to perpetuate the agrarian way of life. At one point he suggested that a freehold qualification for voting would not be incompatible with the rights of man so long as all men had the opportunity to take up 50 acres of land. An egalitarian land policy would stave off indefinitely the spectre of a Europeanized America. As early as 1780, the *Boston Gazette* had addressed itself to this problem and had concluded that an agrarian law, limiting the size of the land-holding of any individual to 1,000 acres, would be the most effective means "whereby we shall maintain the character of a free Republic, prevent monopolies of land . . . and prevent [the] fate of the Clans of Scotland."[35]

The reflections of Samuel Adams illustrate the attention patriots were giving at this time to the problem which those who, in the words of Henry Van Schaack, had "kindled the flame of war and directed popular zeal through the whole course of it," now faced as a consequence of their acts.[36] Samuel Adams prescribed at various times a system of public education ("for the Kingdoms of the earth have not been gov-

[33] *Pennsylvania Gazette*, Feb. 1, 1775.
[34] Tucker, St. George (ed.), *Commentaries on the Laws of England*, I, p. 32.
[35] *Boston Gazette*, June 19, 1780.
[36] Van Schaack, H. C., *Memoirs of the Life of Henry Van Schaack* (Chicago, 1892), p. 96.

erned by Reason"), a return to revealed religion, and a rejection of the skepticism of a David Hume and even the pursuit of asceticism, expressing the desire to see Boston a "christian Sparta."[37]

The function of the Federal Convention was not to theorize, however, but to produce a practical, political solution to the problems of the times by establishing an effective, central government for the new nation. The convention created a form of government both mixed and balanced, allowing all the electors of the lower houses of the various states to elect the members of the House of Representatives. In doing so, the convention recognized that, whatever "inconveniences may attend the democratic principle, it must actuate one part of the government." The important matter of suffrage qualifications was thereby left exclusively to the states. Thus, far from attacking the advance in democratic suffrage since 1776, the Federal Convention confirmed and underwrote it. "Who are the electors of the federal representatives?" queried Hamilton or Madison in Number 57 of the Federalist Papers. "Not the rich, more than the poor; not the learned, more than the ignorant; not the haughty heirs of distinguished names, more than the humble sons of obscure and unpropitious fortune. The electors are to be the great body of the people of the United States."[38] Recognizing that a democratic government must rest upon a compact between that government and the people, the states of Connecticut and New York allowed all adult males to vote for representatives to their ratifying conventions, a right which Massachusetts had conceded in regard to its state constitution.

By its neutrality on the suffrage issue, the Founding Fathers disarmed in advance many who might otherwise have been critical of the Federal Constitution. For this reason, the major criticism in the ratifying conventions was directed against the

[37] Cushing (ed.), *Writings of Samuel Adams*, IV, p. 236.
[38] Ashley, W. J. (ed.), *The Federalist* (Everyman, 1911), p. 291.

creation of a too-powerful central government. It was feared that the forms of directly responsible, republican government in the states could not be extended to the nation as a whole without the creation of more elaborate political organizations. Such organizations, it was thought, would work to the advantage, not of the middle classes and farmers, but of the wealthy and of the cities.[39]

Patrick Henry maintained that the power of Congress to determine the time, place, and manner of congressional elections might lead eventually to disfranchisement of voters because, he said, there was nothing in the constitution which would prohibit the imposition of property qualifications. "According to the mode prescribed," he said, "Congress may tell you that they have a right to make the vote of one gentleman go as far as the votes of one hundred poor men."[40] Elsewhere in the south similar criticism of congressional control over elections was voiced. In North Carolina, this criticism was answered with the observation that the power over the manner of elections did not include the power to determine the voting qualifications, an interpretation already endorsed by James Madison.

As cogent as any criticism made in any of the ratifying conventions was that of one J. Lewis in a letter to the Maryland politician, Joseph H. Nicholson. He wrote Nicholson in the summer of 1789 that he was far from sanguine as to the future of American government because the constitution did not incorporate an agrarian law, limiting the individual ownership of land to 10,000 acres. Without it, he was convinced, the country would find difficult the preservation of equality, so essential, as Montesquieu had said, to the perpetuation of popular government. Without an agrarian law, he predicted,

[39] Kenyon, Cecilia M., "Men of Little Faith," *William and Mary Quarterly* (xii, Jan. 1955), pp. 3-43.

[40] Henry, William H., *Patrick Henry: Life, Correspondence and Speeches* (New York, 1891, 3 vols.), iii, p. 502.

the "Grand Convention must have founded only a temporary Democratical Constitution," for the equality which prevailed would gradually decline and Americans would in time "experience the Inequality that is so universally prevalent in *England, France* and every other *European* state. . . ." The rich would live "like Lords, influence the Elections and be possessed of the sovereign power." Then, he observed, "our glorious struggles for liberty will have been in vain."[41] The Duc de Rochefoucauld, on the other hand, thought that prospects in the United States favored the establishment of a sound constitution, because there were not then in the country those distinctions of birth and place which were the curse of the Old World.

Accompanying or following the creation of the federal government were a considerable number of changes in some of the state constitutions. Many of these were the direct result of the great debates on government in the ratifying conventions. Others came about because some hastily drafted documents proved unsatisfactory in practice and still others, particularly in the south, were induced by growing inequalities in representation caused by startling advances in population. Whatever the reason, the years between 1787 and 1792 were characterized by considerable constitution-making and revision along the seaboard from New Hampshire to Georgia.

In Georgia, three conventions were held in 1788 and 1789 to debate the merits of more representation for the fast-growing upcountry, unicameralism, and the voting qualification. The constitution resulting from the deliberations of 1788 required a 50-pound property qualification.[42] This was quickly criticized on the grounds that it would discourage immigration and anger war veterans as well as "benevolent" citizens who,

[41] Library of Congress, *Joseph H. Nicholson Papers*, I, Lewis to Nicholson, July 29, 1787.
[42] Ware, E. K., *Constitutional History of Georgia* (New York, 1947), pp. 63-70.

even if rich, had faith in the lowly and humble. An advocate of property tests pointed out that those who favored representation based upon ownership of property were scarcely in a position to criticize property tests for voting, that such tests would disqualify few but would nevertheless be the means of excluding from the suffrage the dregs of Europe, a single cargo of which could swamp Georgian electors at the polls. A telling illustration of the danger in allowing foreigners to vote was drawn from Montesquieu's analysis of the connection between foreign influences and the decline of Rome.[43] Despite so spirited a defense of property tests, the constitution of 1789 conceded the vote to all free white males who had paid a tax during the preceding year. The counter-revolution in Georgia, to the extent there was one, had collapsed.

In South Carolina, a similar increase in backcountry population, and related developments, were the background of the convention of 1790. Prior to the sessions, petitions from such areas as Camden County favored the relocation of the capital inland, requested the issuance of a paper money and the erection of additional county courts. The petitions were silent on the suffrage issue. It was understandable, therefore, that the convention changed the suffrage clauses only slightly, permitting all free white male citizens to vote who were owners of a 50-acre freehold, or owners of a town lot, or six months' residents and payers of a 3-shilling sterling tax. Property tests for holding office, however, were revised drastically upward.

The South Carolina property tests proved confusing in practice. In 1791, lessees of Indian lands in York County, under the impression that only freeholders could vote in the state, petitioned the legislature for the right to vote inasmuch as they had "fought for the Cause of Liberty." This and similar petitions drew from an assembly committee the statement that leaseholders had only to pay a 3 shilling tax to vote,[44] but

[43] *Georgia Gazette*, Dec. 11, Dec. 24, 1788.
[44] South Carolina Archives Commission, *Legislative System Petitions*,

many inhabitants remained uncertain of the requirements.

Of interest in state constitutional history during this period is the sharp difference of opinion in Pennsylvania over the merits of the constitution of 1776. Those who defended it called themselves Constitutionalists, those who decried it, Republicans, a distinction interpreted by one contemporary observer as that between democrats and aristocrats.[45] The quarrel was more complex, however. Few Republicans favored reducing the broad suffrage created in theory by the first constitution. They proposed the establishment of an independent executive and judiciary, and a bicameral system of government to destroy concentration of powers in a single-chambered legislature. When they wrote a new one in 1790, the Republicans were wise enough not to change the taxpaying qualification for voting to which Pennsylvanians were strongly attached, as an incident in 1783 had shown. An attempt was made during an election in that year to turn away from the polls a group of young soldiers because they had "no will of their own." One soldier retorted that the government had had no objections to their fighting "& now you have to our voting. This is not just; we have fought for the right of voting & we will now exercise it." The reporter of this incident concluded, "It was not possible to reply to such an argument. The soldiers voted & some say that they actually did gain the victory for their party."[46] The Republicans opposed, however, the efforts of Albert Gallatin and others to further liberalize the suffrage. Constitutionalists and Republicans were essentially in agreement on the suffrage issue. Neither wanted to allow vagabonds or beggars to vote. Both agreed that the vote should be con-

1785-1786; *ibid.*, 1788, for St. John Colleton Petition and 1791 for the Petition of Inhabitants of Indian Lands in York County.

[45] See Brunhouse, R. L., *The Counter-Revolution in Pennsylvania 1776-1790* (Harrisburg, 1942).

[46] N.Y.H.S., *R. R. Livingston Papers*, 1777-1799, P. P. Du Ponceau [?] to R. R. Livingston, Oct. 15, 1783.

fined to the middle class, meaning freeholders, householders, and settled residents.[47]

In one particular, the Republicans could accuse the Constitutionalists of being undemocratic because they were responsible for the clause in the constitution which confined to freeholders voting in the nominating elections for justices of the peace. Second only to the trouble caused by the Test Act was that caused by efforts to restrict these elections to freeholders. According to the records there was great confusion. Elections were held in which non-freehold voters participated, unaware of the legal qualification. Others fully aware of it created fagot votes, as in Washington County in 1789.[48] In some elections not enough freeholders voted, because of the pressure of harvesting crops, to assure the election of their candidates. Many who appeared at the polls were turned away even when they came with their land deeds in their hands if, it was hinted, they gave indication of voting the wrong way.

Thomas Fisher of York thought it "morally impossible for Judges Inspectors & Constables to Determine upon a day of Election who has the Right of a freeholder to vote," because in York there were "so many small tenements, so much buying and selling of them and so many joint interests in houses and lands." It was hard, he said, "in a Land of freedom to Divest or hinder any person to vote because he has not obtained his Deed." Non-freeholders as well as freeholders had a great stake in the quality of justice in a community where there was much litigation among the illiterate country folk.[49] Suffice it to say that the new constitution, under Republican auspices, abolished the freehold qualification and, indeed, the election

[47] *Gazette of the United States*, Jan. 16, 1790.
[48] See Pennsylvania, D.P.R., *Records of the Secretary of the Supreme Executive Council*, Election Returns: Washington and other counties.
[49] *Ibid.*, York County, Sept. 8, 1788.

of nominees for justices of the peace, in favor of a system of nomination by the chief executive.

The counter-revolutionary constitution of Pennsylvania was subject to bitter attack. Tom Paine was still denouncing it in 1805 as "a copy in miniature of the Government of England, established at the conquest of that Country by William of Normandy."[50] The anti-Constitutionalists were identified by a leading statesman as "most of the merchants, most of the monied Men, most of the Gentlemen in the late Army & more of the mob of the Town." The farmers, he said, were the core of the Constitutionalists.[51] Nevertheless, the Republican proposals for constitutional changes won popular support.

Without the flamboyance of Pennsylvania, Delaware and New Hampshire held constitutional conventions in 1791. The New Hampshire convention amended rather than scrapped the constitution of 1784 which had conceded a taxpaying qualification for voting to adult male residents. The Delaware convention, probably influenced by Pennsylvania, gave the vote to adult white male residents if they had paid a state or county tax, and it extended the vote to their sons if they were between twenty-one and twenty-two years of age. It also made mandatory the use of the secret ballot in elections.[52]

No state between the end of the Revolution and the Federal Convention divorced property from voting. There was still only one state, Vermont, where manhood suffrage had been achieved. Nevertheless, those states which shifted to a taxpaying qualification during this period created a very broad electorate indeed. How democratic a taxpaying qualification

[50] Van Der Wyde (ed.), *The Life and Works of Thomas Paine*, x, p. 255.

[51] Historical Society of Pennsylvania, *George Bryan Papers*, 1785-1787, (n.d.).

[52] Turner, L. W., *The Life of William Plumer*, pp. 349-350; Munroe, John A., *Federalist Delaware 1775-1815* (New Brunswick, 1954), p. 190, *passim*.

would be depended wholly upon the incidence of direct taxation in the various states. In New Hampshire, Delaware, Georgia, and North Carolina all adult males were subject to a poll tax or its equivalent. With taxation of adult males almost universal, a taxpaying suffrage was almost universal suffrage. On the other hand, South Carolina did not assess a poll tax. For this reason, the 3-shilling tax requirement made necessary, in law at least, possession by the voter of property which would yield a 3-shilling tax.[53] It would appear, however, that in practice anyone who tendered 3 shillings to a tax collector could vote.

In Pennsylvania, a direct state tax was never collected until 1832. Voters in that state qualified by paying a small county tax, levied six months before election upon property owners or upon all single freemen over twenty-one who did not follow any occupation or calling. The taxpaying qualification was declared by Judge Brackenridge in 1816 an inducement to pay taxes, a means of preventing tumults at elections, and a means of providing a register of voters six months before election. Another judge declared that it was designed to cut down the purchasing of votes just before election by "moneyed men."[54] Whatever the reason, the qualification survived the constitutional revision of 1837 and was not abolished until 1931.

It is clear that the suffrage reforms of the critical period advanced democratic practices and principles considerably. The predominant mood of the period, regardless of how reactionary it may have been in other particulars, was not reactionary by and large in regard to the suffrage. In his old age, Thomas Jefferson looked back upon the contributions which Americans had made to the institutions of government and pronounced them good, and basically Anglo-Saxon. "The

[53] These statements are based upon a collation of the tax statutes of the seaboard states.

[54] Brightly, F. C., *A Collection of Leading Cases of the Law of Elections in the United States* (Philadelphia, 1871), pp. 114-125.

full experiment of a government democratical, but representative was and still is reserved for us," although the idea had been borrowed from the "little specimen formerly existing in the English constitution (but now lost)."[55]

[55] Library of Congress, *Thomas Jefferson Papers*, ccviii, p. 208, to Isaac H. Tiffany.

CHAPTER 8

SUFFRAGE REFORM IN THE
JEFFERSONIAN SOUTH

ALEXIS DE TOCQUEVILLE observed in the 1830's that clearcut
parties had existed in America in the Federalist-Republican
era but not in the America of his day.[1] So far as suffrage reform was concerned, however, the first great political parties
were by no means clearcut. Many Jeffersonians, for example,
would not accept Jefferson's latter-day plan for a general
suffrage whereby all adult males who paid taxes or served in
the militia would be allowed to vote; others supported it
wholeheartedly. Divergent opinions on the suffrage embarrassed the Federalists also. No states better illustrate the com-
plexities of suffrage reform in relation to political parties than
Maryland and South Carolina.

In Maryland, the man chiefly responsible for reviving the
movement for suffrage reform, begun during the Revolution,
was Michael Taney, Federalist representative in the state
legislature and father of Roger B. Taney, later Chief Justice of
the Supreme Court of the United States. It would seem hard to
make much of a case that a great number of Marylanders,
otherwise qualified, were unable to vote in view of the 30-
pound visible estate qualification for voting. Nevertheless, an
estimate of the number of qualified voters in 1788 was 25,000,[2]
which meant possibly that only 55 percent of free white males
were qualified. If this estimate is correct, the possibilities are
either that voting was in practice confined to freeholders (one-
half of adult males were freeholders), or that the 30-pound

---

[1] See Holcombe, A. N., *The Political Parties of Today* (New York,
1925, 2nd ed.), pp. 1-13.
[2] *Maryland Journal*, May 16, 1788.

qualification was determined by tax-book assessments in which only certain kinds of property were assessed, and those at a fraction of their real value. There is documentary evidence of a fairly convincing character, however, that at least by 1800 the 30-pound qualification was divorced from freeholds and from tax assessments. Moreover, depreciation of the state paper money had destroyed the clear estate qualification if old tax-books reflecting sterling values were not used to determine it. However determined (or perhaps not determined), the voting qualification after the Revolution was sustaining an electorate which varied from time to time and place to place from about 50 to 90 percent of adult white males.[3] It is probable that those who could not qualify were the young men, the improvident, and the poor. Young men had indeed attempted to secure a taxpaying qualification at the outbreak of the Revolution but had failed.

It would have been difficult to predict at what point, if any, the issue would be reopened. After the Revolution as before, Maryland politics were largely a matter of interplay between family representatives of the Tilghmans, Lloyds, Pacas, Chases, and, after the repeal of the anti-Catholic laws, the Carrolls. There were significant differences of opinion between them on only a few important issues, such as the merits of paper money and the Federal Constitution.[4] The system of elections was aristocratic but not irresponsible. "The delegates returned," said an English observer, "are generally persons of the greatest consequence in their respective counties; and many of them are perfectly acquainted with the political and commercial interests of their constituents."[5]

Save in times of great popular excitement, elections did not

[3] *Baltimore American*, Sept. 28, 1799; Maryland Senate, *Votes and Proceedings*, 1800, p. 29; Pole, J. R., "Suffrage and Representation in Maryland," *Journal of Southern History* (xxiv, May 1958), pp. 218-228.
[4] Scharf, J. T., *A History of Maryland* (Baltimore, 1879, 3 vols.), ii, pp. 29-32.
[5] Eddis, William, *Letters from America* (London, 1792), p. 126.

stimulate much interest. A contemporary magazine ascribed the indifference of voters to coercion by the rich and powerful under viva voce elections, the absence of a real choice between candidates and programs, and a moral atmosphere like that of English borough elections.[6] On the occasions when political feelings ran high, the laws regulating Maryland elections were flagrantly violated. Foreigners were naturalized just before elections in illegal fashion and allowed to vote. Even Samuel Chase did not hesitate to take advantage of what he termed, and had earlier deplored, the venality of electors. In 1788, he appeared at the polls with 500 voters, of whom it was said that only 110 were legal. In 1792, according to a report, he acted "in so arbitrary & outrageous a manner as a Judge of Election" that Baltimore mechanics were with difficulty restrained from hoisting him into a chair and pitching him into the harbor.[7]

Fundamental criticism of the government and the constitution of Maryland seems seldom to have been made until 1797. One of the few criticisms voiced earlier was published in a Baltimore newspaper and opposed a plan to incorporate Baltimore with a charter which would minimize popular control by viva voce elections and property tests. The newspaper used this criticism as the basis for an attack upon the Maryland constitution. Men in rags had not had a hand in framing the document, said "Rags," although true republican doctrine recognized that they too were of human flesh and blood and had families to support and defend. He prophesied that such inequalities as the state constitution had created would in time destroy liberty.[8]

The first full-scale attack after the Revolution upon Maryland suffrage commenced in 1797 when Michael Taney, Mary-

[6] *The American Museum* (VIII, Dec. 1790), pp. 282-283.
[7] *Maryland Journal*, Oct. 24, 1788; Maryland Historical Society, *O. H. Williams Papers*, VII, p. 633.
[8] *Baltimore Daily Intelligencer*, Feb. 7, 1794.

land aristocrat, Catholic, and ex-student of Jesuit schools on the continent, introduced a bill on December 5 to establish universal manhood suffrage, and thereby make his state the second to divorce property and taxpaying from the suffrage qualification.[9] Taney's intervention is difficult to explain on the basis of the meager evidence now available. Previously, he had taken the "popular" side by voting for paper money. He had voted, however, against efforts to prohibit the practice of primogeniture, and was considered a Federalist because he supported John Adams and Federalist domestic and foreign measures. Possibly, Taney introduced his bill because he believed that the threat of American involvement in a war against France made it just and necessary to appease militia men, some of whose fathers in '76 had not been anxious to fight for the rights of Maryland unless they were given the right to vote. It is possible, of course, that Taney had highly personal or partisan reasons for his support of suffrage reform. His son said that his father's elections to the House of Delegates had excited a taste for politics and political eminence. Why he is identified in the official records as serving only one year in the house remains a mystery.[10]

Taney's bill was one instance, among several, of increased criticism of the constitution. During the same fall, Solomon Ettinger, a Maryland Jew, petitioned the legislature to remove the civil and political disabilities oppressing Jews; about the same time, a group of Washington County inhabitants criticized the existence of only one polling place for each county as greatly inconveniencing the voters and narrowing the popular basis of government. Nicholas Hammond, on the eve of a solid career in Maryland affairs, called for the compiling by tax commissioners of county voter registration lists in order to

[9] Maryland, *Votes and Proceedings of the House of Delegates* (Nov. 1797), p. 57.

[10] Tyler, Samuel, *Memoir of Roger Brooke Taney* (Baltimore, 1872), p. 80.

curb sheriffal abuses and the creation of fagot voters, by which means even "popular topers have been made eligible."[11]

Because the distinction between Federalist and Republican had been drawn only in national and not state politics, the Taney bill created considerable confusion and embarrassment within the ranks of each party. The initiator of the reform was a Federalist in national issues. Some of those opposed to him on these issues were opposed to him on the suffrage also. Marylanders who had supported the Republican position in national issues were sharply divided by the amended version of Taney's bill which would enfranchise all free-born adult males of twenty-one years of age, if resident in a county for one year. The vote in the House of Delegates in favor of the bill, 30 to 21, was not a clearcut party vote. Indeed, Joseph H. Nicholson and Robert Smith, who shortly thereafter became outstanding leaders of Maryland Republicanism, joined Philip Barton Key, ultra-conservative representative of the city of Annapolis who had fought as a loyalist in the Revolution, in voting against the bill.[12]

The senate's rejection of the bill as well as the adverse vote of some of the members of the lower house was the subject of considerable comment and debate before the next election. The result, comments one Maryland historian, was that "those who had opposed it lost favor."[13] Some Republicans explained that they had opposed the bill, not because they were unwilling to enfranchise the poor, but because the first bill would have permitted free Negroes and mulattoes to vote at a time when the public was greatly prejudiced against them because of the recent uprising in Santo Domingo. This was Nicholson's explanation for his vote. He sensed the direction of public opinion and attempted to seize the initiative from his op-

[11] Maryland, Hall of Records, *Executive Council Papers*, Nov. 28, 1797.

[12] Scharf, *op.cit.*, II, p. 609; *Votes and Proceedings of the House of Delegates* (1797), p. 96.

[13] Scharf, *op.cit.*, II, pp. 609-611.

ponents in national affairs in the same way in which, much later, on the occasion of the second British Reform Bill of 1867, it was said of Disraeli that he had caught the Whigs bathing and had run away with their clothes.[14] Nicholson stood sponsor for a reform bill which would meet his objections to enfranchising free Negroes in the session of 1798, at the same time that he was acting as a member of a committee to prepare a new militia bill. His efforts failed to secure the support of the lower house which voted on December 27 to put over the bill to the next session.[15] Another casualty of this session was a bill to "encourage learning and establish a uniform system of education" in the state.

The senate, the seat of Maryland conservatism whether Republican or Federalist, was much opposed to suffrage changes unless they would restrict the suffrage still further. In 1799, it proposed that all voters be required to submit written evidence of their ownership of a 50-acre freehold or the ownership of 30 pounds of property, the latter to be determined by the lists of tax assessments. Use of the tax books to determine the 30-pound qualification would have been distinctly retrogressive, as the opposition press and others pointed out. Property, they claimed, was assessed at only one-quarter of its real value and such important items as crops, provisions, utensils, tools, wearing apparel, home manufactures, stills, grains, tobacco, carriages, and certain sizes of boats were not assessed at all. Quite legitimately, Republicans attacked the measure.[16]

That the principles of late eighteenth-century radical democracy were making a great impact upon Maryland thought is indicated not only by the effort to commit the state to a system of public education but also by other plans conceived in the same spirit. The next session of the legislature was even more

[14] Emory, Frederic, *Queen Anne's County, Maryland: Its Early History and Development* (Baltimore, 1950), p. 367.
[15] *Votes and Proceedings, House of Delegates 1798*, pp. 67-68.
[16] *Baltimore American*, Sept. 28, 1799; Aug. 21, 1801.

active in this regard. Members tried, although unsuccessfully, to remove the religious qualification for officeholding, and they succeeded in passing new election laws which created election districts almost equal in size and population and in establishing the secret ballot. They repulsed efforts to reduce the per diem pay of legislators on the grounds that the exclusion of all but the rich from the legislature would "place the poorer classes of the community entirely in the hands of the rich. . . ."[17]

At this session, a committee composed of three Federalists, one of whom, Philip Barton Key, had been stoutly opposed to suffrage reform, produced a bill which would enfranchise adult white males. The senate rejected it on November 29, 1799.[18] From this time on, the suffrage issue was further confused by the events leading to the presidential elections of 1800, which, in Maryland, involved considerable discussion as to whether presidential electors should be chosen, as the Federalists advocated, on a state-wide basis or by districts, as favored by the Republicans. Jeffersonians who opposed suffrage reform pointed out that in Jefferson's Virginia only freeholders could vote in the counties, and that the poor and middling classes, which by and large were legally qualified in Maryland, were excluded. One Jeffersonian in Ann Arundel County, on the other hand, expressed shocked surprise that there were people who wanted to curb the rights of others to vote, implying that they must be Federalists.[19]

Concerning this election, the Connecticut Federalist, Oliver Wolcott, made some interesting observations. He wrote Fisher Ames that Maryland politics were affected by the habits of slave-owners and that distinctions between rich and poor were felt by each. Nevertheless, the "ancient usage" of aristocrats of paying their respects "to the sovereignty of the people" was

[17] *Votes and Proceedings, House of Delegates 1799*, pp. 15-17.
[18] Senate, *Votes and Proceedings 1799*, pp. 9-10.
[19] *Maryland Gazette*, Aug. 14, 1800; *The Telegraph and Daily Advertizer* (Baltimore), Aug. 16, 1800; July 28, 1800.

being honored again during the election. Candidates on both sides, he said, were travelling through their districts, "exciting the favor of the people they associate with on no other occasion."[20]

Exciting the favor of the people of Maryland had come to mean taking a stand for the principle of a democratic suffrage for whites. Under party pressure, politicians whether sincere or not in their support of suffrage reform, saw that it was worth votes. Thus neither Maryland Federalism nor Republicanism was so much the symbol of resistance to reform as was the senate. The Republican, Robert Smith, and the Federalist, Charles Carroll, might disagree in the senate over national issues but they did not disagree as to the undesirability of suffrage changes. Carroll's assertion, years later, that "a mere Democracy is but a mob" would have received Smith's approval if it had been made at the time both were using their influence in the senate to forestall suffrage reform.[21]

A Republican at one time proposed publicly a bipartisan coalition of anti-reformers to secure the election of representatives who would oppose suffrage reform and other dangerous democratic tendencies. Republicans of Franklin County admitted that not all Federalists were opposed to suffrage reform although they asserted that the passage of a reform bill would be a "blow against Federalism in their county, at least, if not in the state as a whole."[22]

Samuel Chase saw the cross-currents of the political life of his state in a jaundiced and unfavorable light, saying, it was alleged later, that "degenerate sons" of the constitutional fathers of Maryland had been the chief supporters of the recent destructive measures. On the other hand, a Federalist newspaper denounced Jefferson for his alleged unwillingness

[20] Connecticut Historical Society, *Oliver Wolcott Papers*, xxi, Wolcott to Fisher Ames, n.d.

[21] Pierson, G. W., *Tocqueville and Beaumont in America* (New York, 1938), p. 507.

[22] *Republican Advocate* (Frederick Town), Dec. 6, 1802.

to allow any but taxpayers to vote. "When," asked the writer, has "Jefferson shown himself to be the poor man's friend?" On the contrary, he asserted, Jefferson was a "hypocrite and enemy of the people."[23]

Marylanders, irrespective of class, status, or section, were swept along by a movement based upon democratic principles but initiated at the top. Some marvelled at a popular movement led by a number of the substantial citizenry, if not aristocracy, of Maryland. "I am astonished at the popular delusion and madness, that possesses men of property, when I see them assent to a change in our Constitution," said one observer, "and give men without any property the vote."[24] To others, it was natural and right. "I have always thought," wrote one Marylander, "that where a man of high birth and fortune becomes the advocate and the supporter of the rights and liberties of the people, he is deserving our additional esteem." The spectacle of such men in politics, he asserted, was not rare. "Some of the wealthiest lords of England are the greatest supporters of the people's liberties, and the firmest barrier against the encroachment of the crown."[25]

Irrespective of formal party affiliation on broad, national issues, suffrage reformers pressed their program of a democratic suffrage until they won in 1802. Their arguments added nothing new to those advanced earlier. The suffrage qualification in Maryland was attacked as being based upon principles associated with the government against which Marylanders had rebelled in 1776, and as being contrary to a political system based on equal rights. Every child, said a Fredericktown paper, cannot inherit a fortune, but every child should inherit liberty. "It is the duty," it concluded, "of every father to trans-

[23] *American and Commercial Daily Advertiser,* June 13, 1803; *Frederick Town Herald,* Sept. 18, 1802.
[24] *The Republican or Anti-Democrat,* Sept. 29, 1802.
[25] *American and Commercial Daily Advertiser,* May 28, 1803.

mit to his son the right of suffrage."[26] In the wake of the war scare of 1798, the argument was used that men good enough to fight were good enough to vote, with customary effect. "Who stood in the ranks as soldiers and fought the battles of the revolutionary war?" demanded the Fredericktown *Hornet.* "Is not the poor man now bound to do military duty? And do not the farmers and mechanics now fill the ranks of the militia companies? The soldier is as much entitled to vote as the Captain of the company or the Colonel of the regiment."[27] Another newspaper reminded its readers that suffrage is the parent of representation.

Reformers urged the people of Maryland to disprove the contention that man "is a being formed only to be ruled by the will of others and not his own."[28] This implied that henceforth elections would no longer be considered social occasions, as many Frederick Federalists still considered them. "A Farmer" warned the voters that they thought "meat, bread, and whiskey" were translatable into votes and already had held a barbecue at a mill where "an old bull, a 12 yr. old ram and a boar which had run wild in the woods" had been consumed. "The freemen of Frederick," asserted the farmer, "will never sell their liberty for a meal of victuals."[29] The frame of mind of Marylanders was described in almost alarmist terms by the *Federalist Gazette.* "The truth is," it said on August 9, 1800, "the people of Maryland have become too saucy and are really beginning to fancy themselves equal to their superiors." Some Marylanders found congenial the spirit of the Levellers and others of the Puritan Revolution. On December 24, 1800, *The Telegraph and Daily Advertiser of Baltimore* published a long excerpt from Marchamont Nedham's *Excellencie of a Free*

[26] *The Hornet* (M. Bartgis, Editor), I, no. 6, 1802.
[27] *Ibid.,* I, no. 7.
[28] *The Baltimore Telegraph,* Nov. 8, 1800, quoting *Bartgis' Republican Gazette.*
[29] *The Hornet,* I, no. 15.

State. One can surmise what Nedham's principle were when it recalled that John Adams bore an exceptionally strong dislike for his political ideas.

The Maryland senate recognized that further resistance to the movement for suffrage reform was unwise, if not useless. Nicholson had been elected to the United States House of Representatives and the new reform leader in the lower house was Edward Lloyd, Jr., the son of Edward Lloyd of Wye House on the eastern shore, who had been the co-author of the bitterly partisan Sedition Act of 1798. Lloyd Jr. later became the Republican governor of the state. His suffrage bill passed the House of Delegates on December 3, 1800, by a vote of 57 to 11, after its supporters had repulsed efforts to delete the word "white" from the bill or to amend it so as to confine the franchise to the owners of 30 pounds property.[30] The senate refused to accept this bill, countering it with a revised version of its proposals of 1799 which the house rejected. The house declared that the senate proposal would disfranchise many persons entitled to vote under the constitution, and that members of the house were "guardians of the rights and privileges of the people" which should not be frustrated by or made dependent upon any "partial assessment law" which the legislature might pass in the future."[31] Refusing to retreat from its fundamental position, the senate proposed to allow all persons, otherwise qualified, to vote if they possessed assessable property of 10 dollars. This qualification the senate considered wise because it feared the time would come, as it had before in history, when a large number of people would be without property, virtue, or knowledge to resist the demagogue. Moreover, the senate maintained that the state of natural liberty did not necessarily include the liberty to vote. Here the issue rested."[32]

[30] *House of Delegates, Votes and Proceedings 1800*, pp. 51-52.
[31] *Senate, Votes and Proceedings, 1800*, p. 36.
[32] *Ibid.*, pp. 42-43.

Clearly, the suffrage reformers had to find a way to swing
the senate into line or give up the fight to secure the passage
of their bill in two successive legislatures, which was the only
way of amending the constitution at this time. They had been
holding in reserve, however, until all other means of persuad-
ing the senate had failed, a stratagem which would almost certainly prove effective. In December of 1801, the house played
its trump card. Suffrage reformers threatened to demand the
calling of a constitutional convention to make the senate an
elective body, at a time when criticism of it was steadily increasing. Only shortly before, *The National Aegis* of Worcester
County had excoriated the senators as independent of the people's will and asserted that they might as well be selected for
life as to be chosen by the current indirect method.[33] The
mere threat of calling a convention was sufficient to force
senate acceptance of a bill allowing all free white adult males,
if twelve months resident in a county, to vote by ballot in
elections for sheriffs, delegates, and other state officials.[34] The
conservatives felt that a bird in hand was worth two in any
Blackstonian bush. They tacitly agreed to accept universal
white suffrage in return for the maintenance of the senate as
it had existed previously and the continued ascendancy of
eastern Maryland in state affairs.

Politicians who had been opposed to reform were not immediately forgiven and forgotten. During the elections of 1802,
in such counties as Frederick and Cumberland, every effort
was made to smoke out the representatives who had failed to
show any enthusiasm for, or to vote for the bill. Reformers,
who called themselves "Democrats," held a meeting in Cumberland County on August 30, 1802, to protest the vote of two
of their representatives against the bill. In Frederick County,
a newspaper campaign was instituted against the four county

[33] Quoted in *The Hornet*, I, no. 47.
[34] *House of Delegates, Votes and Proceedings 1801*, pp. 73, 90, 109.

representatives who were designated "Republicans." To stand even a chance of being re-elected in the fall of 1802, they were forced to declare their attachment to suffrage reform. Because they refused to state unequivocally that they favored the second passage of the bill, their opponents accused them "of shallow and pitiful artifice" and of endeavoring to cheat themselves into power.[35] The election in Frederick was very spirited. Over 4,000 votes were cast, a number which represented a considerable increase over previous elections, with a "Democratic" majority of 219. "Republicans" laid the cause of their defeat to demagogues, better organization by their opponents, indifference of their own supporters, and partiality of judges of elections. It might be added as another reason for "Republican" defeat, that the "Democrats," sponsors of suffrage reform, did not hesitate to make use of property tests to keep from the polls those who might vote against them in this election.

The suffrage bill was confirmed in the 1802 session of the legislature, with the senate concurring unanimously. The success of the reformers and the discomfiture of the conservatives embittered Maryland politics considerably. Samuel Chase, then a United States Supreme Court Judge, excoriated the bill so unmercifully that, at the time of his impeachment, his opponents incorporated as the 8th article of the proceedings against him, the "inflammatory" speech he had made to a grand jury in which he sought to "excite" the people against reform, saying that it would lead to mobocratic rule.[36] James McHenry, a Federalist, wrote Oliver Wolcott that Maryland, "having established universal suffrage may expect its highest honors will come in due course."[37] Years later, Charles Carroll still nursed resentment against those democratic ideas which,

[35] *The Hornet*, i, no. 11.
[36] *Annals of the Congress of the United States*, 14th Congress, 2nd Session, p. 146.
[37] *Wolcott Papers*, xx, McHenry to Wolcott, March 31, 1804.

although they had helped to bring Catholic emancipation, had also destroyed his political career after 1800. "Those who grew up under the *old regime*," declared a Marylander in 1831, "may object with that disposition which is natural to man, to prefer the institutions with which his youth is familiar and to describe [sic] degeneracy to the present, just in proportion as he himself begins to be numbered with the past."[38]

Democratic sentiment was not exhausted with the triumph of suffrage reform. During the years immediately after, democratically minded Republicans and Federalists joined in efforts to secure popular election of the governor, senators, and justices of the Levy Courts; to increase the representation of Baltimore; to abolish the religious qualification for office; to make illegal a tax for the support of the Christian religion; and to repeal property tests for office. Active in trying to secure the passage of some of these bills was John H. Thomas, a Federalist representative from Frederick County. The efforts of Thomas and others were directed to securing the passage of another suffrage amendment in order to remove the ambiguity of the first. The amendment of 1802 had failed to make clear that voters in state elections could also vote in elections for members of the Federal House of Representatives and for the presidential electors. As a result, a special amendment was added to the constitution in 1810 to remove this ambiguity. By this time, the reform movement inaugurated by Michael Taney in 1797 had spent its force. Probably the actual increase of enfranchisement was not as great as warranted by the amount of time and attention given to suffrage reform.[39]

Meanwhile, a comparable situation was developing in South Carolina. Between 1808 and 1810, South Carolina Republicanism was pushed in the direction of democratic suffrage by the

[38] McMahon, J. V. L., *Historical View of the Government of Maryland* (Baltimore, 1831), p. 447.

[39] *Maryland Gazette*, Nov. 14, 1810; Thorpe, *op.cit.*, III, 1705; Pole, J. R., "Suffrage and Representation in Maryland," *The Journal of Southern History*, pp. 218-228.

force of circumstances over which it had little or no control. As in Maryland, many Republicans opposed suffrage reform, agreeing with the remnants of Carolinian Federalism that it would be a mistake. Perhaps South Carolina would not have provided a thoroughly democratic alternative to the freehold and taxpaying qualification of the constitution of 1790 if it had not been for the war scare at the time of the Chesapeake affair of 1807. It is a fact, however, that there was some discussion in 1807 of the status of the militia, one newspaper advocating the creation of a volunteer standing army composed of "men of property."[40] That such a discussion was not considered academic is illustrated by an announcement in the *Carolina Gazette* of January 29, 1808, that war was expected. It was perhaps more than a merely fortuitous circumstance that a military man, Major James Miles of Prince William Parish, was responsible for the introduction of the first suffrage reform bill in June of 1808.[41]

Inclining opinion toward suffrage reform was the very unfavorable public reaction to the numerous violations of the suffrage and election laws. Complaints reached the legislature that mulattoes and minors voted, that some persons voted two or three times at a single election, that others voted upon the payment of a small tax just before voting (by which means a property test was converted into a voting tax), that there were more votes found in voting boxes than there were voters at elections, and that polls were opened and closed capriciously. Some persons voted unaware that they were not legally entitled to do so. A committee reported on a petition from Williamsburg County in 1796 that many, including war veterans, had voted "rather from want of information of the Constitution & Existing Law of the State, than from audacity, or in-

[40] *Carolina Gazette*, Oct. 16, 1807.
[41] *South Carolina Journals*, 1807-1808, p. 165.

tentionally violating the same. . . ."[42] One man who voted in a St. Paul's Parish election of 1796 expressed surprise that something comparable to universal manhood suffrage was not the law of the state. "I went to the Election," he explained, "as any other man wud [sic], supposing I was entitled to vote."[43] The impression of laxity in the policing of property and tax-paying tests, the fact that the early records are virtually barren of complaints against them show why the great issue in South Carolina until 1808 was representation and not the suffrage.[44] The beneficial effects of an abundance of land and the encouragement of immigration by a liberal land policy during the eighteenth century extended well into the nineteenth.[45] South Carolina politics were more sectional than social in the early nineteenth century.

The beginning of the criticism of the suffrage laws coincides not only with the war scare of 1807 but also with an attack from the backcountry upon the xenophobia of the low country nabobs, particularly around Charleston. If the contentions of David Ramsay, historian of Charleston, are at all typical, the well-to-do, sophisticated element in Carolinian society was fearful that it would be overborne, not by the native poor, but by foreigners from across the seas and by Tarheelers pouring into the state across the northern border. In 1802, Ramsay wrote a treatise upon the distinction between citizens and inhabitants of foreign birth which asserted, if interpreted correctly, that no one should be allowed to vote who had not taken the Revolutionary oath of allegiance to the state or was a descendant of those who had.[46] This interpretation of Ram-

[42] Numerous petitions exist in the collection designated *Legislative System, Elections* in the South Carolina Archives Commission, Columbia. See Petition of Sundry Inhabitants of Williamsburg County, 1796.

[43] *Ibid.*, St. Paul's Parish, 1796.

[44] Wolfe, John B., *Jeffersonian Democracy in South Carolina* (Chapel Hill, 1940), p. 47.

[45] Meriwether, R. K., *Expansion of South Carolina* (Kingsport, Tennessee, 1940).

[46] South Carolina Historical Society, Charleston, *Original Manuscript of David Ramsay*, 1802.

say's proposal is supported by the fact that election officials of Marlborough District were applying residence and oath requirements, for which there were no provisions in the constitution, against persons not descended from some who had taken the oath.[47]

There had been signs of the development of an advanced democratic philosophy among Carolinian Republicans since about 1800. One reflection was the creation of South Carolina College in 1801, which was considered necessary to provide superior educational facilities, particularly for the upcountry. Other reforms envisaged the creation of more polling places to render voting more convenient, the election rather than the appointment of a number of state officials, and the abolition of property tests for officeholding. With regard to suffrage, one proposal showed how uniquely southern was the setting for the movement. Charleston papers in 1808 and 1809 not only cited the writings of Abraham Bishop, the Connecticut suffrage reformer, the democratic aspirations of the Society of United Irishmen, and the writings of John Horne Tooke, the British reformer, but also pointed out that men liable to work on the roads, to serve in the militia, and to be members of the slave patrol did not have the franchise.[48] Arguments used more frequently in the north were printed in a peculiar newspaper published in Charleston, known as the *Strength of the People*, which relied on staple quotations from Paine and from works dealing with the French Revolution.

A distinctly sectional aim of the upcountry Republicans was to secure more equitable representation in the legislature, a grievance antedating the Revolution and still very acute. About 1796, the citizens of Abbeville County complained with truth that four-fifths of the free people in the state controlled only one-third of the membership of the lower house. In 1808, this

[47] South Carolina Archives Commission, *Legislative System, Elections*, Petition, Nov. 15, 1808; *House Journals* (Ms.), pp. 66-68.
[48] *Carolina Gazette*, June 17, 1808; *The Times* (Charleston), Jan. 18, 1809.

grievance was alleviated considerably by a compromise between the two sections, by which the upcountry secured a majority of the lower house, the low country maintaining its control of the upper house.

During the same year in which this fundamental compromise was achieved, the suffrage issue was interjected into the legislature. The struggle which resulted has been as much underplayed as the seriousness of the Chartist upheaval of 1848 in Britain. On June 23, 1808, Major Miles introduced a resolution that the constitution be amended in such a way as to "exclude the pecuniary qualification" for voters for both houses. The committee to which the resolution was referred drafted a bill which, on June 29, passed by a vote of 66 to 28. William Dayton, Nathaniel Hayward, William Lowndes, Langdon Cheves, Thomas Pinckney, Jr., and other well-known personages voted no.[49] Opponents were relieved when the senate refused to pass the bill, thus frustrating for the time the effort of reform leaders to begin a process of amending the constitution as Maryland reformers had done.

The senate had only begun to feel the pressure from the house. In 1809, the reform bill, drafted by a committee of which young John C. Calhoun was a member, was passed in the house by a vote of 88 to 22. The senate, more circumspect than that of Maryland, accepted it by a vote of 24 to 6.[50] Because it was now necessary for the legislature to pass the act again in the next session, the election of 1810 was greatly concerned with the merits of suffrage reform as well as with the voting records of the members on the suffrage bill.

Important newspapers, including the *Charleston Courier*, chose to ignore the issue completely. Nevertheless, a comparison of the membership of the legislature of 1809 with that of

---

[49] South Carolina Archives Commission, *House Journals* (Ms.), 1807-1808, pp. 165, 195-196.

[50] S.C.A.C., *House Journals*, 1809, pp. 23-24.

1810 shows a turnover of about 50 percent,[51] a phenomenon in Carolina history and the basis for the observation of a leading Republican opponent of the bill. Judge Charles J. Colcock said on December 8, 1810, that "a complete revolution in publick offices has taken place."[52] The Charleston papers referred only obliquely to the struggle within the Republican party. "A Republican Elector" supported the candidacy of one individual, saying that he was "a fit Representative to oppose the perilous innovations that are meditated in our political system."[53]

Perilous or not, the bill passed the house in 1810 by a vote of 100 to 9 and the senate by a vote of 32 to 6.[54] Henceforth, all persons hitherto qualified to vote could continue to do so, and the franchise was extended to all free white male adult citizens resident for two years in the state. Within the limits of a two-year residency requirement, universal white manhood suffrage had been achieved.

In later years, opponents of John C. Calhoun endeavored to associate him with those who had opposed a democratic suffrage in South Carolina. He was accused in the northern press of saying that universal suffrage was an evil in his state. Fitzwilliam Byrdsall, Loco Foco Democrat, wrote Calhoun in 1842 that it was clear to him from the evidence that Calhoun's opinions were very different and that his vote in the Carolina affair had been a "glorious democratic fact" in his favor.[55] It is true, however, that many Carolinians had a low opinion of universal white suffrage. In 1816, a woman reproached William Lowndes for voting for the protective tariff, branding it the greatest evil since universal suffrage.

[51] S.C.A.C., *House Journals*, 1808, pp. 1-4; 1810, pp. 1-2.

[52] O'Neall, J. B., *Biographical Sketches of the Bench and Bar of South Carolina* (Charleston, 1859, 2 vols.), I, pp. 125-126.

[53] *City Gazette*, Dec. 31, 1810.

[54] *Ibid.*, Dec. 20, 1810.

[55] American Historical Association, *Correspondence of John C. Calhoun* (Washington, D.C., 1899, 2 vols.), II, p. 861.

Carolinians opposed to the suffrage had greatly exaggerated the probable effects of the reform bill. Judge James H. Hammond declared in 1850 that the government of the state was controlled by an aristocracy in the legislature which, he said, was the real center of power. "The people," he maintained, "have none beyond electing members of the legislature—a power very negligently exercised from time immemorial."[56] Even the hopes of reformers that scandalous abuses in voting would be rectified and that representative government would be invigorated were proved misplaced.

Nonetheless, suffrage reform in South Carolina, following the reform in Maryland, meant that of the five states along the southern seaboard only Virginia and North Carolina failed to sustain a democratic suffrage for white adult males, either by universal suffrage or by a taxpaying qualification. If they were frank, Republicans had to concede that reform was far from being a strict party triumph.

[56] Quoted in Meigs, William M., *The Life of John C. Calhoun* (New York, 1917, 2 vols.), I, pp. 106-112, 107n.

NORTHERN SUFFRAGE IN THE JEFFERSONIAN AGE

REPUBLICANS fought more strenuously for suffrage reform in the north than they did in the south, partly because they were endeavoring to increase their strength in a territory where Federalism for many years was as much a "natural" phenomenon as Republicanism in the south. They strove also to perfect a party machine to deliver the votes to their candidates and, where the convictions of party leaders were favorable, they tried to broaden the basis for their popular support by suffrage and other reforms. Federalists reacted by creating or perfecting their own party organization so as to meet the Republicans on their own ground. In self-defense, some Federalists shortsightedly opposed suffrage reform, and to this extent they isolated themselves from the main stream of suffrage thought and gave credence to Republican accusations that the Federalist party as a whole was undemocratic.

The advantages to the Republicans of fighting for suffrage reform were evident in the situation in New York about 1800. In the elections of that year the Republicans had swept the state, thanks to the unpopularity of Federalist measures and to the allegedly tireless efforts of Republicans to stimulate voter interest. John Jay complained that Federalists were too interested in professional and personal concerns for the good of their party, whereas their opponents were united and did not spare time, trouble, or expense. Jay exaggerated the indifference of Federalism in this and in prior elections. New York Federalists had been pioneers in the creation of party machinery to win county, state, and federal elections. The Federalist and Republican parties were alike also in that they were highly personal machines, as had been those of the De Lancey and Livingston factions before the Revolution. Theodore Sedgwick, Yankee Federalist, went so far as to say that the "line of division" by which the parties were separated elsewhere was "more obscurely marked" in New York and that the people were "more under the dominion of personal influence."[1]

The activities of the Federalist Ebenezer Foote of Newburgh exemplifies this phase of Federalist activity. By 1795, he presided over a machine which was operating effectively on a county basis; he employed circulars to stimulate the voters' enthusiasm and made provision for the use of carriages to convey his adherents to the polls.[2] In self-defense, Republicans had to follow suit and create comparable forms of organization, such as those which existed in Delaware County by 1810. A meeting of the Republican Committee of Correspondence on January 10 of that year agreed to divide the county into at least three, but not more than eight, districts and to appoint for each some "young and active person" who would have a "personal communication with every elector" for the purpose of determining his political sympathies. On the basis of these interviews, lists of Republicans and Federalists could be made for the convenience and information of the county organization.[3]

New York Federalists did not hesitate to use their power as manorial lords to coerce their tenants, a power which some of them considered as much a part of the social and political order as the continued deference of their tenants. If Rufus King is to be believed, James Duane thought he had a right to be elected perpetually to the assembly. To assure his chance to exercise this right, he exerted whatever pressure he could as

[1] New York Historical Society, *Rufus King Papers,* xxxi, Sedgwick to King, Aug. 24, 1802.
[2] New York State Library, Manuscript Division, *Ebenezer Foote Papers.*
[3] N.Y.S.L., Manuscript Division, *Samuel A. Law Papers.*

a landlord. Similarly, William Cooper, Federalist boss of Otsego County and father of James Fenimore Cooper, was so violently partisan when Jay ran for governor in 1792 that he threw all discretion to the winds, threatening tenants and debtors with ruin if they did not vote as they were told. He told one man that he would be arrested and jailed if he were to challenge the legality of some of the votes.[4]

Federalist power in Otsego County was not to be compared, however, with the power of Federalist Stephen Van Rensselaer of Rensselaerwyck. Fascinated, if indeed not envious of him, Republicans pilloried him, and truthfully, as the "overgrown landlord, who is troubled at the name of *free* election. . . ."[5] As early as 1794, he wrote his lieutenant at Canajoharie, recommending that he prepare a number of ballots to be distributed among the voters and that he employ a friend or two to attend each poll. If necessary, he agreed to pay the travelling expenses of those who otherwise would have foregone the right to vote. By 1801 he was said to be promising his tenants that he would renounce his right to a quarter of the sale price of a tenancy if the tenant would vote as he directed. His friends, it was said, in his name threatened recalcitrant voters with eviction if they were in arrears of their rent.

Both Federalists and Republicans were often willing to democratize the suffrage during elections, if only secretly and informally, by allowing unqualified persons to vote. While Republicans accused Cooper of allowing non-freeholders to vote in 1792, the Federalist Ebenezer Foote was unhappy to discover in 1809 that in Franklin "every person over 21" was brought to the polls and "forced to vote by Democratic runners."[6] The challenging of voters on the grounds that they were not qualified was more frequent when a contest had

---

[4] *Journals of the House of Assembly of the State of New York 1792*, pp. 70-93, 188-203.

[5] N.Y.S.L., Manuscript Division, *John Williams Papers*, III, p. 187, "A Farmer."

[6] N.Y.S.L., *Foote Papers*, Amos Douglas to Foote, April 28, 1809.

excited strong partisan feelings. On one such occasion, crusty Jeremiah Schuyler, when he learned of the death of the Democrat Major Nicholas Snyder, was heard to say, "Another God Damned Democrat has gone to Hell, and I wish they were all there."[7] In an exciting election of 1786, tenants of Duane were chagrined when they were challenged as unqualified to vote for the senate and for governor. Their explanation was simple. "Had we bin all of one mind," said one, "thair would have bin no objections to our vots."[8]

During the Jeffersonian era, Republicans never made an issue on a statewide basis of the freehold and leasehold qualifications for voting in New York, despite the fact that they were patently undemocratic in principle and in practice. In Amenia, for example, in the election of 1801, only 162 persons voted for governor while 206 were qualified to vote for assemblymen. In the 1783 election in the Poughkeepsie Precinct, there were 92 voters, of whom 5 were not qualified to vote for senators and the governor. These five included two barbers, a cord-wainer, a plumber, and a sailor, showing that some wage workers, artisans, and shopkeepers could not meet the freehold qualification.[9] Deeming the suffrage clauses of the constitution undemocratic, Republicans held a meeting at Vosburgh's Inn in Hoosick on February 11, 1811, and resolved that all who paid taxes or served in the militia should be allowed to vote.[10]

There was considerable difference of opinion among Republicans as to what stand the party should take on suffrage. Should Republicans support a taxpaying or militia qualification? Were the propertyless a potential source of danger and disorder or should the party support the vote, for whites at

[7] N.Y.H.S., *Miscellaneous Manuscripts*, July 5, 1808.

[8] N.Y.H.S., *James Duane Papers*, vi, John Meyers to Duane, May 1, 1786.

[9] N.Y.S.L., *Amenia, Poll Book*, 1800-1801; N.Y.P.L., *Tomlinson Collection*, Poll Lists for Poughkeepsie Precinct, April 29, 1783.

[10] N.Y.S.L., *Miscellaneous Manuscripts*, Hoosick.

least, as a natural right? Probably Federalists and Republicans were more often than not agreed that the freehold test guaranteed the security of liberty, order, and property. Young Martin Van Buren, the future Democratic leader, was nursed intellectually on the ideas of Blackstone and the younger Jefferson, as much so as the future Chancellor of the state of New York, James Kent.[11]

Where prevailing suffrage qualifications interfered greatly with party success, Republicans occasionally opposed them as a matter of self-defense, particularly in the city of New York, where, in municipal elections, voting was confined to the freemen of the corporation and to 20-pound freeholders. City Federalism was the beneficiary of this qualification. In control of the corporation, Federalists refused to admit as freemen humble carters and laboring people to the extent they had previously, preferring to enfranchise merchants instead. The result was that in 1800 13 percent of the total population could vote in state elections but only 5 percent in municipal ones.[12] Furthermore, landowners could vote in every ward where they owned property. With voting still by viva voce, with Federalists able to control the appointment of the inspectors of elections in a way highly satisfying to themselves, the Republicans had additional reasons for attacking the property tests in the city. They did not at first attack the qualification as such, however. They created the Tontine Association to manufacture fagot votes and beat the Federalists at their own game.[13] The Tontine Association was very active during the election of 1801. One of its most zealous members was Daniel D. Tompkins, future Republican governor.

Only when Federalist election inspectors refused to accept

[11] Remini, Robert V., *Martin Van Buren and the Making of the Democratic Party* (New York, 1959), pp. 30-42.

[12] Pomerantz, S. I., *New York, an American City: 1783-1823* (New York, 1938), pp. 26-27, 64-70.

[13] *Ibid.*, p. 134; *New York Evening Post*, Dec. 15, 1801, Jan. 15, 1802.

the Republican fagot votes did Republicans attack the city charter and advocate a lowering of the voting qualifications in charter elections. Defenders of the charter quoted the suffrage principles of Blackstone and reminded Republicans that John Locke had incorporated (as was then believed) a freehold qualification in the constitution he wrote for the Carolinas in 1662. Republicans argued that Locke had been forced to make the Carolina constitution according to "a monarchical plan" and that actually he had been the first writer to define the grand principles of civil government. They made Blackstone a defender of their own principles by quoting out of context his statement that the right to make laws resided in the people at large.[14]

Not being philosophically inclined, a number of carters merely told the Federalist mayor and alderman of the city that, although poor, they had been entrusted with the defense of the country during the late war. Furthermore, if allowing non-freeholders who were not freemen to vote in city elections were really dangerous, they said, they also would be opposed to it. The proof that this practice was not dangerous was the fact that non-freeholders had been voting for years in state elections without any maleffects.[15] Aside from the merits of this argument, Republicans were convinced that suffrage reform would bring many desirable results. It would help reduce the scandalous and lavish expenditure of a rotten borough administration, thereby bringing down the tax rate to reasonable levels.

Republicans found it hard to agree, however, on the program of reform. Some would have been contented with a bill to permit all persons qualified since 1801 to vote in town elections (that is, taxpayers, freeholders, or renters of a $5 tenement) to vote also in charter elections. It proved impossible to secure such a bill. The bill which passed in 1804 gave the

14 *American Citizen*, April 10, July 28, Oct. 26, Nov. 17, 1801.
15 *Ibid.*, Oct. 28, 1801.

vote to all adult male citizens renting a tenement worth $25 a year.[16] It also abolished plural voting and established a secret ballot in city elections; the latter was extended to town elections in 1809.

Suffrage reform proved very important in subsequent electoral successes. Federalists were forced more than ever to seek the favor of the voters, appealing especially to the free Negroes as the Republicans catered to the immigrants whether naturalized or not. Republicans took keen satisfaction in their conviction that reform had freed them from a petty aristocracy and that tradesmen, mechanics, and carters had been granted a second Declaration of Independence. Their only disappointment with the reform bill was its failure to make the office of mayor elective.

A Republican more ardently dedicated to suffrage democracy than any in New York at this time was Abraham Bishop of Connecticut. Perhaps more than any other man, he was responsible for propelling Connecticut into the modern age of democratic republicanism. Son of a deacon of the Congregational Church in New Haven, graduate of Yale, class of 1778, he became a lawyer in 1785. In 1787 he went to Europe, where he spent almost two years. His European experiences, particularly those in France, proved the turning point in his life. He returned to the United States a different man.[17] The *Connecticut Courant* said that Bishop had been "educated in a family respectable for order and religion, and till his departure from college, was a youth of decent manners and sober morals."[18]

---

[16] Pomerantz, *op.cit.*, pp. 143-147; N.Y.S.L., Manuscript Division, *Assembly Papers*, Miscellaneous, VI, p. 48.

[17] See Purcell, R. J., *Connecticut in Transition, 1775-1818* (Washington, D.C., 1918); Robinson, W. A., *Jeffersonian Democracy in New England* (New Haven, 1916); Stamps, Norman, *Political Parties in Connecticut 1789-1819* (unpub. Ph.D. thesis, Yale University, 1952); and Dexter, F. B., "Abraham Bishop of Connecticut and His Writings," Massachusetts Historical Society, *Proceedings* (2nd Series, XIX, 1905), pp. 190-199.

[18] *Connecticut Courant*, Aug. 16, 1802.

Fired with zeal for the rights of man, inspired with the vision of a world of liberty and equality, he returned to a state the antithesis of revolutionary France. Connecticut had weathered the American Revolution without any major structural changes and as late as 1800 could still be designated with much truth as the land of steady habits. Among them were a multiple church establishment, which had remained unchanged since the passage of the Certificate Law of 1791, and a one-party system of Federalism in which Congregational ministers, in consultation with party leaders, determined policy and controlled nominations. The structure of government, resting upon a charter of Restoration times, remained in most fundamentals unaltered as late as 1800.

Likewise, Connecticut suffrage laws had been left untouched by the Revolution. The legal requirement of ownership of a freehold worth 40 shillings a year, or the possession of personal property assessed at 40 pounds, had been translated into terms of American currency in 1796, the freehold worth $7 a year, the personal property assessed for $134.[19] Once admitted to the freemanship, a person retained the rights of a freeman for the rest of his life, unless deprived of them by the highest court. In law at least, a man who was not a freeman might vote in town meeting if he were the owner of a freehold worth $9 or possessed personal property assessed at $150. The personal-property qualification was extremely difficult to meet because most of the personal property which made up an average household was not subject to taxes after the Revolution. Town officials could easily determine the annual value of each freehold because the legislature assigned an annual value per acre for the various kinds of land, crop land, and other, in the state. The tax assessors kept records of them for each taxpayer. From these records, it was possible to determine the annual value of every freehold.

[19] *Acts and Laws of the State of Connecticut in America* (Hartford, 1796), pp. 414-415.

By 1800, if not before, it was becoming difficult to meet the freehold qualification. In East Guilford, now known as Madison, the number of adult male residents who could meet the freehold qualification for the freemanship dropped from 79 percent in 1740 to 65 percent in 1800. In Kent, situated in the extreme western part of the state, the same phenomenon has been observed, those qualifying by ownership of property dropping from 79 percent in 1751 to 63 percent in 1796.[20] Whereas in Kent only 3 percent of adult male residents would never in their lives be able to qualify prior to 1796, after that year 11 percent of adult males would not. So far as the law was concerned, it was becoming more difficult for men to qualify for freemanship. Probably, as modern political parties developed in Connecticut, more attention was given to the enforcement of suffrage laws, thus cutting down the number of voters drawn from the poorer and younger men to whom the Republicans directed their appeal with increasing success.

Even if the suffrage laws had been more democratic, it is not at all probable that popular participation in elections would have been greater during the early national period. Almost all commentators prior to 1800 noted how little interest was displayed in voting. In 1793, it was said that the governor was chosen by 5 percent of the legal voters. As late as 1800, Oliver Wolcott wrote Fisher Ames that in Connecticut it was not considered proper to discuss public men or measures in the newspapers. Fisher Ames had for some years, he said, been happy to know that "folly," i.e., Republicanism, was not a "fashion" in Connecticut.[21] Men in public affairs often held office for years; for example between 1783 and 1801 only one assistant failed to be reelected. The Federalists of Connecticut had as yet no reason to explore some of the practical conse-

[20] Williamson, C., "The Connecticut Property Test and the East Guilford Voter: 1800," *The Connecticut Historical Society Bulletin* (xix, Oct. 1954), pp. 101-104.

[21] C.H.S., *Oliver Wolcott Papers*, xxi, 1800: xviii, Ames to Wolcott, Nov. 4, 1796.

quences of their own republican theory that, in the last analysis, the people were the rulers, because the people of Connecticut had seldom if ever questioned their rule.

Thanks to the work of Abraham Bishop, Ephraim Kirby, Gideon Granger, and others, there was established in Connecticut just prior to the presidential election of 1800 a strong Republican organization to elect Jefferson. Within a short time they had created an authoritarian machine controlled from the top which, radiating from the residences of party leaders, was able to penetrate every town. Supplementing the party organization as a means of attracting votes was the employment of newspapers, magazines, and public mass meetings.[22] The burden of the Republicans' argument was that theirs was the party of democracy. As Bishop wrote in a pamphlet on "Political Delusion," he would use the terms "republican and democrat" synonymously throughout "because the men who maintained the principles of 1776, are characterized by one or other of these names in different parts of the country."[23]

As important as his efforts to elect Jefferson was Bishop's program for Connecticut. He proposed to write a genuine constitution for the state in which the republican principles of separation of the powers of government between the executive, the legislature, and the judiciary would be recognized as well as the total separation of church and state. Furthermore, the tax structure was to be reformed by lessening the burden on male polls, and the suffrage laws were to be amended.

Federalist spokesmen sneered at the demand for suffrage reform as the product exclusively of Republican desire for election to public office, an "excellent hobby horse." Nevertheless, conviction as well as desire for votes figured in the Repub-

[22] Stamps, *op.cit.*, pp. 75-99.
[23] Bishop, Abraham, *An Oration on the Extent of and Power of Political Delusion* (Newark, 1800, 2nd ed.), p. 7n.

lican demands that property be divorced from voting. Drawing upon the full arsenal of suffrage reform arguments, they found it unnecessary to add any new ones. Possibly a greater appeal was made at this time to the philosophy of natural rights as the basis for a democratic suffrage than had been made previously. Man, said the reformers, was not born with a deed in his hand or gold in his pocket. Man was man and who, indeed, was more? They argued also that there was more virtue in the poor than in the rich, for "the Bible says hath not God chosen the poor of this world, rich in faith?"[24]

Federalists fought the reformers partly because they feared the loss of their power as the standing order of Connecticut if the demands for reform were successful. Nevertheless, they were mistaken in opposing suffrage reform and in ignoring the advice of a perspicacious Federalist, John Felch, of Canterbury, who wrote Jonathan Trumbull on September 3, 1803, that the leaders of a certain party had been "very clamorous" to reform the voting qualification and that, "without any inconvenience to the public," freemanship could be extended to taxpayers and militia men. "Be that as it may," he concluded, "it is a popular theme, and I believe they will gain more proselyters [sic] by it, than they would by the *Timely* admission of such to the franchise." A general revision of the civil code "would cripple this Hobby and many others."[25]

Federalists defended the existing qualifications as democratic. They said that with the diffusion of landownership among a majority of adult males and with the relative absence of tenantry, a majority already were voting or could vote. Indeed in Connecticut, they declared, even paupers voted and suffrage was more widespread than in several states which "in name

[24] *Connecticut Republican Magazine* (i, no. 4, 1802), p. 155; *American Mercury*, April 28, 1803.

[25] Connecticut Historical Society, *Jonathan Trumbull Correspondence*, Sept. 12, 1803.

and profession are highly democratic."[26] As a result, they continued, extremes between rich and poor were virtually nonexistent in their state, a state in which power was vested in the middle class. "This middle state," said one newspaper, "has in all ages and countries, and even by God himself been declared to be the state most favorable." Federalist papers told their readers that men influenced by the "fatal error" of France in allowing too many to vote and by the pernicious ideas of Tom Paine were deplorably active in Connecticut. They claimed that Plato, Aristotle, Harrington, Locke, Hume, and Montesquieu were opposed to universal suffrage. The French had had the great misfortune of having repudiated in 1792 the voices of experience in these matters. "From France, that hot bed of Jacobinism and licentiousness, this pestilence of democracy, which threatens our ruin, first sprang," declared "A True Republican."[27]

While opposed to increasing the number of voters in Connecticut by suffrage reform, Federalists were not averse to increasing the number of votes cast in their behalf by whatever means were available. They created fagot votes and used other means to manufacture voters. They perfected a political organization remarkably similar to the Republicans'. They attempted to reduce the number of Republican voters by intimidation. To effect this aim, they secured in 1801 the passage of an act regulating elections for assistants and for members of the United States House of Representatives. While the act authorized the continued use of the secret ballot in elections for governor and town representative, it became known as the Stand Up Law because it required that in other elections voters raise their hands or stand up when publicly polled. Federalists defended the act as being in large measure a reform bill because it abandoned the extremely cumbersome,

[26] *Independent Republican and Miscellaneous Magazine* (Newburyport, Mass.), August 1805, pp. 12-13.
[27] *Windham Herald*, April 23, 1801; *The Visitor* (New Haven), March 29, 1803; *Connecticut Courant*, March 9, 1803.

lengthy, and involved methods previously used in these elections. Nevertheless, it outraged Republicans in Connecticut and elsewhere. "The annals of American legislation do not probably contain a more dangerous precedent," exclaimed one critic.[28] Federalists in the 1802 session of the assembly refused to accept a secret ballot for all elections, showing that the objective of reform was not more important than that of exposing Republican voters to Federalist unpleasantries at election time. In 1813, Federalists resumed their efforts to limit the size of the electorate by passing a bill requiring that the freehold qualification should mean the possession of a freehold free of mortgage, and that the personal-property qualification exclude the $60 valuation placed on each poll.

Reminiscent of the Sedition Act of 1798 were Federalist efforts to limit free speech on the suffrage issue by invoking the state law against sedition. In 1802, Seth Wetmore was fined $100 by the Connecticut Supreme Court for sedition, on the grounds that he had advocated "equal representation which we fought for in the Revolution and universal suffrage." The *Albany Register*, scandalized by Wetmore's conviction, declared that British patriots who had defended the American cause in their country had been advocates of universal suffrage for their own countrymen, and had remained so. With such an example, had not an American the right to labor for suffrage extension "where he thinks it too much restricted for the public good?"[29]

The Supreme Court of Connecticut thought otherwise, as did the legislature when it assumed responsibility for preserving the old suffrage laws against Republican attacks. On October 29, 1802, John T. Peters of Hebron introduced a bill to allow all adult male citizens to vote if liable to pay taxes, or if excused from paying them, if they were also certified by

[28] *The National Intelligencer*, Nov. 16, 1801.
[29] *The National Intelligencer*, Oct. 8, 1802; *Albany Register*, Sept. 28, 1803.

the selectmen and civil authorities as being of good character. He argued, with quotations from Lord Camden and the Whigs of 1775, that taxation and representation should go together. He said that in the town of Woodbury all young men were admitted as freemen and that this was general throughout the state. Peters was saying, in effect, that the property tests should be abolished because they were already meaningless in many towns. He noted that Yale graduates were allowed to vote on the strength of their diplomas and, finally, that Pennsylvania and New Hampshire seemed to experience little or no difficulty with their taxpaying qualifications.

The opposition endeavored to stifle even debate on the bill by "coughing, sneezing [and the] shuffling of feet." One leading opponent, Noah Webster, tried at least to present his own constructive alternative. He proposed to create an electorate modelled upon the distribution of voting power among common stockholders in joint stock companies which varied with the extent of their investment in company stock. According to his plan, each taxpayer would cast one vote, those on tax lists at $100 to $200 would cast two votes, and those listed at more than $200 three votes. All ministers of the gospel would be given three, irrespective of their assessments on the tax list.[30] His proposal was far from popular with Republicans, one of whom said that if one person were worth more than another, the burden of his militia services should be increased proportionately, allowing the poor "to stay home on military day and earn money."[31]

During a debate carried on in the press, Noah Webster wrote that he feared a taxpaying qualification would permit foreigners to vote before they had become thoroughly assimilated. He admitted that there were few foreigners in the state

[30] *Connecticut Journal*, Nov. 24, 1802; *American Mercury*, Nov. 18, 1802; *New Haven Visitor*, Jan. 11, 1803.
[31] *American Mercury*, Feb. 10, 1803.

at the time, but thought that there would be many more in the future. Rome, he said, appealing to Montesquieu, had fallen because she had allowed foreigners to exercise undue influence in her government. Reformers rejected this argument, saying that Webster's source was a "patrician historian or one under patrician influence," implying that for this reason Montesquieu's analysis could be ignored with safety.[32] Those who, unlike Webster, did not wish to admit even taxpayers to a share in elections were indignant at the argument that taxation without representation was tyranny. Asserting in Blackstonian phrases that the suffrage was a matter of expediency and not of right, one newspaper claimed that the "Patriots of '76" had no idea, when they used the argument against the British, "that the State legislature had no right to tax the people, because some, who paid taxes, had not a vote; and some others who did not pay did vote."[33]

Although a Republican paper was not far wrong in asserting that the Republicans and moderate Federalists agreed on all fundamentals, the Republicans could not rally a sufficient number of Federalists to pass the suffrage bill in 1802. It was defeated by a vote of 118 to 58, a predominantly party vote. Republican failure at this time should not obscure the fact that their campaign of education and their party organization was causing a political awakening among a people as conservative as any in America. One indication of their substantial progress was the fact that the number of votes for governor increased 70 percent between 1804 and 1806.[34] If reform had not been affiliated nationally with that Republicanism responsible for the hated Embargo and other acts anathematized in New England, it might have succeeded years before it finally did in 1817 and 1818.

[32] *Ibid.*, March 10, 1803.
[33] *Connecticut Courant*, March 2, 1803.
[34] Stamps, *op.cit.*, p. 112.

The same reversal of Republican fortunes was largely responsible for the decline of Massachusetts Republicanism as the nation approached the brink of war against Great Britain. From about 1800 until the Embargo Act, Massachusetts Federalists, like those of Connecticut, had been increasingly apprehensive for the future of the American form of government, the more so as voters had been supporting the Republicans. It seemed to Federalists that events no longer were confirming Hamilton's assertion in 1788 that "the tendency of the people's suffrage will be to elevate merit even from obscurity."[35]

Angered and saddened by the election of Jefferson in 1800, Federalists nevertheless became as convinced as he of the necessity for preserving America as a land of farmers and of property widely diffused. Unlike Jefferson, however, many Federalists became conservative if not reactionary in their opinions. "We know too much for mobs and massacres," sighed Fisher Ames, "and too much, we might add, for subordination to any good civil government."[36] As early as 1796, he wrote Oliver Wolcott that at a recent meeting in Dedham "almost every gentleman was there & acted with me, but a word about Liberty & putting bridles in the People's mouths routed us all."[37] Other Federalists sympathized with their New York kin who deprecated the wicked practice of reading the Declaration of Independence. Fisher Ames was convinced that Jefferson believed in extreme democratic principles and he accused James Madison of having "a strange vein of absurdity in his head."[38] John Adams, shocked by the lack of patriotism of many Europeans who helped the French to

[35] *The Debates and Proceedings of the Constitutional Convention Assembled at Poughkeepsie on 7 June, 1788* (facsimile ed., Poughkeepsie, 1905), p. 39.
[36] Connecticut Historical Society, *Wolcott Papers*, xviii, Ames to Wolcott, Dec. 2, 1802.
[37] *Ibid.*, xviii, Nov. 14, 1796, Ames to Wolcott.
[38] Warren, Charles, *Jacobin and Junto* (Cambridge, 1931), p. 185n.

subvert their country and overthrow their lawful government in the name of liberty, equality, and fraternity, wrote acidly that the "Treachery of the Common People, against their own Countries . . . has given a paralytic stroke to the Wisdom and Courage of Nations."[39]

In this temper, Federalists were prone not only to reassert the necessity for maintaining balanced forms of government and to stress the rights of minorities, sectional and social, but also to call a halt to any further increase in democratic sentiment and institutions. "The spirit of our country," asserted George Cabot in 1801, "is doubtless more democratic than the *form* of our government. . . ." Hitherto, he said, "the former has been restrained by the latter from those excesses to which it naturally tends." He added, however, that he was opposed to any system of government which "excluded the *People from a share.*"[40]

An alarming increase in the strength of Massachusetts Republicans caused Cabot to change his mind. In 1804, three years after he had declared his opposition to limiting the popular will, he advocated that Massachusetts restrict the electorate to well-to-do freeholders. "If no man in New England," he wrote, "could vote for the legislatures, who was not possessed in his own right of two thousand dollars value in land, we could do something better."[41] Other Federalists displayed their fear of foreigners, one of them writing Timothy Dwight that the Pennsylvania constitution was anathema, not only because it did not require a property qualification for voting but also because foreigners were permitted to vote after only two years' residence. He advised Dwight that no

<hr />

[39] Connecticut Historical Society, *Wolcott Papers*, IX, Adams to Wolcott, Oct. 27, 1797.

[40] N.Y.H.S., *Rufus King Papers*, XXXI, Cabot to King, July 30, Nov. 6, 1801.

[41] Lodge, H. C. (ed), *Life and Letters of George Cabot* (Boston, 1878), p. 344.

Irish or English Jacobins should be allowed to vote unless resident ten years and he really doubted if "full blooded Frenchmen should vote at all."[42]

As an outstanding leader of Massachusetts Republicans, Elbridge Gerry was embarrassed by his Federalist opponents who resurrected his remarks to the Federal Convention that the evils of the time flowed from an excess of democracy. Republicans in the state believed, by and large, in a democratic suffrage. Many Federalists also inclined in this direction. One attacked Virginia as "an aristocracy of planters" where no amount of personal property "constitutes a qualification for the electors."[43]

So indifferent were the legislators of Massachusetts to the qualification for state elections that they did not pass an act, as did Connecticut and Rhode Island, recasting the requirement from terms of pounds to terms of dollars. The act of 1782, stating that those rated at 20 pounds or those not assessed who voluntarily paid a tax equal to two-thirds of a single poll tax could vote in town affairs, appears to have been the qualification from this time forward, although the distinction between state and town electors was drawn in at least one election. The act was afterward justified as a means of enforcing the payment of taxes, beyond that on the poll, rather than as a means of restricting the electorate. In Boston, it was hard to determine the real number of ratable polls because some men avoided both the payment of taxes and their militia obligations by threatening their landlords to move elsewhere if their names were turned in to the tax assessors.[44] Boston was accused of increasing the number of its representatives from 32 to 37, in 1809, by the simple expedient of hav-

[42] Massachusetts Historical Society, *Timothy Pickering Papers*, xxviii, p. 387.
[43] *A Defense of the Legislature of Massachusetts, or the Rights of New England Vindicated* (Boston, 1804), p. 10.
[44] *Boston Gazette*, April 24, 1809.

ing assessors take into consideration *"hundreds of poor people"* who they knew paid no tax.[45] The Registration Act of 1800, probably modelled upon the short-lived County Registration Act passed by the British Parliament in 1785, appears to have been a dead letter, although the town fathers of at least Brookfield conscientiously prepared lists of qualified voters.

Overt complaints were directed against abuses of electoral procedures and, by Federalists, against the resourcefulness of Republicans in finding means within the law to increase the size of their vote. Federalists complained that their opponents called out the militia for training on election day, that they created fagot votes where possible, and that in a Salem election they printed eagles on the ballots in the expectation that voters would use them because they displayed the arms of the United States. The Republican moderators of town electoral meetings in Petersham were accused of abusing the trust reposed in them, and of having permitted "to pass unnoticed the most outrageous, indecent and disorderly behavior, such as repeated shouts, clapping of hands and profane swearing...."[46] The people of Roxbury were so violently partisan that Federalists sat on one side of the hall, Republicans on another. The townsfolk of Roxbury became so angry over the question of sending representatives to the legislature, solely at the town's expense, that an effort was made to invoke the distinction between town and state qualifications. The result was a fight between the two partisans, followed by a "violent scuffle" which caused several to leap for the doors.[47]

There are excellent reasons, therefore, for believing that property as such did not figure greatly in Massachusetts elec-

[45] *Independent Chronicle*, May 22, 1809.
[46] *Hampshire Federalist* (Springfield), May 3, 1810.
[47] Cushing, L. S., Storey, Charles W., Josselyn, L., *Reports of Controverted Elections in the House of Representatives of the Commonwealth of Massachusetts from 1780 to 1852* (Boston, 1853), p. 160.

tions and that Federalists faced not a theory but a condition
bordering on universal suffrage. The mildness of their plan to
reduce the size of their opponents' vote by excluding non-
taxpayers from the suffrage indicates their acute awareness of
the folly of acting upon Cabot's proposal to create a freeholder
electorate. In 1809, they sponsored an act which required that
collectors of taxes make lists of electors upon which the names
of all freeholders would appear, as well as the names of those
who had paid taxes of any sort or kind at least once during the
three preceding years. Only those whose names appeared on
this list could vote in town affairs. As town electors were more
often than not state electors as well, this act was designed to
cut down the Republican vote in all elections.[48] The act
aroused Republicans. They accused Federalists of endeavoring to disfranchise young men who had not recently paid
their taxes but who now were eager to vote. The *Independent
Chronicle* did not attack the taxpaying qualification as much
as it did the unfair use which Federalists would make of the
admittedly frequent evasions of taxes by young and poor Republicans. Federalists defended the act on the grounds that
taxation and representation were inseparable but it proved
impossible to defend even on these grounds. Republicans
asked the voters to support them because their opponents had
attempted to deprive the young men of their vote.[49]

Chastened Federalists retired from the scene with a bill
which repealed the obnoxious legislation before the election
of 1810. The *Berkshire Reporter* was correct in saying that the
repeal was a "compliment to the feelings of democrats" and
that the legislature had shown itself unwilling to "give *offense*
to *the* weaker brethren." An act of 1811, passed under Republican auspices, was a break with legislation extending as far

[48] *The Public and General Laws of the Commonwealth of Massachusetts,* IV (Boston, 1816), pp. 95-96.
[49] *Boston Patriot,* March 28, 1810.

back as 1692 in that it allowed all adult male citizens, resident in a town one year, and liable to be taxed, to vote in town elections. If taxed on property or on their polls, they could vote in other town affairs. It is difficult to understand, except on the grounds of partisanship or ignorance, a statement made in 1812 in a Vermont newspaper that in Massachusetts the property qualification for voting and holding office deprived thousands of their rights.[50]

While Massachusetts Republicans had to contend only with a taxpaying qualification, their fellows in Rhode Island contended with a 40-pound freehold qualification for voting. An act passed in 1798 restated the qualification in terms of dollars, $134 instead of 40 pounds, showing that the legislature intended to enforce it. Despite their emphasis in Rhode Island on the Jeffersonian belief that the cultivators of the soil were the most virtuous, valuable, and vigorous citizens, Republicans found it expedient to attack the freehold qualification, a program which under the pressure of the Dorr War was finally successful in 1842.

Stimulated by the success of the South Carolina reform of 1810, by criticism of the freehold qualification for voting for the senate and the governor in New York, by thorough acquaintance with the earlier movement in Connecticut and the agitation of suffrage matters in Massachusetts in 1809 and 1810, a suffrage reform movement got under way, if abortively, in 1811. Republicans saw that reform was desirable because Federalists manufactured votes by splitting freeholds for election purposes, by which means they often cast more votes in towns than Republicans, because paupers were allowed to vote and because freeholds not worth $134 were deliberately overvalued to allow their owners to vote. Negroes and possessors of life leases were voting also.[51] Federalism

---

[50] *The North Star* (Danville, Vermont), Aug. 15, 1812.
[51] *Rhode Island Republican*, April 16, May 9, July 17, 1811.

represented an aristocracy, charged Republicans, which had developed quite unnaturally in the "home of civil and religious liberty" and one-half of the citizenry were not legally qualified to vote. Citing Paine, Franklin, and the *Connecticut Republican Magazine*, the *Rhode Island Republican* advocated that all those having a "sufficient, evident common interest in and attachment to society" should be allowed to vote, meaning all taxpayers, militia men, and road workers. Republicans tried to convince Rhode Islanders that it was the Federalists who opposed "a free suffrage for the people."[52] Nevertheless, they deprecated the fact that men of their own party upheld the old charter and that the party had failed to make suffrage reform an issue at the state convention of March 1811. This convention was held about the time that a suffrage reform bill, having passed the senate, was held up in the house. Obviously, suffrage reform was a minority sentiment in both parties at this time. Largely for this reason, the freehold qualification survived in Rhode Island well into the nineteenth century.

Whereas in New York, Connecticut, Massachusetts, and Rhode Island, the suffrage issue was related to reformist convictions and to political expediency, it would be difficult to assert that these factors were present to an equal extent in the changes in New Jersey suffrage in 1807. With possibly 70 percent of adult males voting in 1790, suffrage reform was not likely to be much of an issue.[53] As a result, reform in New Jersey was fairly unique. Chief among the demands hitherto made in relation to voting had been one to bring the poll closer to the voter because "true principles of Republicanism and of genuine Liberty requires [sic] that elections should be brought as near to every Man's Door as possible so that the

[52] *Ibid.*, Feb. 21, May 29, 1811.
[53] Pole, J. R., "The Suffrage in New Jersey, 1790-1807," *Proceedings of the New Jersey Historical Society* (LXXI, Jan. 1953), pp. 39-61.

genuine voice of the People may be taken. . . ."[54] The concession of township polling in 1797 met this criticism. Subject to criticism also were the admitted excesses of partisanship, as revealed in the complaints concerning an election held in Trenton. At this election, said critics, men under age voted, as had some Philadelphians, Negroes, slaves, aliens, married women, and persons not worth 50 pounds.[55] The confusion, vagueness, and looseness of the suffrage clause of the constitution and the general indifference to proper enforcement rendered it generally a dead letter. Even tests for officeholding were ignored.

One Federalist, William Griffith, fussed considerably over the jungle-like confusion in the state, and had advocated a taxpaying qualification as a desirable simplification of existing rules and regulations. He was unable to excite much enthusiasm for his proposal until an extraordinary election in Essex County in 1807 made clear the necessity for clarifying and purifying the suffrage. The object of this election had been to determine whether the county seat should be located in Newark or in Elizabeth. Local patriotism and self-interest got the better of the moral and legal scruples of the community, irrespective of party affiliation. In the election, the people of Newark alone cast more votes than had ever been cast in the county as a whole. It was, as an historian has written, a saturnalia of corruption and abuse.[56]

This election demonstrated the necessity of removing the ambiguities and confusions from the constitutional qualifications. As a result, suffrage concerns figured importantly in the assembly of 1807. Declaring that the number of corrupt elections since 1798, the number of aliens, Negroes, and women who were voting, as well as the great diversity in

[54] New Jersey State Library, *AM 1,976* (1793).
[55] New Jersey State Library, *AM 1,979* (1802).
[56] Pole, J. R., "The Suffrage in New Jersey, 1790-1807," *op.cit.*, pp. 55-58; *Sentinel of Freedom*, April 14, 21, 1807; Aug. 25, 1807.

means used to determine the value of the property tests had created an intolerable situation, a newspaper said that means had to be found to prevent the good people of the state from falling prey to a "Second Bonaparte."[57]

The legislature responded by passing an act to clarify the constitutional requirement. Under the provisions of this act, all free white male citizens worth 50 pounds could vote. However, any person otherwise qualified, who had paid a state or county tax, or had his name enrolled upon a tax duplicate for the last state or county tax, would be deemed to be worth 50 pounds.[58] The bill had the support not only of Republicans but also of the Federalist members of the legislature. The creation of a taxpaying qualification established on a legal basis a very broad franchise. Few, if any, householders would escape the tax collector. Single men *with* horses were taxed and single men *without* horses. As elsewhere, an approximation of universal taxation created an approximation of universal suffrage.

While suffrage reform in New Jersey was something of a special case, the history of suffrage since the beginning of the two-party system shows, as George Cabot said, that the country was more democratic than its institutions. A democratic suffrage philosophy was not the monopoly of either of the two great parties, because they shared a common inheritance of democratic ideas from the Revolutionary period. *The National Intelligencer*, a Republican organ, declared, apropos the change in the voting qualification in New York City, that it was "ardently to be desired that but one opinion may ere long prevail on this point among the Republicans of the United States."[59]

[57] *The True American*, Nov. 23, 1807.
[58] Bloomfield, J., *Laws of the State of New Jersey* (Trenton, 1811), p. 34.
[59] *Republican Watch-Tower*, April 21, 1804, quoting *The National Intelligencer*.

 CHAPTER 10

HARD FEELINGS ABOUT
THE SUFFRAGE

IN BRITAIN and in Europe, the Napoleonic Wars were followed by a period of reaction against war and revolution, and against the democratic principles which many thought were responsible for both. British historians have long agreed that the sequence of events from 1789 to 1815 postponed the reform of British suffrage and representation until 1832, when the great Reform Bill was passed. The conservative reaction was reflected here and there in America but it made little or no impression upon majority opinion in Connecticut, Massachusetts, and New York, where constitutional revision reopened the issue of the suffrage. Conservatives thought they had the better of the arguments, but they did not have the votes to sustain them.

The reasons for the further attrition of suffrage conservatism differed somewhat from state to state. Federalism in Connecticut, for example, had been dealt a series of blows since about 1812 from which it never recovered. Firstly, the Federalists' lack of patriotism during the war was widely condemned; secondly, they failed to appease the religious grievances of a large number of citizens and, in general, showed themselves incapable of adjusting their thought to the changing times. Federalism was weakened further as the result of criticism within the party of the power of Congregational ministers in state affairs. Lay Federalists were less disposed to accept without question the advice, so freely tendered, of leading Congregational ministers on nominations to office and on other secular matters. Lyman Beecher asserted

182

that the refusal of Federalist laymen to accept the nominees of the ministers for governor in 1811 "shook the stability of the standing order and the Federal Party in the state" and, in effect, broke the charm which the ministers had held for generations over laymen.[1]

Demands for reform increased to the point where it was possible to unite all the elements which had grievances against the standing order. The fusion of the reform elements took place at a meeting of Republicans and Episcopalians at New Haven in February 1816. Reformers agreed to a program which included pledges to separate church and state, reform the suffrage, repeal the Stand Up Law, shift the incidence of taxation from polls to real property, and achieve full publicity for legislative debates and proceedings, a practice conceded in Britain only shortly before the American Revolution and by the United States Congress as late as 1793.

Oliver Wolcott, ex-Federalist, farmer, manufacturer, and Congregationalist, assumed the leadership of a more heterogeneous Republican party than that of Abraham Bishop's time. To appeal to all reformers, it was called the Toleration Party or the Union Reform Ticket. The party exerted all its efforts in 1817 to win control of the state government in order to assure the calling of a constitutional convention which would carry through reform.[2]

The first order of business for Republicans after their success in the elections of 1817 was the repeal of the Stand Up Law. A friend of Oliver Wolcott strongly advised him to attack the law because it was outrageous that men "called freemen" had to vote publicly before the civil authorities and established clergy, both of whom were active in elections. Connecticut would not know true freedom, he said, until it

[1] Beecher, Charles (ed.), *Autobiography, Correspondence etc. of Lyman Beecher, D.D.* (New York, 1864, 2 vols.), I, p. 259.

[2] Purcell, *op.cit.*, pp. 333-335; Stamps, *op.cit.*, pp. 228-232.

enjoyed the secret ballot in all elections.[3] Much to the point was Republican conviction that the law cost them about one-fourth of their potential voting strength. The property tests, the failure of Federalist-dominated towns to qualify as many Republican freemen as they did Federalists, and the "criminal neglect" of voting were responsible, according to Connecticut Republicans, for the fact that only about one person in ten voted in their state, whereas about one in six voted in Massachusetts, New Hampshire, and Vermont.[4]

Federalists defended the old order, particularly the Stand Up Law, saying that its repeal would force the return to the cumbersome methods of nominating the assistants which had been abandoned by some towns in favor of those of the Stand Up Law long before it had been passed. Republicans remained unconvinced and, in the fall of 1817, it was repealed.[5]

Another reform adopted in 1817 increased Republican strength. Believing that the most important element of the population unable to qualify under existing legislation were young men, reformers gave the vote to all free males over twenty-one who paid taxes or served in the militia. Although this act was in part an electoral stratagem, it also stemmed from the conviction that in any act so fundamental as the writing of a constitution virtually all adult males should have a say. It was because of this conviction that all adult males had been permitted to vote for members of the state convention to ratify the Federal Constitution.[6] Federalists opposed the act publicly as much as they dared. They denounced it as a wicked device of Connecticut Jacobinism, adopted only when Republicans suspected that a majority of qualified freemen would not vote for reform.[7]

[3] *Wolcott Papers*, xlv, anonymous letter, April 21, 1817, to Wolcott.
[4] *American Mercury*, April 2, 1817.
[5] Purcell, *op.cit.*, pp. 363-364.
[6] Stamps, *op.cit.*, p. 250; Purcell, *op.cit.*, p. 372.
[7] *Connecticut Mirror*, Nov. 2, 1818.

Federalists tried to discredit reform not only by associating it with Jacobinism but also by confounding it with the British reform movement. Commenting upon the Union and Reform Ticket of 1817, the *Connecticut Mirror* said that this "charming name appears to be of English origin, and is thought will inherit all the virtues of its family relations in that country."[8] Agreeing with Lyman Beecher that Connecticut Republicans included nearly all the smaller sects, "besides the Sabbath-breakers, rum-selling tippling folk, infidels and ruff-scuff generally," Federalists spokesmen were certain that the Republic had degenerated under the leadership of Jefferson.[9] Cromwell's military dictatorship was as much the inevitable outcome of English democracy as Napoleon's dictatorship was the outcome of French democracy, declared the *Connecticut Courant*, and asserted that both Englishmen and Frenchmen preferred a military dictatorship to the "plague of democracy, from which they had escaped." A dictatorship, it implied, would be preferable to democracy in Connecticut.[10]

Here, as elsewhere, Federalists appealed to the writings of Thomas Jefferson when it suited their purposes. They tried to infer from what he had written that all was well in Connecticut, quoting his alleged statement that Connecticut was "the Athens of America."[11] Some Federalists introduced the argument that their state was basically a democracy in the true sense of the word because the people, rightly conceived, already comprised the majority of the voters. Drawing a distinction between *the people* and *the populace*, the *Courant* declared that *the people* were actually the middle class. In Connecticut, this middle class was descended from Englishmen who had triumphed at the time of the Glorious Revolution. It was midway between "the great ones" and the popu-

8 *Ibid.*, Aug. 18, 1817.
9 Beecher, Charles (ed.), *Autobiography of Lyman Beecher*, i, p. 342.
10 *Connecticut Courant*, Feb. 27, 1816.
11 *Ibid.*, July 8, 1817.

lace, which elsewhere in the world, particularly in Africa and Asia, was alarmingly large.[12]

In reply, Republicans revived the arguments of Abraham Bishop, but they recognized also that changing times had produced new problems, all of which had a bearing upon the suffrage reform movement. One of these was the result of the growth of manufacturing which had been stimulated by the Embargo and War of 1812 and now sought protection by federal tariff legislation. Henry Clay, sponsor of the American system, advocated a protective tariff not only to help small manufacturers struggling against British competition but also to create a home market in the east for the surplus farm products of the west. In Philadelphia, Matthew Carey, fresh from reading Richard Malthus' *Essay on Population,* supported tariff protection as the means by which American manufacturers could pay higher wages to their working people than were paid in Europe, thereby forestalling Malthus' gloomy predictions concerning the future of an industrial society.

Connecticut's suffrage reformers were sensitive to this problem and aware of its bearing upon the suffrage because Connecticut was becoming a center of manufacturing. Hitherto, the Blackstonian argument that employees of manufacturing establishments should not be allowed to vote because they were overly dependent upon their employers had been a theoretical one for Americans in general. This argument was relevant only in an industrial society such as Britain or in certain societies on the European continent. The debates in America over the tariff showed, however, that the tempo of industrialism in the United States was quickening. The fears of suffrage conservatives for the future had, for the first time, real substance. The Connecticut legislature listened with at-

[12] *Connecticut Courant,* quoted in *The American Star* (Petersburg, Va.), Aug. 16, 1817.

tention, no doubt, to Matthew Griswold when he described in Blackstonian terms how manufacturing would in time change the face of America and produce a shock to the electoral system.[13]

In an important development in suffrage thought, Republicans, some of whom were engaged like Wolcott in manufacturing, repudiated the Blackstonian argument and advocated a taxpaying qualification. *Niles' Register*, a national spokesman for the manufacturing interest, said that property tests themselves led to an aristocracy while a personal-property test or universal suffrage led to election frauds. Only a taxpaying qualification was free of these undesirable accompaniments. A proper and just handling of the suffrage, it maintained, was the bulwark against social instability and radicalism. Industrialism, in effect, was incompatible neither with order nor a broad suffrage. "If the suffrage is rightfully considered," *Niles' Register* said in 1820, "it is hardly possible that any serious contention can arise among the people of a free state." Needless to say, the journal approved the repeal of the Stand Up Law, declaring that Connecticut needed a constitution to secure "equal rights."[14]

At this time, Connecticut was not only undergoing changes resulting from the growth of manufacturing but was also being affected by the growth of the New West. Young men and others had already left Connecticut to help found Vermont and had contributed greatly to the peopling of the Western Reserve. One suffrage reformer argued that political reform at home might prevent further emigration. The *Connecticut Register* declared that, if men continued victims of the Stand Up Law and other injustices, they would "emigrate to the west and your state would lose its name in the nation."[15]

[13] *American Mercury*, June 9, 1818.
[14] *Niles' Register*, Oct. 21, 1820; Oct. 25, 1817; Nov. 22, 1817.
[15] *Connecticut Register*, Oct. 3, 1818.

Lastly, Republicans were aware of the necessity for the reform of the militia. In Washington, John C. Calhoun, as Secretary of War, was endeavoring to create a militia system which would prove more effective in future wars. Reformers in Connecticut thought that the militia of their state had been ineffective in the War of 1812 because young men were not very concerned about protecting a state in whose government they had no share, and they argued that at least all adult males active in the militia should be allowed to vote. A New Haven paper declared in 1816 that it was as honorable to qualify a man as a freeman as it was to equip him to fight, as honorable to assist him in getting to the polls as in getting him to a military review.[16]

In one particular only were proponents and opponents of reform in agreement. Both had had considerable acquaintance with the abuse of the franchise by illegal voting and they wanted a realistic and enforceable election law. The elections of 1817 and 1818 had witnessed extraordinary exertions on both sides to win by fair means or foul. One observer declared, in view of the practices of those elections, that Connecticut had a corrupt version of universal suffrage and that almost any change would be for the better.[17] Partly for this reason, the suffrage clause of the constitution, conceding the vote to adult white males of "good character," resident six months in a town, who were $7 freeholders or militiamen or state taxpayers, was considered by many a successful effort to purge the suffrage of undesirable and overly democratic elements. Indeed, the *Connecticut Herald* denied on September 28, 1818, that the constitution rested upon universal manhood suffrage, saying that the illegal practices which had prevailed before had "approached far nearer to universal suffrage than the . . . suffrage article of the Constitution."

[16] *Columbian Register* (New Haven), Nov. 2, 1816.
[17] *American Mercury*, June 9, 1818.

Nevertheless, the provision of the constitution and the act of 1821, which removed the theoretical distinction between the freeman qualification and the qualification for non-freemen for voting in town affairs, brought the law into conformity with the practice in towns at various times, i.e., voting by males who were resident taxpayers. If the growth of parties caused a more stringent enforcement of the laws than previously, it is a distinct possibility that in actual practice the suffrage was less "democratic" after 1818 than it had been in the eighteenth century. At all events, the numbers voting in elections declined rather than increased after the reform was instituted. Moreover, the requirement that voters be citizens indicated an increase in legal precision and a suspicion of foreigners. Oliver Wolcott, for one, shared the growing bias of his generation against immigrants. During 1803 he had written Fisher Ames that the landowners of Pennsylvania had unwisely stimulated the rapid settlement of their colony by offering citizenship on easy terms "till at length the powers of Government, have been transformed to a Class of People, too heterogeneous . . . & too violent and ignorant to use with moderation."[18]

The citizenship requirement came just one year after Chief Justice Marshall, in the case of Chirac v. Chirac, had laid down the dictum that naturalization lay exclusively in the sphere of federal competence.[19] Henceforth, states which inserted citizenship clauses had reference to citizenship gained under federal statutes rather than those which some states had inherited from colonial times. Another indication that the convention was more prejudiced about race than about class was its confinement of the suffrage to persons who were white.

[18] *Wolcott Papers*, xxi, Jan. 24, 1803.
[19] Roche, John P., *The Early Development of United States Citizenship* (Ithaca, 1949), pp. 6, 7, 7n.

For a number of reasons, therefore, the constitution in its suffrage and other clauses was a moderate document for which even Federalists could vote. Indeed, their aid was almost indispensable in achieving the adoption of a constitution which aroused criticism because it did not meet demands for universal suffrage or for a redistricting of seats in the legislature. The adoption of the constitution, however, caused a slump in reform interest as indicated by the decline in voting. "In Connecticut," said the *National Advocate* of New York, "they disarmed the poorer classes by taking them into the body politic."[20] A taxpaying qualification in Connecticut, as in many other states, was almost manhood suffrage, so long as males of voting age were almost all polled.

The success of Connecticut reform helped to generate elsewhere in the northeast a questioning of the effectiveness, utility, and justice of state constitutions which had existed since the close of the Revolution without much modification. In Massachusetts, for example, the press kept the public informed of developments in Connecticut. However, when Massachusetts decided on constitutional revision and reform, the immediate occasion was the decision of the people of the District of Maine to set up their own state.[21] In 1819 the separation was formalized. Maine drafted a constitution which conceded universal manhood suffrage in state elections and a taxpaying qualification in town meetings, thus writing into law an approximation of the prevailing practice in Massachusetts, as Vermont had legalized the loose practices prevailing in her parent state, Connecticut, before the Revolution.[22]

One year after Maine became a separate state, a notable convention met in Boston. The suffrage was an important sub-

[20] *National Advocate*, Aug. 18, 1821.
[21] *Boston Daily Advertiser*, July 17, 20, 21, 1819.
[22] Thorpe, *op.cit.*, III, pp. 1,646-1,664.

ject of its debate, particularly during the exchange of views between old John Adams, the chairman of the convention, and the young Daniel Webster. The last Federalist president of the United States could not abandon his adherence to the Blackstonian school. He had declared himself against a tax-paying qualification in 1811 and, as late as 1816, he was shocked by the venality of British elections.[23] He knew, more-over, that Massachusetts was changing, and in his opinion not always for the better. Another prominent citizen, Josiah Quincy, was alarmed by the increase in paupers, writing Oliver Wolcott that "the poor come in shoals from Nova Scotia & Ireland; and we must find some means to reduce the num-ber or we shall all be candidates for the alms house."[24] A Boston paper averred that pauperism was increasing more rapidly in Massachusetts than in Britain and that the increase was due to alcoholism, early and improvident marriages, and an irrational system of outdoor poor relief like that against which liberal British economists railed.[25] Manufacturing was aggravating rather than ameliorating the situation. The paral-lel between old and New England seemed too marked to ignore. Massachusetts seemed just a step or two behind Britain.

For these reasons, John Adams was convinced more stub-bornly than ever that the future happiness and welfare of the American people rested not only upon a system of checks and balances but also upon sound suffrage principle and practice. It is therefore understandable that he abandoned his impar-tial role as chairman of the convention long enough to make known his views, now reactionary even for Federalism. The French Revolution, he said sarcastically, was a "perfect and complete" example of the "utility and excellence of universal

---

[23] Library of Congress, *Thomas Jefferson Papers*, ccviii, to Jefferson, Dec. 16, 1816.
[24] *Wolcott Papers*, xlvii, March 11, 1821.
[25] *Boston Intelligencer and Evening Gazette*, March 17, 1821.

suffrage." Its British advocates, he exclaimed, were "ruining themselves."[26]

In one of the more notable addresses of the convention, Daniel Webster answered the old gentleman obliquely. He spoke as a man greatly influenced by the seventeenth-century English theorist, James Harrington, whose most famous assertion was that dominion follows property, and also by ideas bearing a Jeffersonian stamp. Acknowledging that, where there were great extremes between the propertied and the non-propertied, universal suffrage would indeed be dangerous, Webster went on to say that in this country "the people possess the property more emphatically than it could be said of the people of any country," and that the real task of statesmen was to see that property was distributed in such a way as to give the "great majority of society an interest in defending it."[27] Only where great inequalities in property existed would universal suffrage be a menace to property, liberty, and order.

The majority of the members of the convention were in agreement with Webster, and for this reason the suffrage debate was not so important as the issue of representation. Webster was an advocate of representation, not on the basis of population exclusively but on the basis of taxation as well, particularly in the senate. He was not fearful of a liberal suffrage in the future as much as he was concerned about a more equitable representation for commercial and manufacturing interests and a better balance between the various interests in the state. New York's *National Advocate* of July 21, 1821, published a brilliant analysis of Webster's role at the convention. Claiming that celebrated men were more "attentive to local interests than to great principles of free government," it said that no one at the convention had displayed

[26] *Journals of the Debates and Proceedings in the Convention of Delegates . . . 1820* (Boston, rev. ed., 1853), p. 278.
[27] *Ibid.*, pp. 312-315.

more ingenuity than Webster, "for while he was apparently advocating the Agrarian, or rather, freehold plan of government, and seemed disposed to lodge the power with the agriculturalists he was actually laboring to secure to the commercial portion of the commonwealth the power in the senate. This complexion," the paper exclaimed, "was probably thrown over his reflections, to obtain the votes of the country members."

Webster failed to secure the adoption of his plan of representation, but he collaborated successfully in the plan for suffrage by which taxpayers could vote if qualified by age, residence, and citizenship. He maintained that no one who did not contribute to the support of government should be allowed to vote, a principle very different from that underlying universal suffrage and a logical position for one who advocated representation based upon taxation for the senate.

When the convention composed an address to the people, it supported the suffrage clause with the observation that it would "relieve Selectmen from much perplexity, and will enable them easily to distinguish between those who have a right to vote and those who do not."[28] Newspaper discussion of the suffrage clause was so slight as to indicate that the general torpor of opinion about constitutional matters in general extended to suffrage matters. Only one newspaper hailed it as a triumph for the rights of man and as of "more importance in principle than all the others put together."[29] On November 1, 1820, the *Essex Register* of Salem approved the clause, declaring that a property qualification was an encouragement to fraud in times of political excitement, "and these are the only times when any qualifications are necessary, for it is only at such times that they are attended to. If there was any way by which no one but those who would exercise their judgment freely, and without influence or cor-

[28] *Ibid.*, p. 625.   [29] *Boston Statesman*, April 16, 1821.

ruption should be admitted to the vote, we would most gladly subscribe to it. But we are satisfied no such way exists—we therefore must, most certainly open the door of universal suffrage." Because adult males without property were liable to a poll tax and, if overlooked by the tax assessors, had the right to demand that they be taxed, suffrage without reference to property had been effected without being expressly recognized by law. In the light of the suffrage history of Massachusetts, it may be said that the document altered, but not essentially, the old qualification.

Response to the qualification was not wholly favorable, however. In answer to the comments of some who were disappointed that unmarried women who owned property or paid taxes could not vote, "Gracchus" replied that they had disobeyed God's injunction to multiply and subdue the earth. Aristotle's authority was invoked because he had written that women were less fit to govern than men. The provision of the constitution which allowed minors enrolled in the militia to vote in militia elections was attacked on the grounds that some masters would be obliged to train under their apprentices, "to the great detriment of the principle of subordination established from the beginning of the world."[30] These criticisms had little effect. The suffrage clause was ratified by a vote of 18,702 to 10,150.

In the same year, the Boston town-meeting form of government was finally abandoned in favor of a city form of government, the suffrage being extended to all taxpayers. Two years later, the last propertied distinction between voters in town affairs and state voters was abolished. The simplification of the suffrage thus achieved did not increase popular participation in government, unless the electorate received an unusual political stimulus. For example, votes for governor declined from 53,297 in 1820 to 49,086 in 1821, shot up to

[30] *Independent Chronicle*, Sept. 20, Sept. 23, 1820.

73,051 in 1824, then dropped to 40,338 in 1826.[31] Lack of interest, for whatever reason, rather than lack of enfranchisement has been the vital fact in Massachusetts electoral history. It is doubtful if the right to vote in Massachusetts just before the Civil War was any more widely shared than it had been before the American Revolution, despite the "democratization" of the suffrage.[32] Only one person in six of the total population was a legal voter in 1857.

A quite different pattern of enfranchisement, or unenfranchisement, prevailed in New York, where, in 1821, a convention distinguished by the presence of many notable Americans was the seat of one of the great suffrage debates in American history. The desire, long dormant, to revise or to scrap the Revolutionary constitution was stimulated by the efforts of British reformers to liberalize the franchise in Britain. New York and Albany papers reported mass meetings addressed by Orator Hunt and others in Manchester, Smithfield, and Leeds. William Cobbett's *Political Register* was quoted. Finally, accounts in the press of the Connecticut and Massachusetts conventions also encouraged criticism of New York's political institutions. Many persons favorably impressed by what was happening in nearby eastern states met in conventions to demand reform in Washington County in 1817 and in Montgomery County in 1820. The members of the latter convention were said to be watching the outcome of the Massachusetts deliberations "with anxious solicitude."[33]

Some New Yorkers were critical of revisionism wherever it might occur and happy to learn that it had not been as extreme as feared. Rufus King, for example, was pleased that Massachusetts had rejected universal suffrage. The *New York Evening Post* declared that scenes of "mobocratic gallantry"

---

[31] Massachusetts Archives, *Abstracts of Votes.*
[32] *Manual for the Use of the General Court* . . . (Boston, 1860), p. 13.
[33] *Albany Argus*, June 24, 1817; Feb. 9, 1821.

which had occurred recently in some British cities were an inevitable result of the demagoguery of men like Burdett and Hunt.[34] The *Albany Daily Advertiser* expressed the hope on May 3, 1817, that the morals of Connecticut would not be destroyed "in the whirlpool of democratic liberty and Jacobin frenzy."

A major impulse for revision of New York's constitution came from the great changes taking place in the character of the population of the state. Not only did Yankee merchants move into the port of New York early in the nineteenth century to engage in trade, but Yankees also came over the barrier of the Berkshires and the Green Mountains to settle upstate New York. Whereas in 1777 two-thirds of the population of New York lived south of Albany, in 1820 the figure was only one-third.[35] Furthermore, the nature of this population was changing the state and its political outlook because Yankees, coming from states which had not since the Revolution known a balanced form of government or, with the exception of Rhode Island, a freehold qualification for voting, or even much enforcement of the suffrage laws, found New York's constitution undemocratic. Of the 107 members of the constitutional convention which met in Albany in 1821, 31 had been born in Connecticut and 7 in Massachusetts.[36] Contemporaries realized the significance of these facts. Rufus King, Federalist turned Republican, wrote Christopher Gore that the population of the state was "nearly divided between the old and the new Inhabitants—the latter are out of New England where laws, customs, and usages differ from those of

[34] *Ibid.*, Aug. 21, 1818.

[35] Young, Helen I., *A Study of the Constitutional Convention of New York State in 1821* (unpub. Ph.D. thesis, Yale University, 1910), pp. 2-3, 11.

[36] Carter, N. H., Stone, W. L., Gould, M.T.C., *Reports of the Proceedings and Debates of the Convention of 1821* (Albany, 1821), pp. 687-689.

N York."[37] James Wadsworth, a major landowner of the Gene-
see, declared flatly in 1821 that "whatever abstract opinions
old Inhabitants on the Hudson may entertain on the subject
of civil government," it should not be overlooked that "we
are a Republic surrounded by sister republics, whose Constitutions are more liberal than our own—and the common
people of those republics have acquired a general intelligence
& a sense of moral obligation which guaranty to their governments a stability & a fidelity . . . which ours does not possess.
You cannot retard, you cannot stay, the progress of these
liberal provisions for the improvement of the people of this
state."[38]

In New York, suffrage became a much more important issue
than it had been in either Connecticut or Massachusetts, and
for good reason. The existence of a balanced form of government resting upon a dual electorate, composed of 20-pound
freeholders and 40-shilling renters for the assembly, and 100-
pound freeholders for the senate and for governor, was threatened. By 1821, the total electorate of both classes comprised
14.76 percent of the total population, or approximately 78
percent of adult males. Only 38.7 percent of all electors could
vote legally, however, for governor and the senate. In New
York City, about 62 percent of the total male population
could vote legally while only 24 percent could vote for senators and governor.[39] Critics found it impossible to understand
why the New York founding fathers, in a convention elected
by the mass of the people, created such complex and undemocratic suffrage qualifications. One observer declared that it
was due to the colonial aristocracy of New York whose allegiance to the Revolution would have been jeopardized if

[37] *Rufus King Papers*, Oct. 14, 1821.
[38] *Ibid.*, James Wadsworth to William A. Duer, Dec. 31, 1821.
[39] See Hough, F. B., *Census of Electors of the State of New York*
(Albany, 1857), p. x.

an overly democratic government had been established. Also, it was said that, without residence and property tests, Tories, Hessians, and other undesirables would have made more difficult the election of safe and sound Whigs.[40] The *National Advocate* had another explanation: the founding fathers knew the rights of man in theory but they had yet to learn them by practice. "Whatever the cause for the suffrage clauses of the constitution, they must go," said the newspaper. "We are not a government of the people while such disabilities exist. . . ."[41] Arguments based on natural rights, now platitudinous, were used here as elsewhere by reformers, and at various meetings held on July 4, 1820, to advocate suffrage reform there were demands to extend the franchise to militia men and taxpayers.

Practical no less than theoretical considerations figured in the burden of arguments against the existing suffrage laws. "Republican Young Men," comprising a group which could least easily meet the qualifications, held a meeting at Saratoga on January 22, 1821, and criticized the constitution for limiting the suffrage and not placing more local offices at the disposal of the electorate.[42] As fundamental was the argument that the suffrage laws meant different things in different parts of the state. Evidence was presented that in some places all adult male residents on tax lists were being permitted to vote, that the distinction between the voters for the assembly and for the senate and governor broke down under the impact of party ambition, that fagot voting was widespread, and that with no sure method of determining who could or could not qualify, many persons, when tendered the elector's oath, perjured themselves, unwittingly or not. One observer commented that to extend the franchise "would leave us just where we are now; since every man who can be trusted with

[40] *Oneida Observer*, quoted in *Albany Argus*, Dec. 20, 1820.
[41] *National Advocate*, June 21, June 30, July 9, 1821.
[42] *New York American*, Feb. 15, 1821.

198

a deed, is made a freeholder long enough to vote in elections worth the expense of such a contest."[43]

An added complication arose from the difficulty of determining what kinds of leases should be considered freeholds. By statute, only leases for an indefinite number of years had been declared freeholds. A contemporary analysis showed, however, that different rules obtained in different parts of the state, probably all different from the law, and that in most cases long-term leaseholds were considered freeholds.[44] The confusion in those parts of New York where the manor system survived, until swept away in the aftermath of the Anti-Rent War of the 1840's, was comparable to the situation in the extreme western part of the state, where the Holland Land Company and other great absentee landowning interests disposed of lands by a peculiar method.[45] The company refused to give title deeds to lands until the purchaser had paid for them in full. Not having deeds to their lands, the early settlers were unable to qualify as voters for governor and senate, or serve legally on juries or fulfill other important duties in local government. The agent of the company, Joseph Ellicott, was faced with an ugly situation when, in the election of 1807, Federalists challenged the right of settlers from Vermont, accustomed to universal manhood suffrage, to vote on the grounds that they were not freeholders. Some of these, exasperated at having come as far as twenty miles to vote, employed their fists, as a contemporary account said, and voted.[46]

This problem was met in various ways. Election officials might ignore the qualification, a deed might be given for that part of the land which had been improved, or payments under contract might be interpreted as creating an equity in the

---

[43] *The Columbian*, Dec. 22, 1820.   [44] *Albany Argus*, June 1, 1821.
[45] See Evans, Paul D., *The Holland Land Company* (Buffalo, 1924).
[46] Chazanof, William, *The Political Influence of Joseph Ellicott in Western New York, 1802-1821* (unpub. Ph.D. thesis, Syracuse University, 1950), pp. 107-108.

freehold sufficient to enable the purchaser to vote. Elsewhere, it was said, those persons buying land in installments were not voting. One can appreciate the comment of a contemporary that the requirements for qualification of the freehold voter, being so much "matters of law, fact, and opinion, frequently render the right so questionable, as to excite an opposition which can only be removed by the oath of the party."[47] Disputes over assembly voters were much less numerous, because it was relatively easy to determine who was a renter and a taxpayer. The outmoded character of the freehold qualification is indicated further by the fact that a man who owned ten feet of ground worth 100 pounds voted, while a middle-class man worth a million, an honest mechanic, or prosperous merchant could not vote.[48]

At all events, one critic branded the freehold qualification as the product of Norman lawyers. "In this enlightened age, and in this republican country," he said, the rights of free men "should not be tested by the refinements and subtleties of Norman jurisprudence."[49] Furthermore, the distinction between assembly and other voters did not serve any useful purpose in a country where property was so diffused, where for a long time the freeholders would be in the ascendancy, and where the poor of today were the rich of the morrow. Even bicameralism, as a feature of balanced government, he argued, could be abandoned if its worth were disproved.

The leading politicians of the two major opposing factions in New York, the Clintonians and the Bucktails, understood the issue of democracy at stake but understood also the partisan issues and interests involved. Van Buren and other Bucktails hoped that associating themselves with reform would enable them to persuade the electors to turn De Witt

[47] *Albany Argus*, June 1, 1821.
[48] *National Advocate*, June 14, 1821; *Albany Argus*, March 20, 1821.
[49] *Albany Argus*, June 1, 1821.

Clinton out of office and vote the Bucktails in. Clinton, on his part, was said to be in a dilemma because he relied greatly on freehold votes but at the same time wanted reform, to the extent at least of eliminating the Council of Appointment and consolidating power over patronage matters in the hands of the governor. Clinton knew that the Bucktails had felt their defeat at the polls, as a friend wrote him in May of 1820, "to the pith of their bones and to the core of their hearts but are recovering from their dismay and hope to revolutionize everything. . . ."[50] So far as suffrage was concerned, only Van Buren's mouthpiece, the *Albany Argus*, advocated universal suffrage. Nevertheless, all factions accused each other of harboring elements opposed to suffrage reform in a way which determined that it would not be a clearcut party issue.

When the bill to submit the question of a convention was drafted, the effort of its sponsor to use the Massachusetts plan of 1780, allowing universal white manhood suffrage, was turned down in favor of a freehold, taxpaying, or militia qualification, thus breaching only in a cautious way the constitutional requirement of 1777. The resulting election was the most openly democratic since the stirring elections just before the Revolution. *The Columbian* was correct in stating that for the first time all young men, twenty-one to thirty years of age, had the privilege of voting; it urged them to use it well. The *Argus* exhorted the "brave and generous youth of Albany" to go to the polls with the same alacrity with which they reached for their muskets.[51] Whereas only 93,437 votes had been cast for governor in the election of 1820, 144,247 were cast on the question of having a convention in 1821, of whom only 34,891 voted in opposition. Whether or not this increase was due in any considerable

[50] Columbia University, *De Witt Clinton Papers*, IV, p. 49, Charles G. Harris [?] to Clinton, May 24, 1820.
[51] *The Columbian*, June 18, 1821; *Albany Argus*, Extra, 1821.

degree to the enfranchisement of 30,000 young men, otherwise unqualified by property tests to vote, has not been determined.[52]

Suffice it to say that the election of 1821 breached the suffrage barriers of 1777. The sequel showed that Van Buren had been substantially correct when, during the convention, he opposed universal suffrage, partly on Blackstonian and Jeffersonian grounds and partly on the grounds that the experiment, once tried, would be irrevocable. A qualification allowing adult white male citizens to vote, if taxpayers or militia men, was actually the qualification written into the constitution of 1821. Chief Justice Spencer's efforts, with quotations from Jefferson about the virtues of the cultivators of the earth, to preserve the freehold qualification for the senate were vitiated by the retort that Jefferson had changed his mind on the suffrage issue. James Kent, upholder of Blackstonian and even Jeffersonian principles, found that agrarianism was criticized by a defender of the working classes.[53] Daniel D. Tomkins asserted that there was more honesty and integrity to be found in them than in the higher classes, and paid his respects to the emphasis of the classical economists upon the crucial role of labor in the creation of capital.[54] Disavowing an intention to enfranchise the poor, Samuel Young, American Ricardian, said that he favored the enfranchisement of "the intermediate class," and that the time when America would have to wrestle with the problems of an urban proletariat in the grip of Malthusian laws was far distant. "Chill penury," he declared, in a quotation from Oliver Goldsmith's *Deserted Village*, was not a characteristic of the country. So long as there was an abundance of land and a relative absence of land speculation, it never would be.[55]

[52] *Albany Argus*, Aug. 22, 1821.
[53] Carter, Stone and Gould, *op.cit.*, pp. 215, 236, 220-221.
[54] *Ibid.*, pp. 238-239.　　　　[55] *Ibid.*, p. 274.

The New York City delegation was particularly sensitive to Kent's dicta. If we can believe Rufus King, only two members of the New York delegation, Nathan Sanford and Jacob Radcliff, favored a more democratic suffrage than that which was adopted.[56] The others were opposed to a broader franchise not only because they were sincerely convinced that Kent had the correct vision of the American future, but because they found their city suffering from the tribulations of early nineteenth-century urbanism. The cry that pauperism was on the increase was often raised in the city's conservative press. Moreover, property owners in the city were alarmed at the mounting municipal tax burden which they associated with the modest rent-paying qualification for voting in the city since 1804, and which they said that Tammany Hall exploited. On February 2, 1821, the *New York Evening Post* declared that the doctrine that all men are created free and equal had created enormous mischief, pointing in particular to the fact that the poor performance of the Corporation of New York was the result of applying to government the principle of no taxation without representation, without proper safeguards. It suggested that a special governing board composed exclusively of freeholders be established, to be elected by persons qualified to vote in city affairs. Another proposal was to create a chamber of landowners in which only landowners could sit or vote.[57]

A proposal more friendly and more sympathetic to the problems of workers in city factories was made several years later, one indicating an indebtedness to Robert Owen's schemes for a social democracy within the framework of the institution of private property. Declaring that a new kind of feudalism had emerged in which wealthy manufacturers were in a position to control hundreds of votes, the proposal envisaged as

[56] *King Papers*, Rufus King to Charles King, Sept. 30, 1821.
[57] *National Advocate*, March 15, 1821.

necessary the planning of the growth of manufacturing, itself eminently desirable, in such a way as to prevent society's suffering from its disadvantages. This could be achieved by creating a joint stock company of small capitalists, each one of whom would have a part of the factory under his general supervision, each part being managed directly by men elected by the "free suffrage of all." Universal suffrage in factories would prevent the workers from being subjected to degradation, as they were in England, and provide them with a political education equal to that of the agricultural classes.[58]

Despite their concern as to what the future might hold, sensible men regardless of political ties accepted suffrage reform as inevitable, if for no other reason. Rufus King probably expressed majority opinion when he advocated acceptance of the new constitution on the grounds that it would make for repose and stability. Its rejection, he thought, would shake the very foundations of society. It was impossible to prevent the lowering of the voting qualification, he said, and added, "One of the things last learned is the Duty of every Government to concur in & approve measures which they could not if they would hinder—in this way things are stopped from going to Extremes. . . ."[59]

The belief of many New Yorkers that they were at a historic turning point is not justified by the immediate consequences of the suffrage reform of 1821. The proportion of electors for assemblymen among the adult male population increased only from about 78 percent to 90 percent.[60] This was not, in Carlyle's phrase, "shooting Niagara." Those who had agreed to a taxpaying or a militia qualification for voting had hoped that it closed the suffrage debate indefinitely. Nevertheless, that universal suffrage which almost all New York reformers

[58] *Ibid.*, July 25, 1825.
[59] *King Papers*, King to (?), Dec. 19, 1821.
[60] Hough, F. B., *op.cit.*, p. x.

had disavowed was conceded in the form of an amendment to the constitution in 1826. In contrast to Maryland, where there was an uproar over the suffrage in 1800, New York was not aroused to any extent over the issue.

The transition from taxpaying to universal suffrage was achieved without even much comment in the press. The reasons lay in the mundane problems to which a simplified, but still complex qualification had given rise. In the first place, a taxpaying qualification encouraged numerous frauds at the polls. In the Sixth Ward of New York, for example, a voter was challenged on the ground that he was not a taxpayer. The collector of taxes consulted his books and asserted that he was. When the books were examined closely after election, it was determined that he was not a voter and that the collector had lied. Whether or not renters who paid taxes on the property they occupied should be deemed taxpayers, in the meaning of the constitution, was determined only by a law passed in 1823. As late as 1825, the senate was wrestling with the problem of clarifying the taxpaying qualification of lessees and lessors. Where tenants paid the taxes, a landlord might lose his vote. Where the landlord paid them, the tenant, who was often a laborer or mechanic, might lose his, unless he were otherwise qualified by the constitution. The *Argus* claimed that 500 men had lost the franchise in 1823 because they had been exempted from militia duties, having served with the volunteer fire department. Governor Joseph C. Yates had, therefore, ample reason for declaring, in his message of January 1823, that difficulties had arisen at the polls over the proper interpretation of the suffrage clauses of the new constitution, implying that something should be done.[61]

Suffrage extension, on the grounds of preventing fraud and injustice, as much as on the grounds that it was a necessary step toward suffrage democracy, became a political issue in

[61] *Albany Argus*, Jan. 10, 1823.

the gubernatorial campaign of 1824. The Republicans chose to capitalize on the roles which Samuel Young and Erastus Root had played as suffrage reformers in the convention by selecting them as their candidates for governor and lieutenant-governor to run against De Witt Clinton and his running mate. During the campaign, opponents of Clinton attacked him for his opposition to the calling of the convention, and the candidate for lieutenant-governor for his conservative views on suffrage in the past. The Clintonians were quick to repudiate their past equivocations, but no more so than the Republicans. To such an extent did both factions stand for further simplification and purification of the suffrage that there was little real choice on the matter in the election.

As the victor in the campaign, Clinton honored his commitments to the electorate and his own convictions, privately expressed before election, that the suffrage needed to be "more carefully defined and more liberally extended." He recommended in January 1825 that because the existing qualification did not include all citizens it should be revised. He indicated that perhaps universal suffrage would be necessary because the state tax, which had recently been reduced from 2 mills to ½ mill on the dollar, might soon be eliminated completely. If it were, the taxpaying qualification would be a major disfranchiser and would virtually restrict the electorate to those who served in the militia, a palpable absurdity. For this reason, as well as others, Clinton advocated a qualification based solely on citizenship, age, and residence.[62] His common-sense approach appealed to New Yorkers. Amid cries that Republicans, rather than Clintonians, had been the first to advocate suffrage reform, the amendment eliminating the taxpaying qualification became a part of the constitution in 1826. With remarkable swiftness, the minority opinion of 1821 had become the majority conviction by 1826. The spectacular

[62] *Ibid.*, Jan. 7, 1825.

lack of resistance to further reform in 1826 is reasonable when it is borne in mind that the proportion of the population qualified to vote increased only 1 percent.[63]

The suffrage reforms in Connecticut, Massachusetts, and New York brought to an end an often harsh and strident debate on the suffrage. The contribution which these reforms made to the practice of a democratic suffrage has been exaggerated, but not their contribution to that conception essential to American nationalism that this country was very different from Europe, and that the suffrage conservatism of Europe, from Aristotle forward, had little meaning in the United States. In this country, there would be no repetition of European developments, no matter what else might take place. The *National Advocate* illustrated the divorce of American suffrage thought from Europe when it criticized Daniel Webster for not having declared his independence from James Harrington. "In forming our government," it said, "we may borrow some of Mr. Harrington's notions here and reject them there. . . . A free people will adopt that form of government which please the majority, without regard to what might have pleased nations in other times and in other conditions."[64]

[63] Hough, F. B., *op.cit.*, p. xliii.
[64] *National Advocate*, July 24, 1821.

CHAPTER 11

SUFFRAGE IN THE NEW WEST

In several of his more famous writings, Frederick Jackson Turner developed the theory that the growth of American democracy, as it was known in the nineteenth century, was due to the influence of the frontier. Discussing this growth with reference to the suffrage, he said in his *Rise of the New West*, "It was only as the interior of the country developed that suffrage restrictions gradually gave way in the direction of manhood suffrage."[1] *The Frontier in American History* restated this theme: "The wind of Democracy blew so strongly from the west, that even in the older states of New York, Massachusetts, Connecticut and Virginia, conventions were called which liberalized the constitutions by strengthening the democratic basis of the state."[2]

Turner implied that a major motive for suffrage reform in the east was the prevention of a drain of population to the west. Nevertheless, the facts of seaboard suffrage reform do not support this thesis; although this argument was used, as in Connecticut, it was never a major issue there or anywhere. By 1812, the states of Vermont, Maryland, and South Carolina had divorced property from the suffrage as a result of movements which owed very little, if anything, to the frontier spirit. A freehold qualification survived along the seaboard only in Rhode Island and in Virginia in all state elections, and in New York and North Carolina in some but not all. The remaining seaboard states, with the exception of Connecticut and Massachusetts (in law, at least), based their adult male

[1] Turner, F. J., *The Rise of the New West* (New York, 1906), p. 175.
[2] Turner, F. J., *The Frontier in American History* (New York, 1920), p. 250.

electorate upon a taxpaying qualification which amounted almost to universal manhood suffrage wherever all adult males were subject to the payment of a poll tax. It must be borne in mind also that, except perhaps in times of high political excitement, adult male suffrage prevailed wherever there was laxity in or indifference to strict enforcement of the suffrage laws. Furthermore, the extent of suffrage democracy in the west has been exaggerated. Ohio and Louisiana confined the suffrage to taxpayers, Tennessee to freeholders unless the voter had been resident in the county for six months.[3] As late as 1812, only one state of the New West, Kentucky, had eliminated all property or taxpaying qualifications. If this analysis is correct, Turner had the western cart before the eastern horse.

By no means all contemporary observers endeavored, like Turner, to draw a distinction between eastern and western developments or attributed to the west the decisive role in democratic reform. In 1806, Benjamin H. Latrobe, the great architect, acknowledged that eastern suffrage reform was sweeping the country. "After the adoption of the Federal Constitution," he wrote, "the extension of the right of suffrage in the States to a majority of all the adult male citizens, planted a germ which had [sic] gradually evolved and has spread actual and practical democracy and political equality over the whole union."[4] Three years later, a Massachusetts pamphleteer, while discussing the merits of a contested election for the United States House of Representatives, asserted that in the eastern states "elections are so popular as to amount almost to universal suffrage."[5]

[3] See Thorpe, *op.cit.*, III, pp. 1,264-1,277; v, pp. 2,897-2,913; III, pp. 1,380-1,392; VI, pp. 3,414-3,425.
[4] Maryland Historical Society, *Latrobe Letterbook*, 1806, p. 623.
[5] Baylies, William, *A View of the Proceedings of the House of Representatives of the United States in the Case of the Plymouth Election* (Boston, 1809), p. 18.

It would be difficult to show that easterners believed that western constitutions before or after the War of 1812 offered any novelties worth incorporating into their own constitutions. Regarding the constitution of Mississippi of 1817, a Massachusetts newspaper made a revealing comment. "It is . . . so similar," it said, "to the constitutions of many of the other states, that its perusal does not excite much interest."[6] As might be expected, eastern reformers and conservatives alike found their principles reflected in the various constitutions of the New West. Connecticut conservatives, for example, praised the taxpaying suffrage requirement of the Ohio constitution because it excluded from voting men who were not property owners. When reformers urged the east to borrow from the west, as they sometimes did, western principles were often rejected as being appropriate to a frontier society but unsuited to an older, more sophisticated seaboard society. Judge Van Ness of the New York constitutional convention of 1821 rejected arguments that New York should pattern its institutions upon the democratic precedents of the west, saying that the state of New York did not stand in need of being instructed by every petty new state beyond the Alleghenies.[7] On their part, eastern reformers took comfort from the fact that Missouri had voted for universal manhood suffrage when it was admitted to the Union in 1822. Obviously, western precedents could be used to underwrite either position taken in the east.

In one particular, however, circumstances of frontier life did render inexpedient property tests for voting. In a new country, the process of surveying land and granting titles is likely to be laborious and long-drawn out, and to lag behind the more urgent demands and needs of the settlers. Such was the case when the British created the Province of West

---

[6] *Worcester Spy*, quoted in *Albany Gazette*, Oct. 11, 1817.
[7] Carter, Stone and Gould, *op.cit.*, p. 270.

Florida after the Seven Years' War. In this colony, the freehold qualification for voting proved impractical because there were too few freeholders to sustain a genuinely representative government. As a result, the British were obliged to choose between abandoning self-government entirely or admitting all householders to the suffrage.[8] They chose the latter.

Virginia faced a comparable problem in dealing with the elections by which Kentucky was set off as a separate state in 1792. When Virginia had created Kentucky County in 1776, it had extended to it its own freehold qualification for voting. This qualification had to be abandoned if there were to be more than a small number of voters, because the enormous amount of litigation over land titles made it difficult for settlers to secure deeds.[9] Moreover, at this time the only really effective organs of government were the militia companies. For this reason, the Danville Convention of 1785, designed to treat with Virginia for statehood, was elected by the militia men on the basis of one delegate per militia company.[10] This breach of the freehold qualification in Virginia elections led to still another, whereby free white male inhabitants were allowed to vote in subsequent elections for constitutional conventions. The connection between these changes and the fact that Kentucky entered the union with a constitution conceding universal manhood suffrage is undoubtedly very close. Not all Kentuckians were happy over these developments. The Political Club of Danville, a group composed of a number of lawyers and others who had come from Virginia, opposed universal suffrage at a club meeting in 1787. The members voted that "some other qualification besides freedom ought to

[8] Howard, C. N., *British Development of West Florida 1763-1769* (Berkeley, 1947), pp. 43-44.

[9] Hening, *Statutes*, xii, p. 37.

[10] Brown, John M., "The Political Beginnings of Kentucky," *Filson Club Publications*, no. 6 (Louisville, 1889), p. 61, passim.

be required."[11] The debate had no effect, however, upon opinion at large or even upon the constitutional convention. Virginia had permitted the breach of the freehold qualification for very practical reasons. Here, as elsewhere, a return to the past was impossible.

Equally pragmatic considerations caused the federal government to abandon the 50-acre freehold qualification for voting in the western territories, a qualification inherited from the old Continental Congress. Some territorial officials, including the governor of Ohio Territory, Arthur St. Clair, favored its retention. St. Clair was a strong believer in Blackstonianism. "I do not count independence and wealth always together," he said, "but I pronounce poverty and dependence to be inseparable." For this reason, he heartily disapproved of the Pennsylvania constitution because it did not require a property test for voting.[12]

When the time came to hold elections for the first legislature of Ohio territory, however, it was found that few persons were qualified under the 50-acre freehold clause because their titles to lands, particularly in the Symnes Purchase, had not yet been granted. The majority of freeholders were owners of relatively small town lots. In order to create enough voters so that genuine elections could be held, the federal government in 1798 enfranchised owners of town lots which were worth as much as 50-acre freeholds.[13] St. Clair was opposed to giving the vote to buyers of Symnes Purchase lands on the grounds that until they secured title they would not act as free agents. The only reason he upheld a freehold qualification, and ballot rather than viva voce elections, he said, was to prevent undue representation for the landlord interest.

[11] Speed, Thomas, "The Political Club, Danville, Ky., 1786-90," *Filson Club Publications*, IX (Louisville, 1894), p. 125.

[12] Smith, W. H., "A Familiar Talk about Monarchists and Jacobins," *Ohio Archaeological and Historical Publications*, II, pp. 187-215.

[13] Smith, W. H. (ed.), *St. Clair Papers* (Cincinnati, 1882, 2 vols.), II, pp. 436-438.

Similar problems beset the inhabitants of Mississippi Territory about this time. The legislature complained to the Congress in 1804 that the 50-acre qualification deprived persons of considerable property of the right to vote, and requested that all persons, otherwise qualified, who had paid a tax six months previous to the election be allowed to vote. The legitimacy of the request was unchallengeable in the light of a situation in which, it was convincingly stated, only 236 persons out of 4,444 could vote in the territory, a source of chagrin to the Federalist governor, Winthrop Sargent.[14] As a temporary expedient, pre-emptioners were enfranchised in 1807. The inhabitants of Indiana Territory were in a similar predicament and joined the Mississippians in requesting Congress to reconsider the 50-acre qualification.

At this time, Congress was unwilling to abandon the freehold concept. Instead, it passed two acts early in 1808 by which all free adult males in Indiana and all free adult white males in Mississippi who had a 50-acre freehold or an equitable freehold or who owned a town lot worth $100 could vote.[15] Dissatisfied with the small extent of reform, partly because some hoped that a democratic suffrage would attract settlers to their territory, residents of Indiana renewed their efforts to secure a broader franchise. Despite their gratitude, they said, for the concession already made, they hoped that Congress would extend the vote to all taxpayers or militia men.[16] In response to these requests, Congress, having defeated an effort to prohibit squatters from voting, abandoned the freehold qualification in 1811 and substituted for it a tax-paying one-year residency requirement.

A comparable situation prevailed in Illinois, where a num-

[14] Sydnor, C. S., *A Gentleman of the Old Natchez Region* (Durham, 1938), p. 27.
[15] Carter, Clarence E., *The Territorial Papers of the United States* (Washington, D.C., 1934-58, 20 vols.), VII, p. 526; I, pp. 411n, 616-618.
[16] Carter, *op.cit.*, VII, pp. 690-691; VIII, pp. 111-112, 112n.

ber of residents asserted that only 200 or 300 persons were bona fide freeholders of the territory. Governor Ninian Edwards corroborated their statements.[17] In 1812, Congress recognized the impracticability of a freehold qualification under these circumstances and abandoned it. Two years later, Congress gave up the freehold qualification in Mississippi, following an analysis of the electoral situation which purported to show that many well-to-do individuals, owners of slaves and large numbers of cattle, were unable to meet the property test and that it had been debased by the dishonesty and corruption involved in the creation of a number of fagot voters.

Suffrage change was a product also of the democratic convictions of the residents of the territories at a time when these convictions were becoming more widespread. For example, a number of southerners living in Vincennes petitioned Governor William Henry Harrison in 1802 that they be permitted to bring slaves into the territory, that public education be provided, and that the suffrage qualifications be changed because, as they existed in freehold form, they were "subversive of the liberties" of the citizens and tended to give too much weight to wealth.[18] Nevertheless, neither they nor other petitioners from the territories requested, at this time, as did seaboard reformers in Maryland and South Carolina, adult male suffrage. Previous to 1814, they were content to ask for a taxpaying and militia qualification. Mississippi reformers in 1814 requested in the language of Jefferson, "general suffrage," that is, a taxpaying and militia qualification. In 1817, William Lattimore, the territorial delegate to Congress, secured the passage of an act to establish a taxpaying electorate, which he trusted would be popular with Mississippians.[19]

[17] Carter, *op.cit.*, xvi, pp. 199-202.

[18] Indiana Historical Society, *Collections*, vii (1922), pp. 62-67.

[19] *The Washington Republican and Natchez Intelligencer*, April 9, 1817.

The real import of the democratic direction of the suffrage change in the New West is hard to determine. In the first place, suffrage laws, as in the east, could very well be ignored by all parties. In Alabama Territory, universal white suffrage was practiced in at least one election in 1818, when the candidates consented to allowing all adult males to vote. Secondly, it may be questioned whether a genuine democracy was possible in relatively primitive communities on the frontier, where the situation can be likened to that prevailing before the Revolution in Georgia and South Carolina. At that time, neither of these colonies had been welded into a cohesive or organic whole. In practice, power was exercised by small groups in and around Charleston or Savannah, the franchise was neglected because it was not highly valued, and election to office was either avoided or refused. Whether in pre-Revolutionary Nova Scotia or in post-Revolutionary Vermont or Tennessee, the frontier did not provide an environment conducive to a responsible, and to that extent, democratic government for a new region inhabited by a scattering of people. A newspaper attack on territorial government quoted Rousseau on this score. "Countries thinly inhabited," Rousseau had written in his *Social Contract*, "are the most proper places for tyrants; wild beasts reign only in deserts."[20] Governor St. Clair had already come to this conclusion and feared oligarchical government. He hoped that the secret ballot might prove a partial corrective in the Northwest Territory.

An argument against a free land policy which would have shocked Jefferson was advanced by a westerner to the Secretary of the Treasury in 1810. In his opinion, free land was an undesirable policy because it would cause a rush of the poor to the territories where their votes would be garnered by cheap politicians.[21] Such fears were not totally groundless. Territorial governors were denounced as being as tyrannical

[20] Carter, *op.cit.*, vii, pp. 135-140.   [21] *Ibid.*, viii, pp. 59-60.

as royal governors of the British North American colonies and were even accused of attempting to control elections, as were other territorial officials. In an election in Missouri Territory in 1817, timid males were herded to the polls in the presence of troops, in the familiar atmosphere of liquor fumes and glinting daggers and pistols. The election was branded more despotic than those in England.[22] As in the east, sheriffs proved capricious in enforcing the voting qualifications, interpreting them one way here and another there. Viva voce elections denied voters protection against those who would intimidate them. Popular participation in territorial elections was lessened by the use of the county as the electoral unit.

Indiana reformers, like those of the seaboard, saw clearly that suffrage reform, *per se*, was not enough, that reform of electoral procedures was of equal importance. For this reason, when they achieved a taxpaying militia qualification in 1811, they sought also, and with success, to curb the abuses of sheriffal authority by turning over the supervision of elections to judges of the County Courts of Common Pleas, as well as to increase voter participation by abandoning the county in favor of the township as the polling unit. This last reform was possibly a greater factor in enfranchising the population of Indiana than the abandonment of the freehold qualification.[23]

While the rapid withering of the freehold qualification was effecting an approximation of suffrage democracy in the New West, the prospect of further reform developed as the time came for each of the territories to emerge from the tutelage of the federal government as a full-fledged state of the union. The speed with which some of them earned the right to statehood was the result of partisan politics. Tennessee was ad-

[22] *Missouri Gazette,* Aug. 9, 1817.
[23] Barnhart, J. D., "The Democratization of Indiana Territory," *Indiana Magazine of History* (XLIII, March 1947), pp. 1-21.

mitted hastily in 1796 against Federalist wishes to delay statehood and thus cut down the size of the Republican vote. The
admission of Ohio when its population was less than the
60,000 required to qualify as a state is the best illustration of
the purely political considerations underlying the movement
for statehood in some parts of the country. Republicans
wanted more votes.[24]

Whatever the immediate reason, the territorial voters were
given eight different opportunities between 1796 and 1821 to
elect delegates to conventions for the writing of state constitutions prior to admission to the union. Suffrage questions
were bound to be discussed and determined in these conventions because it had been the practice since the Revolution
to incorporate state and county electoral qualifications in
constitutions. Like those who framed the seaboard documents,
the men responsible for writing those of the New West came
to their conventions with considerable knowledge of the existing constitutions of the various states. If it is true, as the
president of the Florida Convention of 1838 asserted, that the
members of that body were without books on constitutional
law, without knowledge of history, near or remote, and un-
familiar with the opinions of the great lawyers, this convention was indeed unique.[25]

Actually, western conventions drew liberally upon the institutions and practices of the seaboard. Westerners appeared
to be most satisfied when their fundamental instruments of
government were as much as possible like those with which
they had been familiar. The inhabitants of Wayne County in
Michigan Territory, for example, requested of Lewis Cass
that they be governed by the laws of New York, Massachu-

[24] *The Visitor* (New Haven), Jan. 25, 1803; *St. Clair Papers*, I, pp.
228-230; Combs, W. H., and Cole, W. E., *Tennessee: A Political Study*
(Knoxville, 1940), p. 11.
[25] Hoskins, F. W., "The St. Joseph Constitution," *Florida Historical
Society Quarterly Proceedings* (XVI, April 1938), pp. 242-250.

setts, Virginia, Ohio, and Vermont.[26] On the occasion of the meeting of the first territorial legislature of Iowa, members were said to be collecting copies of the statutes of as many states as they could, each trying to secure the incorporation of as many of the laws of his home state as possible.[27] Western constitution makers borrowed from the eastern states and from each other. Tennessee relied heavily upon Pennsylvania and North Carolina; Ohio on Tennessee, Pennsylvania, and Kentucky; Illinois and Indiana on Ohio and Kentucky. Alabama borrowed from her neighbor Mississippi.

The new constitutions borrowed not only from other documents, but also from the various schools of political thought which these documents represented. Western newspapers helped to familiarize their readers with the ideas or even with fragments of the writings of Thomas Paine, Algernon Sidney, James Harrington, John Locke, Jean Jacques Rousseau, Voltaire, and William Cobbett. They also published reports of the reformist activities of Sir Francis Burdett and Major John Cartwright in Britain.[28] The more conservative suffrage thought of the seaboard was represented as well. William C. C. Claiborne, future governor of Mississippi Territory, left Richmond for Tennessee with his copies of the *Revised Statutes of Virginia* and the writings of Blackstone. As late as the 1830's in Illinois and the 1840's in Louisiana, Blackstonianism had its supporters.

Nevertheless, the suffrage qualifications of the states admitted to the union between 1796 and 1821 incorporated the democratic ideas which had been the conscious inheritance

[26] Rowland, D. (ed.), *The Mississippi Territorial Archives: 1799-1803* (Nashville, 1905), p. 338; *Detroit Gazette*, April 24, 1818.

[27] *The Annals of Iowa: A Historical Quarterly* (III, 3rd Series, 1897-1899), pp. 337, 337n.

[28] *The Orleans Gazette*, April 30, 1806; *Kentucky Gazette*, Sept. 1, 1787; *Missouri Gazette*, Aug. 1, 1812, Dec. 30, 1815; *The Mississippi Republican*, April 29, May 30, 1812.

of the American people since the Revolution. Of the eight states admitted during this period, three required the payment of taxes for voting. The remainder conceded adult manhood suffrage to whites only because, as a resident of Michigan said, Indians and Negroes were excluded from the "great North American Family."[29]

The Congress, in exercising its power over the territories, followed the same trend. It permitted taxpayers to elect members of the various state conventions until the passage of the Enabling Act under which Alabama wrote its constitution in 1819. With this act, the federal government abandoned even this slight concession to the property concept in voting. So long as many western territories levied poll taxes, either permanently or for short periods, a shift from taxpaying to manhood suffrage probably had less real significance than the prior abandonment by Congress of the freehold qualification. Perhaps this situation accounts for the failure of even Republicans in Ohio to be interested in universal suffrage, even for whites, early in the nineteenth century. Yet western suffrage reform was not devoid of meaning for the future. The marked rise of tenantry in the midwest from the 1830's forward would have brought about a reversal of the long-term trend toward a democratic suffrage if the freehold and taxpaying tests, in their original form, had not been eliminated.[30]

As along the seaboard, the issue of elections based upon the level of county, township, or district and the question of the secret ballot were matters of great importance in the New West. In Indiana written ballots were used from 1811 forward, and in Illinois from 1813. In Illinois, however, a sharp struggle over this issue lasted from 1813 to 1829. Defenders of open voting stated frankly that it enabled candidates to

[29] Carter, *op.cit.*, XI, p. 730.
[30] Gates, P. W., "Land Policy and Tenancy in the Prairie States," *The Journal of Economic History* (I, May 1941), pp. 60-82.

pledge a man before election. Critics attacked the practice on the grounds that it was a survival of British tyranny. Advocates of the secret ballot were defeated and in 1829 Illinois returned to public voting. This state was thus in the exceptional position on an issue of which the merits and justice had been proved in the popular mind elsewhere.[31]

Western constitutions reflected those of the east also in the distinctions between the suffrage qualifications for state and local elections, distinctions which survived in some western and southern states as late as the Civil War. Even Alabama, with universal white manhood suffrage, occasionally refused, as in the case of the act incorporating Dadeville in 1837, to allow any but householders and freeholders to vote in town elections.[32] Kentucky in similar acts often required that voters in town elections be payers of taxes either on their polls or on their property. Louisville, when incorporated in 1828, extended the vote in local elections to persons qualified to vote for members of the legislature. Four years later, however, the act was amended in such a way as to eliminate all who did not pay taxes.[33] Similarly, Tennessee frequently refused to create as liberal suffrage provisions for local as for state elections. Ashport, under its charter of 1839, allowed only freeholders and taxpaying residents to vote in local elections. Memphis required by an act of 1853 that only city taxpayers could vote in city elections.[34] When St. Louis, Missouri, was incorporated in 1822, only taxpayers, otherwise qualified, were allowed to vote. As late as 1835, towns were being incorpo-

[31] Carter, op.cit., VI, pp. 36-39; Pease, T. C., The Frontier State, 1818-1848 (Springfield, 1918), p. 39.

[32] Acts Passed at the Called Session of the General Assembly of the State of Alabama (Tuscaloosa, 1837), p. 35.

[33] Acts Passed at the First Session of the 40th General Assembly for the Commonwealth of Kentucky (Frankfort, 1832), pp. 199-200.

[34] Acts of the State of Tennessee, Passed at the 1st Session of the 30th General Assembly . . . (Nashville, 1854), p. 297.

rated in the state which confined town elections to persons who had paid local taxes.[35]

States lying north of the Ohio were no different from those to the south. Indiana, for example, required that voters in the borough of Vincennes be householders or freeholders and in the city of Jeffersonville that they be taxpayers.[36] As late as 1837 in Illinois, a taxpaying qualification in local elections was still popular.[37] When Chicago was given city status in 1837, the electorate was confined to the taxpayers in order to identify the suffrage with sound fiscal policies. Blackstone was the authority cited.[38]

The philosophy underlying a state's denial of the suffrage in local elections to all those qualified to vote in state elections was never better expressed than by Albert Gallatin when he wrote Lafayette in 1833 that he had never known any evil to arise from universal suffrage in Pennsylvania state elections. In elections for municipal officers who had no power over persons, but great power over taxation and expenditures, however, Gallatin maintained that only those who made a financial contribution to the community should be allowed to vote.[39] The last stand of the principle of "no representation without taxation" was in the sphere of local elections. A late variant of this principle was Iowa's requirement that only city taxpayers could vote in those town affairs which concerned taxation or the borrowing of money.

In view of the extent to which western suffrage history was a recapitulation of the suffrage history of the eastern sea-

[35] *The Revised Statutes of the State of Missouri* (St. Louis, 1835), p. 603.

[36] *Laws of a Local Nature* . . . (Indianapolis, 1836), pp. 32-33; *Laws of a Local Nature* . . . (Indianapolis, 1839), p. 18.

[37] *Laws of the State of Illinois* . . . (Vandalia, 1837), pp. 18-19.

[38] Sparling, S. E., *Municipal History and Present Organization of the City of Chicago* (Madison, 1898), p. 29; Pierce, Bessie L., *A History of Chicago, 1673-1848* (New York, 1937), pp. 333-335.

[39] Adams, Henry, *The Life of Albert Gallatin* (New York, 1943), pp. 654-655.

board, it is difficult to believe that the New West was unique or that it made any new contribution to the growth of suffrage democracy. The *Iowa Capitol Republican*, in reporting suffrage developments in Iowa, recognized that the issue of suffrage democracy was not sectional but national, and an expression of the philosophy of the natural rights of man. During the sessions of the constitutional convention of 1846, the *Republican* wrote, "The friends of equal rights throughout the country will rejoice to learn of the progress that the principles of universal suffrage have made in Iowa."[40]

[40] Shambaugh, B. F. (ed.), *Fragments of the Debates of the Iowa Constitutional Conventions of 1844 and 1846* (Iowa City, 1900), p. 341.

CHAPTER 12

SUFFRAGE AND PRO-SLAVERY

WHEN ANDREW JACKSON was inaugurated President of the United States in 1829, only two of the states comprising that section of the country where he had been born required a freehold qualification for voting in any elections, North Carolina and Virginia. Some of the leading spokesmen of southern Republicanism had never been happy with the lack of suffrage democracy in these two states. Nathaniel Macon, who lived long enough to become an elder statesman of North Carolina, wrote an Ohio politician in 1802 that he believed that every man should vote who was married, whether or not he was a freeholder.[1] Jefferson, of course, favored by this time what he called "general suffrage," a taxpaying or militia-based suffrage.

Outside Virginia, observers of many different political persuasions found it strange that the Old Dominion, which had produced so many great figures and contributed so greatly in other ways to the country, should be so backward on the issue of the suffrage. The only change since the Revolution had occurred in 1785, when the unimproved land requirement for freeholders was reduced from 100 to 50 acres. "That nursery of everything that is great, the cradle of WASHINGTON himself," declared the *National Advocate* of New York on July 15, 1825, "has not even a child to offer to the Republic on the side of free suffrage."[2] Virginia was a beacon to conservatives and proof to cynics and reformers that, when politicians were the "ins," they had no need to exploit the suffrage issue for political gain.

[1] *St. Clair Papers*, II, pp. 590-591.
[2] *National Advocate*, July 15, 1825.

Suffrage problems in Virginia were somewhat more complicated than reformers considered them. It has not been possible
to demonstrate any popular demand on the part of non-freeholders for enfranchisement until after the War of 1812. The
ownership of land was so widespread and the definition of
freehold so loose as to encompass most leaseholds of the kind
employed in the eighteenth and early nineteenth centuries,
and the grievance was therefore confined to a minority composed of the very poorest classes and younger men. An early
petition for constitutional reform from inhabitants of Augusta
County did not even mention suffrage. The major grievance
in Virginia was the issue of representation. Probably Nathaniel
Beverley Tucker was nearer the truth than Jefferson when he
criticized Jefferson's statement, made in his *Notes on Virginia*,
that a majority of adult males were unenfranchised. On the
contrary, Tucker said, few could not achieve the status of
freeholder and, if it were true that Virginia had an aristocracy
of planters as northerners charged, it was the most harmless
aristocracy conceivable. As late as 1859, among agricultural
heads of families in various parts of the state, only about 30
to 42 percent were not landowners.[3]

What criticism of the suffrage was made before the end of
the eighteenth century came from members of the Virginia
aristocracy. The democratic convictions of some of these aristocrats were offended by a formal freehold qualification for
voting. This was true not only of Jefferson and of John Taylor
of Caroline, but also of James Madison, father of the Federal
Constitution. In 1785 he acknowledged that the governments
established at the time of the Revolution had sacrificed the
rights of persons to the rights of property, and that the poor
were sacrificed to the rich. Three years later he wrote a draft
for a new constitution for his state. In it he dealt with the

---

[3] Fields, Emmett B., *The Agricultural Population of Virginia, 1850-
1860* (unpub. Ph.D. thesis, Vanderbilt University, 1953), pp. 87-88.

suffrage, arguing that a middle ground should be found between "the theory of free government and the lessons of experience." Looking upon the property tests for voting in a different perspective than earlier, he implied that, at the time of the Revolution, Virginians had not conceived that one right had been sacrificed to another because a distinction between rich and poor had little meaning in America. To whatever extent it had meaning, a balanced form of government, as in New York or North Carolina, would provide an effective remedy against the political dangers of poverty. He opposed the institution of property tests for officeholding, he said, because comparable tests in Britain had proven hard to enforce and, in any event, electors generally preferred to choose men with, rather than without, property.[4] Finally, he asserted, the secret ballot would prevent the abuse of power.

The suffrage reform movement in Madison's state did not really get under way until the nineteenth century. The first half of this century witnessed the abandonment of the freehold qualification in 1830 and the achievement of universal white manhood suffrage in 1851. The first phase of this movement was associated closely with reform in other states. A flurry of protests at the beginning of the century can be correlated with the suffrage reform movement in Maryland at this time.[5] As late as 1829, sentiment for reform was strongest among Virginians who lived closest to the Maryland line. Even reform movements taking place at a considerable distance from Virginia had their effect. A suffrage reform meeting in Providence, Rhode Island, was held up to Virginians as the example which they should follow.[6] As the nation became committed to suffrage democracy, the moral pressure

[4] Library of Congress, *Madison Papers*, x, Observations of a Draft for a Constitution for Virginia.

[5] Chandler, J. A. C., *The History of Suffrage in Virginia* (Baltimore, 1901), pp. 24-25.

[6] *Richmond Enquirer*, Feb. 14, 1829.

upon Virginia naturally increased. A national aspiration tended to become a national problem and one which might require a national solution. One visitor to Virginia implied this when he advised Virginians that their property tests for voting violated the privileges and immunities clause of the Federal Constitution.[7]

Virginia felt the influence also of events in Europe. A Richmond newspaper reported that William Cobbett spoke of the certainty of universal suffrage "without universal confusion" even in big cities.[8] A meeting of non-freeholders in 1829 gave rise to a newspaper discussion of the desirability of a physical force party like that advocated by some Britons, to carry Virginia for reform.[9] Virginia newspapers published accounts of important events in British politics, including plans in 1829 to grant parliamentary representation to Manchester, Leeds, and Birmingham.[10] John Marshall was not far from the truth when he blamed events beyond Virginia's borders for the abandonment of the freehold qualification.

As in other states, the necessity for preparing for or waging war was an important source of reform sentiment. Virginians were employing the timeworn argument that men who were good enough to fight were good enough to vote. Some reformers wanted to give the franchise to all males over eighteen years of age. Although this demand arose before the War of 1812, its most striking manifestation occurred after the war was over. At Harrisonburg on June 21, 1815, a most remarkable meeting was held, composed almost wholly of non-freeholders.[11] A committee was appointed at this meeting to prepare a petition for suffrage reform which was printed and circulated throughout various parts of the state for the signa-

[7] "A Stranger," *Constitutional Whig*, Nov. 24, 1829.
[8] *Ibid.*, July 25, Sept. 25, 1829.
[9] *Constitutional Whig*, Aug. 4, 1829.
[10] *Phenix Gazette* (Alexandria), Sept. 24, 1829.
[11] Virginia State Library, *Legislative Petitions*, Bath County, 1815.

ture of non-freeholders in particular. Convincing evidence of the interest of non-freeholders in securing the franchise was the response from Rockingham in Bath County, where sixteen men signed the petition, all of whom were non-freeholders.[12] Unlike the famous Staunton Convention of 1816, which dealt with the grievance of under-representation, the Harrisonburg Convention centered its attention exclusively upon the suffrage issue. It referred pointedly to the fact that militia men had fought because they had sincerely believed they had a permanent interest in the community, although Virginia suffrage legislation rested upon contrary assumptions. If militia men had acted on these assumptions, they would not have fought and the state would have been defeated. Members of the convention remonstrated also "agt. the law, which requires the Militia, who are excluded from the right of suffrage, to patrol for the public safety, and to preserve roads & streets, while those who are principally benefited, are in a great measure exempt from any participation in these duties." Finally, they said, the right to vote was a God-given right because "*A Representative Democracy is the ordinance of God.*"[13]

The freehold qualification was undermined not only by its incompatibility with the ideas of the Revolution and with the desire to maintain a high degree of patriotism among young men for the protection of the state from foreign armies and slave insurrections, but also by the changing character of the Virginia system of leasing land. The leasehold system of the state, particularly in the Northern Neck, rested upon leases for life or lives and these leases were deemed freeholds. Such leases were becoming less popular, however, before the end of the eighteenth century. Landlords had begun to regret long and indefinite leases because inflation reduced the real value of their income from fixed rents, as much so as the shift

[12] V.S.L., *Real Property Tax*, Bath County, 1815.
[13] V.S.L., *Legislative Petitions*, Bath County, 1815.

in European manorialism from rent in kind to rent in money had reduced the real income of feudal landlords and hastened the decline of their influence in society and government. George Washington regretted having given leases for an indefinite number of years for a fixed annual income as land values rose and monetary values sank. As a result, the nineteenth century witnessed a shift from a type of lease which qualified the lessee as a freeholder to a modern type of lease, from which the capitalist type, from 1 to 21 years or at will, developed. The new kind of lease did not carry the right to vote even though the lessee occupied a very large farm.[14] As a result of this development, tenancy became enmeshed for the first time with the suffrage reform movement. A meeting of representatives of western counties, held in Richmond in 1828, agreed that suffrage extension to include the leasehold was necessary "because of the change of tenure in the Northern Neck."[15]

Not only was the character of the landed institutions of Virginia undergoing change, but Virginia was becoming more heterogeneous economically. In Richmond and in the extreme western part of the state, commercial and industrial activities were increasing and were changing its character, making it more northern and less southern. Both the city and the west were dissatisfied because neither had as much influence upon the policies of the state as it thought equitable, and by 1824 each wanted an increase of political power so as to make the American system of Henry Clay the Virginia system. The prolonged depression in tobacco culture after the War of 1812 lent a sense of urgency to the movement to diversify the economy of the state and put it on the road to a sound, more broadly based prosperity. Virginia conservatives saw the con-

[14] Bliss, Willard F., "The Rise of Farm Tenancy in Virginia," *Virginia Magazine of History and Biography* (LVIII, Oct. 1950), pp. 427-441.
[15] *Richmond Constitutional Whig*, Dec. 23, 1828.

nection between economic depression and the challenge to their agrarian leadership. In the opinion of one observer, "most of the moral and political aberrations of the people were due to the fact that the farmers were not securing the benefits from improved markets."[16] That sensitive barometer of the industrial way of life, *Niles' Register*, criticized the rotten borough system prevailing in Virginia boroughs and towns where, with the exception of Norfolk and Williamsburg, only freeholders could vote. Laborers would not settle or stay where they were not deemed citizens, it said. Therefore migration from the state had swelled for political as well as economic reasons. "We most earnestly wish," said the *Register* in 1821, "that the state . . . would give us some practical proofs of that republican spirit and vigilance that she so much boasts of."[17]

The most prominent of Virginia's rotten boroughs was Richmond. In this city only freeholders could vote in state elections, although owners of $100 property could vote in local elections. The restrictions upon the size of the electorate in state elections is indicated by the fact that approximately 45 percent of the free adult male residents on the tax lists for real and personal property were not freeholders.[18] In Richmond, the Blackstonian argument against allowing employees or tenants to vote was challenged on the grounds that there were sound economic reasons for their voting for the same men, parties, or measures as their employers or landlords. Tenants and workers, it was argued, were far from unwilling victims of the abuse of landlord and employer power because, actually, their interests were often identical. In effect, Blackstone was accused of having oversimplified the origins of the

[16] N.Y.P.L., *James Barbour Papers*, ii, John Taliaferro to Barbour, Feb. 2, 1829.

[17] *Niles' Register*, Nov. 16, 1816; April 14, 1821.

[18] Virginia State Library, *Richmond Records* (Microfilm) Tax Books, 1829.

alleged dependency of the poor and weak upon the rich and the powerful.[19]

While the issue of representation was distinctly sectional, the issue of suffrage was probably much less so. The *Richmond Enquirer* went so far as to say on October 17, 1829, that it was not a sectional issue at all. If contemporary accounts are taken at face value, there were more demands for suffrage reform in the east than in the west, possibly because, since the Revolution, the east had endeavored to break the pre-Revolutionary habit of ignoring the suffrage laws. In the western part of the state, on the other hand, the suffrage laws were, according to Madison, generally ignored. He wrote in 1829 that he had heard that "west of the Blue Ridge the votes of non-freeholders are often connived at, the candidates finding it unpopular to object to them."[20] Contemporary estimates of the number of persons unqualified to vote about this time are somewhat lower than the estimates of the proportion of adult males who were landowners as late as 1850. Somewhere between 40 and 50 percent of adult white males were voters.

Nevertheless, violations of the election laws took place at times in all sections of the state. Both east and west witnessed a considerable degree of illegal voting and coercion of electors. The west was often accused of creating fagot votes. Where tenancy prevailed, clauses were sometimes inserted in leases whereby tenants bound themselves to vote as their landlords dictated. Other charges of illegal voting involved aliens, males under age, unqualified tenants, owners of 21¾ acres of improved land instead of the required 25, and owners of unimproved land totalling less than 50 acres. Furthermore, there was sometimes confusion over who was or who was not qualified to vote. The town of Charlottesville explained its problem to the assembly in 1805: "Various doubts have arisen,

[19] *Richmond Enquirer*, May 8, 1824.
[20] Library of Congress, *Madison Papers*, LXXXI, Madison to J. C. Cabell, Jan. 5, 1829.

not only with respect to the qualifications of electors, but of the persons to be elected."[21] Intermittent breakdown of the suffrage laws led some individuals to despair of an honest freehold qualification. Frauds were charged particularly against the supporters of Andrew Jackson in 1828.

In ordinary times, elections were likely to be tame affairs which did not bring out the full roster of voters. The use of the county as the only electoral unit was one reason for poor attendance. Inhabitants of the northern part of Accomack County petitioned the assembly in 1825 to provide an additional polling place in their neighborhood because they had to ride thirty miles to the county courthouse, which involved much expense and two days' time lost from farming. Of 800 freeholders in the county, only 500, it was said, actually voted. It was of little value, the petitioners argued, to be legally entitled to vote if the right could not be exercised conveniently.[22] The legislature, like that of New Hampshire, was reluctant to divide the counties, alleging that in time the division of counties would create an unduly large representative body.[23]

An effort just before the constitutional convention of 1829-1830 to equate reform with the protection and perpetuation of slavery introduced a relatively new and henceforth significant element in the suffrage history of the south, and at a time when the western part of Virginia was increasingly critical of the peculiar institution. Indeed, so critical had the western section of the state become that one of the major deterrents to calling a convention was the eastern fear that the west would use any increase of political power to the detriment of slavery. Furthermore, Nat Turner's insurrection only

<hr>

[21] Virginia State Library, *Legislative Petitions*, Albemarle County, Dec. 14, 1805. For a typical contested election, see *Journals of the House of Delegates* (Richmond, 1816), pp. 45-47.

[22] V.S.L., *Legislative Petitions*, Accomack County, Dec. 20, 1825.

[23] *Ibid.*, Dec. 28, 1829.

recently had shaken the complacency of Virginians as to their own personal security. In combination with intermittent criticism from the north, it led some Virginians to consider democratic suffrage doctrine as a means of creating greater unity among all whites, and achieving greater security for slavery. Unenfranchised white men in Virginia and South Carolina had already declared that if they could be trusted with membership in the white patrols they could be trusted with the vote. Nevertheless, the union of pro-slavery and suffrage democracy as a deliberate policy did not develop until 1829.

At this time, Senator Morgan openly avowed white supremacy as a desirable result of political reform. After describing the burdens placed on non-freeholders, he quoted Plato as having said that the government of Athens rested upon the fundamental equality between all classes of Greeks. There was no equality such as this between Virginians, said Morgan. Pointing to Santo Domingo as an example, he said that protection against slave insurrections might well depend upon removing undemocratic discriminations against the various classes of whites. "We ought," he said, "to spread wide the foundation of our government, that all white men have a direct interest in its protection." This had been the policy of Sparta, he concluded, and should be the policy of Virginia. The east, seat of Virginia slavery, could then look confidently to the west for help in time of need.[24] The Jeffersonian emphasis upon the justice and utility of a militia requirement was thereby given a pro-slavery twist. Another Virginian had the same objective, but argued for a purely "Military Arrangement of the Right of Suffrage," by which voters would be required to appear at the polls fully armed and accoutered.[25]

The agitation for reform, having slowly gained momentum

[24] *Richmond Enquirer*, March 27, 1829.
[25] *Constitutional Whig*, Oct. 3, 1829.

after the second Staunton Convention of 1825, proved in time too strong to be ignored with safety. The result was the prolonged convention that met over a number of months spanning the years 1829 and 1830. To this convention were elected such great Virginians as John Marshall, James Monroe, James Madison, and John Randolph of Roanoke. The arguments for suffrage reform, still cast in the European idiom which many Americans were discarding, showed that Mrs. Trollope was premature in lamenting that the older tradition of continental learning in America had atrophied. On the contrary, the debate showed a ready familiarity with the suffrage issue in the times of Cromwell, and acquaintance not only with major political theorists, such as Edmund Burke and Thomas Hobbes, but also with such secondary figures as Bishop Filmer. The convention was equally familiar with suffrage arguments more essentially American which had developed from the Revolutionary crisis. It was the last great convention which was of interest because of its ideas, if for no other reason.[26]

The extremes in suffrage convictions expressed during the convention with such clarity, learning, and fervor were responsible for obscurantism in the various compromises which were written into the constitution. The west was dissatisfied by the compromise over the issue of representation, and the suffrage reformers, having lost a simple taxpaying qualification by a vote of 57 to 37, were confronted subsequently by a suffrage clause as complicated as any in American suffrage history. Shorn of its excessive verbiage, the amendment conceded the vote in state elections to leaseholders and householders, if they were taxpayers and otherwise qualified by age,

[26] Smalley, Donald (ed.), *Frances Trollope, Domestic Manners of the Americans* (New York, 1949), p. 312; *Proceedings and Debates of the Virginia State Convention of 1829-30* (Richmond, 1830).

etc. The amendment did not touch the special voting requirements in Richmond or in other local elections.

The extent of enfranchisement effected by the constitutional
revision has been variously estimated. A contemporary analyst
thought that it was less than anticipated. The *Richmond Whig*
published an estimate that in Virginia there were 78,265 free
white males over twenty-one, of whom only 44,325 were electors previously and that the electorate would be increased
only to 52,325, leaving unenfranchised 25,940 adult white
males.[27] These would have been able to vote if the suffrage
reformers who had advocated a taxpaying qualification had
won. Reformers of the west who had hoped to increase their
voting strength in the legislature were disappointed also. The
suffrage clause, they said, was "not worth the wing of a mos-
quito, whether every man, woman and child, black, white and
mulatto, were permitted to vote according to the Amended
Constitution. Of what use is many voters if they have no
representation; if they have no power beyond the court
yard?"[28] The convention failed also to provide for popular
election of officials from the governor down, to establish the
ballot, and to check the partisanship of sheriffs. The failure
to create election districts, the voters of Fauquier County
declared in 1832, made it difficult for those "recently admitted
to the Right of Suffrage [sic] from giving their votes. . . ."[29]
Suffrage democracy was not a product of this convention. It
was to be delayed until the reforms of 1851.

The renewal of reform sentiment in the early 1850's in Virginia was in part a reflection of the suffrage reform movement
which got under way in North Carolina in 1842 and which
took many years to succeed. The North Carolina movement
was, in turn, inspired partly by the Dorr War in Rhode Island
in 1842. Like Virginia, North Carolina had been backward in

[27] *Richmond Whig*, March 26, 1830.   [28] *Ibid.*, March 5, 1830.
[29] V.S.L., *Legislative Petitions*, Fauquier County, Dec. 18, 1832.

revising the suffrage qualifications for elections. Taxpayers could vote for the lower house and, after 1835, for the governor, but only 50-acre freeholders could vote for the upper house. After New York abandoned its first constitution in 1821, North Carolina, with the balanced form of government which the Revolutionary generation had created for the state, had the sole state government of which a Polybius or a Montesquieu could fully approve.

Given the North Carolina poll tax structure, the taxpaying qualification for the lower house was virtually manhood suffrage. The freehold qualification for the upper house was a different story. Analyses of Bertie County in 1824 show that 72 percent of the free polls were landowners, of whom about 10 percent did not own 50 acres. In senatorial elections, possibly only 50 percent of the electorate for the lower house could vote between 1800 and 1835.[30] As in Virginia, the major demand for constitutional revision prior to 1849 dealt primarily with reform of representation. This was the overriding issue of the convention of 1835. On this occasion, the only changes in the suffrage were the disfranchisement of free Negroes who were taxpayers or 50-acre freeholders, by insertion of the word "white" in the suffrage clause and extension of the vote for governor to the electorate of the lower house. This convention was responsible also for the abandonment of borough representation in the legislature on the grounds that the boroughs were as much the center of venality and fraud as ever had been their English counterparts which

[30] North Carolina Department of Archives and History, *Bertie County Tax Records*, 1824; Vinson, John C., "Electioneering in North Carolina," *North Carolina Historical Review* (xxix, April 1952), pp. 171-188. That the big issue was the senate elections and really no other is demonstrated by Pole, J. R., in *Journal of Southern History* (xxiv, May 1958), pp. 227-228. For a general treatment, see Bassett, J. S., "Suffrage in the State of North Carolina" *American Historical Association Reports*, 1895.

had lost their seats in the British House of Commons by the Reform Bill of 1832.[31]

To the same extent that the Rhode Island suffrage movement is associated with Thomas W. Dorr, that of North Carolina can be associated with the Democratic politician David S. Reid. Democrats and Whigs opposed to suffrage reform liked to believe that his sudden public espousal of a sentiment, admittedly latent in the state, was merely the overt manifestation of his aim to oust the Whigs from their long tenure of office. It is true, of course, that as a politician Reid could not afford to overlook a possible means of restoring to power the Democratic successors of the party of Nathaniel Macon and elect a Democrat, Lewis Cass, President in 1848. In Reid's case, however, if not that of his ultra-conservative colleagues, there was no conflict between partisan politics and his intellectual convictions. His papers show that he was thoroughly familiar with the Dorr War and sympathized with the Loco Foco wing of northern Democracy, which was democratically minded, if indifferent to abolitionism and the evils of slavery.[32] Furthermore, the career of Reid demonstrates his sympathy with the Young America movement, which wanted to expand the area of white democracy and Negro slavery in this hemisphere, particularly in the Caribbean area.[33] Reid, as well as his close associate, W. W. Holden, was from the southern viewpoint safe on the slavery issue. To this extent both were orthodox Democrats. Their orthodoxy, however,

[31] Green, Fletcher M., *Constitutional Development in the South Atlantic States, 1776-1860* (Chapel Hill, 1930), pp. 227-233; *Proceedings and Debates of the Convention of North Carolina* (Raleigh, 1836).

[32] North Carolina Department of Archives and History, *Reid Papers*. See, for example, James Philips to Reid, I, p. 47, Feb. 1, 1842; I, Broadside of Governor Dorr's Appeal to the People before Sentence was Pronounced, p. 107. The best account of the political history of the times is Norton, Clarence C., *The Democratic Party in Ante-Bellum North Carolina* (Chapel Hill, 1930).

[33] Rauch, Basil, *American Interest in Cuba: 1848-1855* (New York, 1948), pp. 237-261.

did not extend to the suffrage issue in the state at a time when there was as much opposition to suffrage reform among Democrats as among Whigs. On the whole, the Democratic party was more popular in the eastern than in the western part of the state, and for this reason it was violently averse to reform of representation and consequent increase of Whig power. Unwilling to endanger party unity, Reid did not advocate the calling of a constitutional convention, thus evoking the bitter criticism of Whig newspapers. The *Raleigh Register* accused him of inconsistency in acquiescing in a plan of representation based on property, while attacking suffrage based on the same principle. "When equal masses of voters claim that they are entitled to equal political power," said the *Register*, "Reid denies the claim because, as he would say, they do not possess an equal amount of property, but when individuals assert it, he grants it, because as between them (says he) property ought not to make any difference."[34]

Whatever the reason, Reid interjected the issue of suffrage when he ran for governor in 1848. The party convention which had nominated him had expressed the Young America spirit in felicitating the French upon their overthrow of Louis Philippe, and had listened with favorable attention to an address by Stephen A. Douglas of Illinois. It was Douglas, Whigs asserted later, who convinced Reid that the suffrage issue could be used to pry his opponents loose from their twelve-year grip of public office.[35] Democrats used arguments which by now had lost their novelty and freshness, save in Rhode Island, to arouse North Carolinians on behalf of democratic suffrage principles. Unwisely, the Whigs interpreted the suffrage issue as merely a cynical bid for power by their opponents. The *Register* denounced it as a "species of miser-

[34] *Raleigh Register*, June 21, 1848.
[35] *Raleigh Standard*, March 9, April 19, 1848; *Raleigh Register*, June 24, 1847.

able political clap trap."[36] Other Whig papers, however, saw the danger of openly opposing suffrage reform. The *Wilmington Commercial* predicted that the man who opposed it would be "stigmatized as a traitor, an aristocrat, or a Tory—or whatever name may be most odious to the people."[37] Some Whigs, convinced that it was true, asserted that 99 out of 100 adult males could easily acquire a freehold. Some said that the well-to-do would be driven from the polls if the franchise were broadened, and accused Reid of inconsistency because he did not attack the property tests for officeholding. He was also accused of being only one step from demanding an "agrarian law," and the restoration of voting rights to free Negroes.[38] Whigs said that the chief problem facing the state was not democracy but poverty.[39]

It is probable that more Democrats agreed with conservative Whigs on the suffrage issue than Reid found to his liking. A correspondent in the *North Carolina Times* denied that his fellow Carolinians who could not vote felt oppressed. In his opinion, Reid was arousing a basically contented people in demagogic fashion with the cry that the landed aristocracy of the state had been oppressive. Democrats of Warren, Edgecombe, and other counties, he said, could not conceal their disapproval of the campaign. "They say with us," he concluded, "Woodman! Spare that tree!"[40]

The Democratic leaders had no intention of doing so. They were gratified by the extent of popular enthusiasm for the stand taken by their major candidates. Holden wrote on August 1, 1848, that among the Whigs he had never seen "such long faces and heard such groanings! Free Suffrage—beg your pardon—equal suffrage is a humbug—is it?"[41] Nevertheless,

[36] *Raleigh Register*, May 20, 1848.
[37] *Wilmington Commercial*, quoted in *Raleigh Register*, June 28, 1848.
[38] *Ibid.*, June 15, 1848.   [39] *Ibid.*, July 29, 1848.
[40] *North Carolina Times*, July 1, 1848.
[41] *Reid Papers*, ii, p. 259, Aug. 1, 1848.

Whigs won the election by the small margin of 864 votes. They had learned their lesson. Although there were wide differences of opinion among them, as among the Democrats, and they were unable to obtain the support of all party members to vote for reform in the legislature, they gave up efforts to forestall suffrage reform. They hoped to secure a convention which would create a taxpaying electorate and, more important, reform of representation. Democrats vigorously opposed the Whig plan, declaring that a convention was unnecessary because the legislature had full legal power to amend the suffrage clause of the constitution. It was the Whigs' turn now to pronounce their party the more democratic. On the issue of the convention, a Whig paper asked, "Does all power reside in the people, or is it vested by our bill of rights in the Legislature?"[42] Democrats had been frank, although indiscreet, it said, in asserting that a convention would give the Whigs unlimited power in the state. Caught in the cross-currents of party politics and sectional jealousies as well as the overshadowing considerations of the coming of a civil war, a taxpaying qualification was not effected until 1857. The suffrage reform movement benefited the Democrats more than the Whigs, giving them control of the state and winning for them the support of the non-slaveowning poorer whites.

More openly avowed were the pro-slavery motives of the Democratic party of Virginia when the dormant suffrage reform movement revived, thanks to the influence of events in North Carolina. The most representative figure in this movement was Henry A. Wise.[43] A defender of poor whites, a supporter of a plan for public education, a believer in suffrage

[42] *North Carolina Star*, Jan. 24, 1851.
[43] Rogers, A. A., "Constitutional Democracy in Ante-Bellum Virginia," *William and Mary Quarterly* (xvi, 2nd Series, July 1936), pp. 399-407; Eaton, C., "Henry A. Wise, a Liberal of the Old South," *Journal of Southern History* (vii, Nov. 1941), pp. 480-494.

democracy, democratically elected officials of local government, and equitable representation of the various sections of the state, Wise was above all a defender of the southern way of life and of the peculiar institution. His kind of liberalism existed only in the southern part of the United States. A removal of all remaining sectional and political grievances within the state, he was convinced, would enable Virginia to concentrate attention upon north-south relations. The *Lynchburg Patriot* dealt frankly with this problem. Reform was necessary, it said, because of the "great idea of common safety which has impressed itself upon the minds of all true Virginians, in contemplation of the ominous and threatening state of our relations with our Northern brethren upon the subject of slavery."[44] Whigs claimed to be as democratic as the Democrats but envied the success of their opponents in attributing to themselves exclusive possession of democratic ideas.

Whigs were willing to accept suffrage reform on the practical grounds that the complicated suffrage clause of the constitution of 1830 had meant, in practice, that officers appointed by the governor had the right to say who was and who was not a legal voter, a situation which was palpably unjust to all parties. Whigs were angered equally by the extent of fagot voting. Furthermore, the qualification was interpreted in some places to mean that any one on the tax books, if otherwise qualified, could vote, an interpretation which entitled the possessor of a mere clock to vote. One contemporary commented that the existing property tests were too small and insignificant to fulfill their initial purpose and implied that they might as well be eliminated.[45]

In other states where a property test had been abandoned, an exclusively taxpaying qualification had helped to smooth

[44] Quoted in *Alexandria Gazette*, Jan. 9, 1850.
[45] *Ibid.*, Feb. 22, May 23, 1850.

the transition from property to democracy. Because by this time the majority of American states were practicing white manhood suffrage or its rough equivalent, Virginia reformers quite naturally advocated it. They appealed not only to the practice of other states but to the ineffectiveness of existing arrangements as well. The *Richmond Whig* carried a communication on July 23, 1850, which advocated a democratic white suffrage. "The present Constitution," the writer explained, "shows that every attempt to impose other restrictions than citizenship and residence produces embarrassment and confusion." In Virginia, as most often in America as a whole, reform was a bipartisan movement. Whigs and Democrats called for a convention to bring the government of their state in line with those of other southern states. Efforts which were made between 1848 and 1851 to require a tax payment, the proceeds to be used either for public improvements or for public education, proved unfeasible. In 1851 Virginia conceded manhood suffrage for state elections and, in the following year, abolished all distinctions between city and town elections on the one hand and state elections on the other.[46] Henceforth, all adult white males, if otherwise qualified, could vote in all elections, although without the secret ballot. Suffrage revision effected a considerable increase in the electorate, possibly as much as 60 percent.[47] Virginia had achieved democracy in suffrage, but in the spirit of Henry A. Wise quite as much as in the spirit of Thomas Jefferson. However motivated, the reforms in North Carolina and Virginia brought to a conclusion the antebellum suffrage reform movement in the south Atlantic states.

[46] See, for example, *Acts of the General Assembly of Virginia* (Richmond, 1852), pp. 241, 251, 255, 260, 283.
[47] Chandler, *op.cit.*, pp. 35-36, 21.

THE RHODE ISLAND EXPLOSION

AT THE HEIGHT of the Dorr War in Rhode Island, the *Manufacturer's and Farmer's Journal* of Providence stated, on January 27, 1842, that a year hence writers would conclude that "the Rhode Island rebellion is a sort of phenomenon in political history, which must forever puzzle the brains of political philosophers to explain." Later writers, including historians, have found it more difficult to explain how a resident of Rhode Island could so lack knowledge and comprehension of the situation in his own state as to make such an assertion. Rhode Island was the only American state which as late as 1840 confined the electorate to the freeholders, if otherwise qualified. For this reason, if for no other, a vigorous movement for suffrage reform was bound to develop. Not since the Revolution had opponents of suffrage reform discovered a preventive for reform fever, always endemic and sometimes epidemic. Rhode Islanders in time were infected. After 1834 the pressure for reform increased considerably and in relevance to the changing character of the little state.

The closest analogy to the Dorr War is undoubtedly the situation in Britain out of which arose the parliamentary reform movement which succeeded with the passage of the first great Reform Bill in 1832. The eighteenth-century reform movement was aborted by the reactionary effects of the French Revolution upon British opinion. It was successfully revived in the nineteenth century because it promised to recognize the facts of industrial life, including the divorce of more people from the land and the growth of manufacturing areas where few or none had existed before. The Industrial

Revolution rendered even less equitable the existing arrangements of suffrage and representation, creating tensions which were relieved by seasonable reforms.

During the first half of the nineteenth century, Rhode Island was becoming a Britain in miniature. Once a predominantly agricultural and commercial community, it was becoming an industrial society.[1] The political results of this transformation were far-reaching. The increase in the landless element of the population, the development of manufacturing establishments in some of the towns, and the redistribution of population which this movement entailed upset the equilibrium in representation and made the $134 freehold qualification much less defensible than before. As a group of North Providence petitioners said in 1829, the population was increasing to the point where the "whole soil would not be sufficient to make voters of a majority of her actual population."[2]

Probably 50 to 75 percent of adult males were able to meet the freehold qualification before the Revolution. So long as the percentage remained relatively constant and so long as eldest sons of freeholders could vote, Rhode Islanders without much difficulty or even hypocrisy could continue to quote, as they did, Roger Williams' statement that Rhode Island was a democracy. The efforts of some Jeffersonian Republicans to secure a taxpaying qualification in 1811 failed partly for this reason. Resistance to reform, which had been successful before the War of 1812, stiffened as it became clearer that the industrial population would be composed, in the future, less of Protestant native stock and more of immigrant groups, Roman Catholic in religion and very different in other ways.

The old New England stock of the small towns, whether

[1] See Brennan, Joseph, *Social Conditions in Industrial Rhode Island, 1820-1860* (Washington, D.C., 1940).
[2] Rhode Island Archive Room, *Petitions not Granted*, May 1829.

Whig or Democratic, was often opposed to suffrage reform if it involved the enfranchisement and increase in political power of a population which did not share its values and interests and which was bound in the course of time to become more powerful. In 1828 one Republican politician quoted John Jay's dictum, as reported by Jay's son, that those who owned the country ought to govern it—referring to the farming element. He warned Republican farmers that the state was filling up with commercial towns, banks, and chartered companies "as variant almost as the various combinations of the alphabet, but all variant in political interests from yours."[3]

For the same reason, farmers, whether Federalist or Republican, Whig or Democrat, often opposed a redistribution of seats in the lower house of the legislature and the abolition of the "rotten boroughs" on the grounds solely that these changes would increase the political power of industrial and moneyed wealth in state affairs, and shift taxation and other important matters of public policy from a rural to an urban orientation.[4] Possibly, if the suffrage reform movement had arisen, as elsewhere, before industrialization and immigration had become "clear and present dangers," it would have been successful without the revolutionary situation by which it finally was effected.

To objective observers, it was becoming questionable how much longer Rhode Islanders would find it expedient or just to ignore the abuses and inequities so essentially a part of their political system. Critics of Rhode Island suffrage were undoubtedly correct in asserting that the freehold qualification was not only undemocratic in theory but becoming more so in practice. In Providence alone, the proportion of adult males who were freemen dropped from over 50 percent in

[3] Rhode Island Historical Society, *Warwick Papers*, x, A Farmer [Jonathan R. Waterman] to the Farmers and Landholders of Rhode Island (March 1828).
[4] *Ibid.*

1790 to about 33 percent in 1832.[5] The fact that 76 percent of all adult males on the Providence tax books for 1840 were property owners is not an accurate reflection of the extent of freeholding among all adult males. Probably the names of a large number of adults did not appear on the tax lists because of the absence of a poll tax at the time, or because they were temporary residents or, as they were called, "birds of passage."[6] In the agricultural towns, probably at least 50 percent of adult males could qualify to vote as freeholders. For the state as a whole, an estimate for 1841 gave 11,239 electors among 26,000 males. It was said that under an "extended suffrage," probably meaning a taxpayer suffrage, 18,139 would be able to vote.[7] If these figures are correct, there is much to be said for reformers who believed that their state was scandalously out of line with the suffrage democracy that existed almost everywhere else in the country.

Electoral procedures, as well as the freehold qualification, came in for a share of criticism. Ezra Stiles' strictures upon Rhode Island as a "licentious republic" could as well have been made with reference to the nineteenth as to the eighteenth century. Eldest sons of freeholders who were by law entitled to vote in towns other than those in which their fathers owned freeholds were granted the right in some towns and not in others. Young men who were not the eldest sons of freeholders were allowed to vote, in many instances, if they would vote as directed. In some towns the Anglo-American practice of creating fagot votes continued well into the nineteenth century. In the 1835 elections a considerable number of votes were manufactured not only by the conveyance of deeds to real property but also by the conveyance of shares of

[5] Stokes, A. K., *The Finances and Administration of Providence, 1636-1901*, pp. 33, 136.

[6] See *List of Persons Assessed in the City Tax of Sixty-Five Thousand Dollars . . .* (Providence, 1840).

[7] *Providence Journal*, May 3, 1841.

stock in companies which held land in freehold.[8] About this time a Rhode Islander explained that in 1810 and 1811 he had favored the taxpaying qualification because he wanted to see an end to the creation of "sham deeds and leases" which "qualified the very Dregs of Society to vote. . . ."[9] Some people found it galling that certain other privileges besides voting were granted to freemen and not to others. For example, no person who was not a freeholder inhabitant of the state could secure any writ of arrest or original summons against any other inhabitant "unless some sufficient freeholder in this State shall endorse on the back of the writ" his full name.[10]

As in Britain, the suffrage issue in Rhode Island was not so important to the political realists as the issue of representation. Residents of such centers as Providence, even when qualified to vote, were convinced that they were not equitably represented in the legislature and that this grievance was the more substantial one. According to the calculations of Providence leaders, a majority of the seats in the lower house was controlled by only a third of the population. A more precise description indicated that, although Providence controlled only four seats or one-eighteenth of the membership of the lower house, it provided revenue to the state in a much greater proportion.[11] Rural politicians won votes among their constituents by pointing out that there had not been a land tax since 1822, and that the burden of state taxes lay on manufacturing enterprises and business interests, a point which caused unfavorable comment on the part of manufacturers.

[8] Archive Room, *Petitions not Granted*, 1828, 1835; John Hay Library, Brown University, *Thomas W. Dorr Papers*, Sullivan Dorr to T. W. Dorr, I, p. 121, May 21, 1835.

[9] *Dorr Papers*, II, p. 129, William Peckham to Dorr, Feb. 3, 1837.

[10] *The Public Laws of the State of Rhode Island and Providence Plantations* (1822), v, pp. 14-15.

[11] Archive Room, *Petitions not Granted*, Memorial of the City Council of Providence, January 1834; *Dorr Papers*, III, Dorr to Jesse Calder, May 4, 1841, p. 55.

Quite naturally, they considered the abolition of "rotten boroughs" as long overdue and as a necessary step in the development of a more favorable opinion in the legislature toward manufacturing. In the opinion of some manufacturers, suffrage reform was not necessary but was acceptable as a democratic gesture if it were not carried to extreme. The unenfranchised and their leaders could scarcely understand this point of view and might have reacted, under appropriate leadership, as did the British Chartists to British Whiggery after 1832.

The man whose political career illustrates the complex character of Rhode Island reform was the man who, by universal acknowledgment, was its outstanding figure, Thomas W. Dorr. Superficially, his career seems inexplicable in the light of his antecedents. Son of Sullivan Dorr, a merchant who made a fortune in the China trade of Massachusetts and became a resident of Providence, Dorr was considered, like Jefferson, a traitor to his class. Few, if acquainted only with the facts of his early life (Exeter, Harvard, and the study of law under James Kent), could have predicted that he would consider himself a leader of the masses, let alone an upholder of the right of revolution, a doctrine no longer so fashionable as it had been in 1776.[12]

The apparent contradictions in his career, however, are easily resolved. His great political enemy, the Democratic leader James Fenner, understood very well what kind of man Dorr was. "Whatever Mr. Dorr does," he was reported to have asserted, "he does from principle."[13] It was absurd to dismiss Dorr as a failure in the practice of law, a man who sought compensation in politics for lack of success in his profession. Actually, Dorr was a very successful lawyer and also a man of

[12] *Dorr Papers*, I, p. 30, Usher Parsons to Joseph Blunt, Jan. 25, 1824; I, p. 48, Dorr to (?).
[13] *Dorr Papers*, IV, J. Albro to Dorr, p. 108, Aug. 11, 1842.

deep and invincible democratic faith. He found democratic principles set at naught in Rhode Island and proposed to do something about it. He took to heart not only the democratic message of the American Revolution but also the democratic orientation of British Chartism, the Canadian Rebellion of 1837, and the revolutionary tradition in contemporary France.

What Dorr's principles were and where they originated is made clear by his correspondence. He praised the democratic spirit he saw in Roger Williams and had the deepest admiration and respect for Thomas Jefferson. He numbered among his friends and acquaintances, particularly after he inclined towards Loco Foco Democracy, John Greenleaf Whittier, George Bancroft, Alexander H. Everett, and the British reformer, Joseph Sturge. After he repudiated his Whig affiliations to become a Democrat and then a Loco Foco, he became a friend of John L. O'Sullivan, Robert R. Rantoul, Orestes Brownson, as well as many other prominent men. Next to suffrage reform, Dorr was most interested in the anti-slavery movement. Events abroad also stimulated his imagination and aroused his enthusiasm, among them the July Revolution in France and the passage of the British Reform Bill in 1832.[14]

Pre-Civil War American reformers in the north spoke the same language and shared the same assumptions. Most of them agreed that men were fundamentally alike, irrespective of race, color, or creed, and that they shared the capacity to improve indefinitely those great moral and rational faculties with which they had been endowed by their Creator. If one could trust man, one could in the long run trust a majority of men. If men were fundamentally good as, according to the true democratic theory of the time they were, there was no inconsistency or danger in making the people sovereign. Nor was it subversive to advocate that the people be allowed to do as they pleased, so long as they enjoyed the crucial moral

[14] See letters in *Dorr Papers*, vols. I, III, IV, V.

sanction of comprising the majority. "It is not only the *Right* but the *Duty* of those now on the stage of action," wrote Dorr, "to change the laws and institutions of government, to keep pace with the progress of knowledge, the light of science, and the amelioration of the condition of society. Nothing is to be considered unchangeable but the inherent and inalienable rights of man."[15]

When in 1834 Dorr entered politics as a Whig and won election to the legislature, he did not have in mind the program of reform for which he later became famous. On the contrary, his opinions at this time were so moderate that he was critical of Britons who thought the Reform Bill insufficiently democratic and who hinted that perhaps a genuine revolution might be desirable. In Dorr's opinion the poor should not be led to think they could help themselves, "without waiting for the slow process of legislation." So far as suffrage reform was concerned, he did not advocate until about 1840 more than a taxpaying qualification. So moderate were his aims that at first he attracted the sympathy of more Whigs than Democrats. He was able even to secure the support of the President of Brown University, Francis Wayland, and leading manufacturers, as well as persons bearing the proud name of Brown.[16]

To press their reform program, Dorr and his associates formed the Constitutional Party in 1834 to agitate for the calling of a specially elected convention to abandon the old royal charter, granted by Charles II, and to write a constitution which would specifically limit the powers of the various branches of the government and incorporate a bill of rights. The aims of the Constitutionalists and others who supported them were so conservative that they became substantially the basis for the constitution which was established by Dorr's

[15] *Ibid.*, II, p. 55, Dorr to Jesse Calder, May 4, 1841.
[16] *Ibid.*, I, pp. 92, 137; II, pp. 25, 141, 175, 241, 251, 287.

enemies after the war was over.[17] The Dorr faction specifically disclaimed any intention of admitting "the rabble" to the vote. A friend warned Dorr that his enemies were misrepresenting his party's position on this matter and that friends of reform thought that the Dorrites were pressing for unqualified universal manhood suffrage and were "completely terror struck."[18]

The Constitutionalists made no progress with their plan of action between 1834 and 1838. During the presidential campaign of 1840, their efforts to focus attention upon suffrage and representation were generally ignored by an electorate interested in the Harrison-Van Buren campaign. Leaders of both the Democratic and Whig parties in the little state were aware that their adherents were divided on the question of internal reform and were happy, as a result, to stress the issues and personalities of an exciting national campaign. The strain on the Constitutionalists proved too great. As an organization, it did not survive the election and was succeeded by the Rhode Island Suffrage Association.

This new organization was new in more than name. It contrasted strongly with the Constitutionalists in the kind of person it attracted, in its aims, and, in time, in its means. Contemporaries were unable to agree as to who was responsible for its initiation. Dorr wrote that it sprang into existence at the hands of voteless men "who did military duty and worked the fire engines."[19] Critics were likely to detect the hand of Democratic politicians who had been greatly aroused during the presidential election by the Whig creation of freeholds and who were therefore convinced that the freehold qualification, with all its attendant abuses, must be abolished. Others suspected that New York Loco Focos had prodded their Rhode Island sympathizers into making the issue of suffrage

[17] Archive Room, *Petitions not Granted*, Petition of towns of Providence etc. in convention, Feb. 22, 1834.
[18] *Ibid.*, Charles B. Peckham to Dorr, March 11, 1836, II, p. 21.
[19] *Providence Journal*, Feb. 17, 1842.

democracy the means of winning the next election. One Rhode Islander, in a cynical summation of events, told the Democrats that they had become reformers in order "to regain lost influence of your party, to swell its numbers and to break down and destroy Whig principles."[20] Nevertheless, some Whigs of Providence and elsewhere considered reform to be as good Whig as Democratic doctrine and were therefore willing to join the Rhode Island Suffrage Association or, at least, to sympathize with it when it became the center of opposition to the status quo. The fact that the organization advocated universal manhood suffrage indicates that it was radical in a sense that the Constitutional Party never was, nor Dorr himself to this time.

The responsibility for the conversion of a reformist organization into a revolutionary one must be shared by anti-reform elements, irrespective of party affiliation. Dorr and his supporters were probably correct in interpreting a state-sponsored call for a constitutional convention, to be held in November of 1841, as evidence of insincerity and opportunism, and no more designed to be the vehicle of genuine reform than previous conventions which had met and done little or nothing. Acting upon this interpretation, Dorr called upon all adult male residents to ignore the freehold qualification and elect members of a constitutional convention which would meet in October 1841. The theory upon which Dorrites justified their action was revolutionary in the sense that it implied that a majority of the people, i.e., adult males, could ignore the existing government under the old charter and displace it with one of their own making.[21] In effect, Rhode Islanders were invited to create a revolution, if only at the polls rather than at the barricades.

Convinced that the delegates to the October convention,

[20] *Ibid.*, Feb. 10, 1842.
[21] See Mowry, A. M., *The Dorr War* (Providence, 1901).

who were chosen by the extra-legal elections, represented a substantial majority of Rhode Islanders, Dorr and his associates settled down to the hard work of producing a modern constitution for their state. The document, known as the People's Charter or Constitution, represented a sharp break with the old charter. The freehold qualification was abandoned, and the suffrage extended to adult white male citizens, if resident in the state one year; the representation of Providence and other large centers in the lower house was increased; voters were required to use a secret ballot and to register in advance of elections; and the office of justice of the peace was made elective. In one or two particulars, however, the People's Constitution was too conservative for a few of the more advanced thinkers at the convention. For example, Negroes, even if otherwise qualified, were not permitted to vote and no person was allowed to vote in any financial matters of the towns or cities unless he were a taxpayer or were rated for the ownership of $150 worth of property. Furthermore, no person could hold any of the more important offices unless he were a taxpayer.[22]

Opponents of the People's Constitution took pleasure in saying that it was "a little too genteel for the workers who had labored in its erection."[23] Even Dorr acknowledged that the document was "not democratic in the broadest sense of the word, but he would not take up time showing it."[24] The more conservative point of view was expressed at the convention by one member who, interrupting a delegate's speech in favor of the franchise for Negroes, said that this convention was "not the Rhode Island Suffrage Association nor a collection of them, but an entirely different body, not to be bound by their acts."[25] Negroes, who considered themselves more American

[22] This constitution is printed in an appendix in Mowry, *op.cit.*
[23] *Providence Journal*, March 14, 1842.
[24] *Ibid.*, Oct. 11, 1842.
[25] *Ibid.*

than the naturalized foreign-born, protested vigorously to Dorr and to the Rhode Island Anti-Slavery Society.

The constitution which resulted from the deliberations of the Landholders Convention in November, on the other hand, was so conservative even to the extent of requiring a freehold qualification for voters that reformers were encouraged to proceed as rapidly as possible to secure ratification of their own constitution and put it into effect by whatever means were at their disposal. Their attempt to do so, of course, failed. Yet from the vantage point of the fall of 1841, men like Dorr thought they had a good opportunity to succeed. In the first place, the Democratic party in the nation was anxious to give the reformers what support it could and to pin the label of reaction upon Whiggery. Secondly, precedents existed in the history of Michigan and of Maryland for the election, without the consent of the existing legislatures, of constitutional conventions which then proceeded to remodel their state governments.[26] Lastly, President Tyler, a states' rights Virginian, might be persuaded that it was not his responsibility, any more than it had been deemed the responsibility of previous presidents in comparable situations, to uphold the old Charter government of Rhode Island by the threat or the use of federal troops. If the administration did not intervene, a peaceful, orderly succession might take place without incident or bloodshed.

The anti-Dorr forces, however, had every intention of asserting their legal authority. From the beginning of the new year in January 1842, they set to work to fragmentize and to destroy the Dorr faction. In February of that year, they redrafted the Landholders Constitution. They decided to abandon the freehold qualification in favor of a personal property qualification for native-born citizens and permitted Negroes to qualify, a point which they stressed in support of

[26] *Daily Express*, Extra, April 17, 1842.

their claim of liberalism. One suffragist thought he had good reason for abandoning Dorrism. "Who will fight for *any* form," demanded one of Dorr's correspondents, "when the substance can be gained by peace?"[27] Dorr acknowledged that the February draft was an advance over the previous one, particularly with regard to the suffrage, but maintained that its failure to concede greater representation for Providence and other centers showed that what the Charter party was granting with one hand it was withholding with the other.

Seeking support wherever it was to be found, the Charter party appealed to basic ethnic, religious, class, and sectional sentiments in the state. It endeavored to associate Dorr with an anti-capitalist philosophy and with the approval of such representatives of the "workies" as Seth Luther. Manufacturers and employers, said Dorr's opponents, had no stake in a movement in which men whose basic interest was in raising wages were influential. If the reformers won, said a spokesman for the Charter party, no one could predict what would happen to the tax rate in Providence and other manufacturing centers.[28] The standard arguments against manhood suffrage of Blackstone and Chancellor Kent were used for whatever effect their declining prestige might have.

Anti-Dorr politicians told the farming population that the real struggle was between "the masses who congregate" in the cities and factory towns and the farmer. For this reason, suffrage and representation reforms would be disastrous to the agricultural and commercial interests. "Farmers of Rhode Island," asked "Country-born," "would it be conducive to the good of the whole that the large towns and factory villages should govern the state?"[29] Other critics of Dorr pointed out

[27] *Dorr Papers*, W. S. Burgess et al. to Dorr, June 25, 1842, IV, p. 87.
[28] *Providence Journal*, Jan. 1, 6, 12; Feb. 28; March 12, 14, 16, 17, 19, 21, 1842. See also *Manufacturer's and Farmer's Journal*, Jan. 3, 4, 13, 1842.
[29] *Providence Journal*, Jan. 4, 1842.

that Rhode Island, unlike New York or Massachusetts, did not have a large agricultural population and that therefore manhood suffrage would be dangerous.

The Charter party warned native-born Protestants that the People's Constitution would admit to the vote naturalized citizens who were often Irish Catholics and would create in Rhode Island a situation similar to New York's in which the Roman Catholic hierarchy exerted great influence. The enfranchisement of immigrant stock, it was said, would create a demand for public support of parochial schools as well as a demand for other Catholic measures, with the result that the home of Roger Williams would fall under the shadow of the cathedral.[30] In short, the anti-Dorr faction, claiming that it upheld the standards of middle-class, agrarian, Protestant, native-born Rhode Islanders, hoped by these arguments to shatter the reform coalition. To an extent this approach was proved sound by subsequent events. Furthermore, the party did not overlook the effect of a threat of arrest and imprisonment for those who would defend or hold office under the People's Constitution. In the spring of 1842 the legislature passed a rigorous act designed to uphold the authority of the existing government, the so-called Algerine Law.

It is difficult to escape the conclusion that these measures lessened popular support of Dorr. Furthermore, he could not count upon the neutrality of the Tyler administration nor even the support, other than platonic, of northern Democrats, save those of Tammany Hall or of the Loco Foco persuasion. The southern wing of the party was totally opposed to the establishment of a people's constitution because it would be, it was feared, a bad and revolutionary example to slaves and wild-eyed abolitionists.[31]

Dorr lost ground also because many of his supporters could

[30] *Ibid.*, March 14, 16, 17, 21, 1842.
[31] *Dorr Papers*, Aaron White to Dorr, June 3, 15, 1842, IV, pp. 80-81.

not justify an act of revolution in the light of the fact that the old Charter party was giving ground on the suffrage issue, and other issues as well. Changing the constitution at the ballot box was different from recourse to the cartridge box. As early as January 1842, Dorr's brother, Henry, a New York lawyer, had warned him against rash acts. Henry thought his brother's plan of action was wrong in terms of principle and expediency. In the first place, he wrote, Dorr had not taken the prudent step of allying himself with some eminent authority, say, John C. Calhoun. Secondly, he said that the movement was bound to be crushed eventually, either at the polls or by force, because, with the exception of Newport and Providence, there was not in Rhode Island the raw material for a revolution *à la française* which would carry Dorr to victory. He warned his brother that his movement might suffer the same defeat as the Chartists of Great Britain.[32]

Dorr ignored his brother's advice. He stood for election as governor in April 1842, considered himself elected by popular mandate but subsequently failed, quite unaccountably, to gain physical possession of the state capitol building in Providence, wasting his forces instead upon a fruitless attack on the arsenal. When this failed, he left for Washington, D.C., to seek help. Unable to obtain a promise, either of aid or neutrality, Dorr returned to Rhode Island and, hoping to rally his followers, stormed Acote Hill on June 28, 1842. These military activities, if they can be dignified as such, did not have the effect he had anticipated. The war was over, and Dorr fled the state.[33]

With Dorr's flight, Rhode Islanders lost an opportunity for many years to effect the kind of reform for which he had stood. The constitution drafted by the Law and Order Party, composed of both Whigs and Democrats, was a document which neither Dorr nor his die-hard supporters could ap-

[32] *Dorr Papers*, III, p. 76.   [33] Mowry, *op.cit.*, p. 215.

prove.[34] Although it was similar to the People's Constitution in that it incorporated a bill of rights, conceded a more equitable plan of representation, and provided special safeguards against the control of town and city finances by the non-propertied or non-taxpaying elements, it was, in its suffrage and electoral clauses, niggardly and begrudging in its concessions. Registration of voters was not accompanied by the secrecy of the ballot. Although the voters were given the opportunity to accept the constitution with or without a clause enfranchising the Negro, they were not offered a similar choice on the question of enfranchising naturalized citizens upon the same terms as native-born whites. One of these suffrage clauses denied the vote to the naturalized citizen unless he were the owner of a $134 freehold. The native-born were given the vote if resident two years in the state and if they had paid taxes of $1 or more or had enrolled in the militia or met their militia responsibilities.[35]

To what extent the new constitution increased the electorate would be very difficult to determine. If the analysis of the electoral figures up to this time, mentioned above, is correct, the shift to a taxpaying qualification increased the electorate from about 11,000 to about 18,000. Possibly, 8,000 adult males could not vote under the taxpaying qualification because they were aliens, temporary residents of the state, or naturalized citizens who had to be freeholders to vote.[36]

Dorr understood the true character of the new constitution. He advised his adherents to vote against a document which required a head tax for voters and a landed qualification for the naturalized citizen, denied the right to a secret ballot, and failed to remedy decisively the inequitable plan of representation. But in the election to ratify the constitution in November 1842 and in the first election of officers in April 1843, the

[34] *Dorr Papers*, IV, Jan. 1842.   [35] Mowry, *op.cit.*, pp. 350-351.
[36] *Providence Journal*, May 3, 1841.

Law and Order Party won handsomely.[37] The reasons for its success lay not only in the strength of ethnic, religious, and class loyalties but also in the means used by the anti-Dorr elements to win. The campaign, particularly for the April election, was one of intimidation and corruption which exceeded any seen before in the state, even during the Ward-Hopkins feud before the Revolution. Given special but temporary rights to vote by a clause in the new constitution, militiamen were escorted to the polls. Employers threatened their employees with retaliation, and landlords their tenants, if they did not vote as they were told. Potential voters, illegal or otherwise, were held virtually incommunicado in factories and other buildings, to be produced under careful surveillance at the polls on election morning, having spent the night feasting and drinking.[38]

The loss of this election broke Dorr's heart. Until the people for whom he had ventured so much failed to support him, Dorr had had a seemingly unquenchable faith that they would show the physical and moral courage necessary to face the challenge of the times. Events after 1841 proved his confidence misplaced. Deeply dejected, Dorr wrote a friend after the election that none of the Dorrites could say what Francis I had said after the Battle of Pavia, "All is lost save honor."[39] He thought that honor, patriotism, and all considerations of a like nature which should "animate a man contending for his just rights" had been thrown away by the suffrage party. "If our party will not fight or vote," he exclaimed, "in God's name what will they do!" In conclusion, he wrote, "I think we could select from the whole a set of slavish, abject, poor-spirited creatures who would do credit to the serfdom of Russia, and who ought to be attached to the soil, and sold and transferred

[37] Mowry, op.cit., p. 241.
[38] Dorr Papers, v, vi, vii. See vi, F. Beckford to Dorr, Jan. 20, 1843.
[39] Ibid., vii, Dorr to Aaron White, Jr., April 27, 1843.

with it, in its various changes of ownership."[40] So depressed was Dorr that he returned to Rhode Island in October and surrendered to the authorities. He was convicted of treason and sentenced to jail for life; he languished there for two years before being pardoned and released.[41]

Thanks to the miscarriage of reform and the unenlightened character of the new government, Rhode Island settled down once more to a state of political apathy. Election statistics show how considerable it was. Whereas in the state elections of 1843, 15,000 had voted, in those of 1850 only 4,000 cast ballots, the latter figure comprising probably only about 20 percent of all adult males.[42] One Democratic newspaper maintained that in 1850 no greater proportion of adult males were voting in Rhode Island than in Great Britain at that time. The major reason for the declining interest in politics lay, according to Democrats, in the fact that suffrage reform, having been effected by those who had been opposed initially to any reform, had created a system "of elections without voters" in which citizens no more thought of voting than the serfs of Russia.[43] It would not be an exaggeration to say that Dorr lost not only the crucial battle but the war as well.

[40] *Ibid.*
[41] Mowry, *op.cit.*, pp. 256-257.
[42] *Providence Post*, July 6, Dec. 17, 1850.
[43] *Republican Herald*, April 6, 1850; *Providence Post*, May 8, 1850.

CHAPTER 14

UNFINISHED BUSINESS

"Be warned . . . ," said the *Workingman's Advocate* of New York on May 7, 1829, "that it is a dangerous thing to sneer at universal suffrage in this republican country." In France, one could speak openly of the canaille, it continued, and in England "of the *mob* and the *swinish multitude*, but this is neither France nor England."[1] Sixteen years later, the *Hartford Times*, a Democratic paper, asserted that the right to a democratic suffrage was no longer the opinion of a sect but was the conviction of an overwhelming majority of the people. "At first scouted as radical and agrarian," it declared on November 15, 1845, "then winning over, one by one, the free and thoughtful; then slowly growing popular with the common people," it was finally "conceded alike by all parties" that property should not be a qualification for voting. Opponents of suffrage, as of democracy, in the words of Alexis de Tocqueville, "hide their heads, and if they wish to rise are forced to borrow their colors."[2]

The fifth decade of the nineteenth century saw Americans so thoroughly wedded to their conception of democracy as resting upon the vote of adult male citizens, preferably white, that it became a vote-getting issue for politicians who attacked their opponents for having been critical of or opposed to manhood suffrage at any time in their careers. As early as the American Revolution, politicians seized every opportunity to use the suffrage issue to discredit their rivals. By the 1840's, when the power of the opposition to suffrage reform was

[1] *Workingman's Advocate*, Nov. 7, 1829.
[2] Tocqueville, Alexis de, *Letters and Reminiscences of Alexis de Tocqueville* (London, 1861), 2 vols., i, p. 311.

routed, the issue was exploited extensively for political advantage.

Because it was probably true that more Whigs than Democrats had reservations about a democratic suffrage and that the Democrats were generally the initiators of reform, Whigs were embarrassed quite often by Democratic attacks. The *Connecticut Courant* complained in 1842 against the practice as unfair and misleading. "If a solitary Whig paper utters a sentiment which can be tortured into opposition to universal suffrage . . . it is at once paraded in the columns of *The* [New Haven] *Times* as full and conclusive evidence that the Whig Party are not only old fashioned Federalists, but full believers in the 'Divine Right of Kings.' "[3] Two years previously, during the campaign of 1840, James Buchanan had attacked the Whig candidate, William Henry Harrison, for having opposed a taxpaying qualification for voting in 1807 when he was territorial governor of Indiana. Webster's position on suffrage in the Massachusetts Convention of 1820 was misconstrued, and he was quoted out of context during this campaign and has been since by many an historian.[4]

Whigs were not alone in suffering obloquy and embarrassment, however. Many distinguished Democrats had at some time in their careers taken a stand against suffrage reform, or were criticized as if they had. When Calhoun was unjustly accused in 1842 of having opposed suffrage reform in South Carolina in 1809, a New York Loco Foco had written him to get the record straight. He rightly contrasted the stand of Calhoun in 1809 with that of Martin Van Buren in the New York Convention of 1821.[5] In the campaign of 1840, Whigs used Van Buren's earlier opposition to universal suffrage to win the votes of democratically minded Americans every-

[3] *Connecticut Courant*, Sept. 26, 1842.
[4] See Schlesinger, A. M., *The Age of Jackson* (New York, 1946), pp. 13-14, for an exception.
[5] See *supra*, p. 202.

where. They attacked him on the grounds that he had said the people were not yet ready for universal suffrage, "thus showing that though for the purpose of gulling us, he now affects democratic principles, he always was a Federalist of the highest tone, a rank aristocrat at best."[6] As late as 1844, Van Buren was still worried about the stand he had once taken. Andrew Jackson was criticized similarly in 1828 because he had been a member of the Tennessee Constitutional Convention of 1796 which combined a freehold with a non-freehold qualification. Thomas Hart Benton seems to have escaped public denunciation, although he had not been initially a supporter of universal manhood suffrage at the time Missouri entered the Union.[7] John A. Quitman of Mississippi hastened in 1832 to explain that his suffrage statements had been "misquoted."[8]

Whigs in self-defense accused not only leading Democrats but also various state Democratic machines of being against suffrage democracy. New York and Vermont Whig newspapers jibed at the Democratic Party in 1839 for not being as democratic as its name implied, citing Virginia's rejection of universal suffrage and the failure of Jackson's own state to abandon property tests for voting, whereas Vermont, a strong Whig state, had long believed in and practiced universal suffrage.[9] Whigs often resented the Democrats' pose as the only sincere adherents of a democratic franchise, preferring to believe the Democrats supported the principle only so long as the people voted them into office. A Connecticut

[6] *By a Workingman, More than a 100 Reasons why William Henry Harrison Should and Will Have the Support of the Democracy for the Presidency of the United States in Preference to Martin Van Buren* (Boston, 1840), p. 9.

[7] Buley, R. C., *The Old Northwest* (Indianapolis, 1950, 2 vols.), II, p. 163; Shoemaker, F. C., *Missouri's Struggle for Statehood, 1804-1821* (Jefferson City, 1916), p. 121.

[8] Claiborne, J. F. H., *Life and Correspondence of John A. Quitman* (New York, 1860, 2 vols.), I, pp. 125-126.

[9] *New York Whig*, quoted in *The Vermont Watchman*, July 1, 1839.

newspaper said that the Democrats had shown by their use of fraudulent votes in 1840 that they were opposed "to a free suffrage except when it sustained them in office."[10] The assertion of the *Detroit Free Press* that the Loco Foco defeat in the city of Baltimore confirmed Jefferson's statement that great cities were sores on the body politic caused considerable amusement for the press of Cleveland. "They were very healthy spots, however," said the *Cleveland Herald and Gazette* on May 7, 1838, "in the eyes of Mr. Jefferson's admirers, when Jacksonianism ruled every city in the land from Detroit to Dog Town." Generally speaking, most Whigs would go along with Democrats on the road to suffrage reform. Daniel Webster hoped that the republic would remain stable under universal suffrage, if the American System effected universal prosperity.

The initiative in suffrage reform remained, however, with the Democrats. They pressed the initial attack, for example, against the taxpaying qualification in those states where it had been adopted as a sound alternative to outright freehold or other property tests. The taxpaying qualification was defended as a sound principle for excluding from the franchise those who, because they did not pay a direct tax, had no stake in keeping governmental expenditures within bounds. No representation without taxation was a sound principle which was implied, it was said, in the Revolutionary slogan, "No taxation without representation." Furthermore, the taxpaying qualification was defended in some states which levied poll taxes as a means of enforcing payment, and its abandonment was considered a threat to the prevailing tax structure and to the state revenue system. Lastly, symbols of personal worth and substance hitherto attached to the freehold qualification had been transferred to the taxpaying qualification.

As might be expected, defense of the taxpaying qualifica-

[10] *Connecticut Courant*, Nov. 26, 1842.

tion did not prove universally popular, although a taxpaying suffrage was revived in the south in various forms after the collapse of Reconstruction. Four states abandoned this qualification before the Civil War, beginning with Mississippi in 1831, whose constitution of 1817 was denounced as "a hot bed of aristocracy" and "an awkward transposition of Blackstone" and hence in need of drastic revision.[11] The immediate reason for the demand for revision was the enthusiasm generated by the French Revolution of July 1830, and the British parliamentary reform movement. Ignoring a newspaper appeal to ground the suffrage upon an income qualification, as in France, the Mississippi convention voted to adopt white manhood suffrage.[12] With that lack of party strife which had characterized reform in their state, the Democrats of New Jersey initiated a successful program to abandon the taxpaying qualification in the constitutional convention which met in 1844.[13]

Meanwhile, a sharp struggle was underway in Connecticut to revise the suffrage qualification of 1817. Democrats had raised the issue of universal suffrage during Jackson's time, but it was the events of the Dorr War in Rhode Island which aroused any degree of really popular reform sentiment. As in the past, Democrats acted as much from motives of political realism as from idealism. They suspected that their Whig opponents were continuing to import voters from other states, and that Whig employers were influencing their employees in the way which Blackstone had deplored. Whigs were not discontented with this state of affairs, but Democrats, needless to say, were very much so. The *Hartford Times* declared that the property test ought to be either more rigidly enforced or abolished. As it existed, it was "a mere burlesque, with dif-

[11] *Natchez Gazette*, July 13, 1831.
[12] *The Mississippian*, Aug. 14, 1809; *The Natchez Gazette*, July 13, 1831.
[13] See McCormick, *op.cit.*, pp. 133-138.

ferent practices prevailing in the different towns of the state."[14] Particularly objectionable was the practice of fagot voting, which continued despite a statute against it in 1819. Convinced that the property tests were a source of greater strength to the Whigs than to their own party, Democrats naturally were more averse than their opponents to the taxpaying and militia qualification established in 1817. Whigs did not oppose the movement to abolish the qualification after 1842. Indeed it was under a Whig administration that the constitutional amendment eliminating the property and taxpaying qualification was ratified in 1844 and 1845. The bill passed the house with a vote of 132 to 12, and the senate unanimously.[15] Of this bill, the *Times* made the statement, "long desired, and long postponed; but it passed, at length, with very little opposition and no excitement. The public mind had become prepared for it, and it was useless to make any clamor. . . ."[16] That both Whigs and Democrats claimed responsibility for the change reveals how bipartisan the movement had become by this time.

In the Louisiana convention of 1845, Democrats employed all the standard arguments of their party, including an appeal to the ideas of Jefferson, as well as to the less-disinterested argument that the existing taxpaying qualification was a great help to the Whigs. One delegate asserted that, in the presidential election of 1844, fraudulent tax receipts were issued to 1,500 persons to qualify them to vote.[17] The taxpaying qualification was termed a farce, with each party purchasing property of small value and creating fagot votes. Efforts made in 1838 to impose a poll tax on all adult free males and thus to

[14] *Hartford Times*, April 13, 1842.
[15] Connecticut, Office of the Secretary of State, *Miscellaneous Manuscripts*, 1845-1846. See also Morse, J. M., *A Neglected Period of Connecticut's History, 1818-1850* (New Haven, 1933), pp. 191-192.
[16] *Hartford Times*, Nov. 15, 1845.
[17] See *Journal of the Proceedings* [of 1845 Convention] (New Orleans, 1845), p. 108.

democratize the taxpaying qualification failed to gain much support, because some feared that it would increase the strength of New Orleans in state politics.[18] While there was a variety of reasons, national and local, for opposition to the taxpaying qualification, one was particularly southern. The desire of suffrage reformers to employ suffrage democracy to buttress slavery was as strong in Louisiana as it had been in Virginia and North Carolina. If the convention were to "elevate every freeman in the state to an equal participation in its government," said one delegate, "and make the broad political distinction between him and the slave . . . you will raise a wall of fire kindled from the united souls of freemen, around our state and its institutions, against the diabolical machinations of abolitionism."[19] Louisiana abandoned the taxpaying test in 1845.

In Ohio, the campaign for suffrage reform and reapportionment was initiated by Democrats. Samuel Medary, a Democratic politician, was leader of the movement for constitutional revision. Resident in Ohio since 1826, Medary had become editor of the *Ohio Statesman* of Columbus, had placed Polk's name in nomination, and had strongly supported, in company with David S. Reid of North Carolina, the presidential aspirations of Lewis Cass in 1848. Medary was impressed, as were most Democrats throughout the country, by Dorr's attempt in Rhode Island to overthrow a legal government in the name of a numerical majority of the voters.[20] Although the people of Ohio did not feel particularly oppressed by the taxpaying qualification, Medary considered it undemocratic and attempted to arouse public sentiment against it. The meeting of a constitutional convention, nevertheless, was not the direct result of great popular demand. Whigs denied that the

---

[18] *Ibid.*, p. 18. [19] *Ibid.*, p. 97.
[20] Dorn, Helen P., "Samuel Medary, Journalist and Politician, 1801-1864," *Ohio State Archaeological and Historical Quarterly* (LII, 1944), pp. 14-38.

people wanted suffrage reform, and that the government, as Democrats said, was considered as oppressive as that of Louis Philippe. They were obliged to conclude, they said, that Medary's "Jacobinism" stemmed from his and his party's desire to recover office. The *Ohio State Journal*, a Whig paper, claimed that Democrats when in power "did nothing but out of power these gentlemen found it necessary to look about for *new* issues, out of which they could make political capital."[21] Unwilling that only the Democrats should benefit from espousal of the suffrage issue, Whigs acquiesced in the attack upon the taxpaying qualification. In its stead, the *Ohio State Journal* advocated in 1850 a literacy test because, although many good people would not be able to meet it, it was preferable to a property test.[22] Whigs favored universal suffrage without distinction of color, which most Democrats did not. In 1851 Ohio rewrote the Jeffersonian Republican constitution of 1801, discarding the taxpaying qualification for voting, and allowing all adult white males to vote, if otherwise qualified.

While suffrage reform was accomplished in these four states, reformers did not succeed in Delaware, Pennsylvania, New Hampshire, Massachusetts, or Rhode Island. In Pennsylvania, members of the convention of 1837, despite some Democratic complaints that persons were left off tax lists by "accident or design," considered the taxpaying test so innocuous, as indeed it was, that it survived the general revision to which the old constitution of 1790 was subjected.[23] Opinion in New Hampshire was similar. The voters turned down an amendment to the constitution in 1851 to abolish the taxpaying qualification in a state which levied a poll tax and thus had universal suffrage in all but name.

[21] *The Weekly Ohio State Journal*, June 13, 1849.
[22] *Ibid.*, March 19, 1850.
[23] *Pennsylvania Archives*, 4th Series, v, p. 453; Agaki, R. H., "The Pennsylvania Constitution of 1838," *Pennsylvania Magazine of History and Biography* (XLVIII, 1924), pp. 301-333.

In contrast to the indifference in Pennsylvania to the abolition of the taxpaying qualification, there was considerable resentment against it in Massachusetts and Rhode Island. The suffrage in Rhode Island remained as restricted as anywhere in the union, thanks to the freehold requirement for the foreign-born and the $1 registry tax requirement for the native-born. Despite the extent of enfranchisement under the constitution of 1842, the voters were less, rather than more, interested in exercising their electoral privileges. In view of the increase of population during the forties, it is especially remarkable that the number of voters decreased so greatly after 1843, as we have seen.[24] The *Providence Post* was not exaggerating when it declared in 1850 that the state constitution was "one of the worst in the country" and "infinitely more calculated to disfranchise than to enfranchise."[25] Whigs were adamant in their opposition to reform. They argued that, in states which had an "unrestricted suffrage," such as Connecticut, New York, and Massachusetts, farmers and landowners comprised a majority which would hold "the fluctuating masses" of the cities in check. In Rhode Island the situation was totally different because the state was rapidly becoming "one great workshop," composed of Catholics, foreigners, Democrats, and other undesirables.[26] Rural, Protestant, native-born Democrats acted like so many Whigs on the suffrage issue, if not on others, delaying even the abandonment of the freehold test for the foreign-born and the $1 registry tax until 1887. Elimination of remaining disabilities was delayed until 1928.[27]

Democrats in Massachusetts were not as timid as those of

[24] See *Providence Post*, July 6, Dec. 17, 1850. See also Williamson, C., "Rhode Island Suffrage Since the Dorr War," *The New England Quarterly* (xxviii, March 1955), pp. 34-50, especially p. 38.

[25] *Providence Post*, May 28, 1850.

[26] *Providence Journal*, Jan. 25, March 25, 1851.

[27] Williamson, C., "Rhode Island Suffrage Since the Dorr War," *op.cit.*, pp. 39-50.

Rhode Island in regard to their taxpaying qualification for voting in state elections. Inspired by the example of the Dorr War, they became increasingly outspoken in their criticism of the voting tests. Partly on the grounds that the qualification was not enforced, partly because persons who had not paid taxes were listed as taxpayers and qualified illegally, Democrats argued that the poll tax, which could qualify the non-propertied to vote and which by custom had been placed at $1.50, should be either reduced to $.75 or $.50 or abolished altogether. The claim was made in 1841 that 12,000 had not voted, either because they had not been assessed for taxes or because they had not voluntarily come forward to pay a tax.[28]

In 1843 Governor Marcus Morton stated in his annual message to the legislature that, to his knowledge, a taxpaying qualification in practice had not prevented anyone from voting in Massachusetts but he implied that those who paid indirect taxes in the consumption of dutiable articles (and that included almost everyone) were logically as much entitled to the right to vote as payers of direct taxes. He was willing to agree with fellow Democrats, however, to a reduction in the poll tax to $.50, rather than its abolition as a democratic gesture.[29] Outspoken opponents of the governor's proposal emphasized the loss of revenue which such a measure would entail, estimated at $150,000 in 1843, and the consequent necessity for increasing taxes on real property, particularly that of farmers.[30] They indicated also that a reduction in the poll tax would help party hacks by reducing the expenses they incurred in paying the poll taxes of factory hands and town paupers. One opponent of the proposal feared that the measure would result in the enfranchisement of drunkards who often were not taxed by the towns in which they lived so that they could not claim legal settlement and hence become

[28] *Boston Post*, Feb. 28, 1843; Jan. 29, 1841.
[29] *Ibid.*, Jan. 31, 1843. [30] *The Atlas* (Boston), Feb. 13, 1843.

town charges. Whatever the reason, a compromise bill to reduce the poll tax to $1 failed to pass the lower house in 1843.[31]

Ten years later, partly as a result of the efforts of Whigs and Democrats to use the secret ballot issue in partisan politics, the Democrats secured the election of a convention to reform the franchise and electoral techniques. In this convention the taxpaying qualification was both attacked and defended. Benjamin F. Hallett, a defender of the working classes, advocated the elimination of the qualification for state elections, citing Benjamin Franklin as his authority.[32] Whigs opposed his plan as a means of relieving politicians, particularly Democrats, from the expense of paying the taxes of persons who otherwise could not vote. When it became clear that the Democrats did not intend to apply their proposals to town and school elections, the Whigs charged them with inconsistency. So conservative were Democrats on this issue that Hallett declared at one point, amid laughter, that he thought he was almost the only *democrat* in the whole convention.[33] Marcus Morton could not but agree, saying that expediency and not conviction had ruled the convention. The final draft of the revised constitution carefully excluded school and town affairs from the clause giving the vote to all adult male citizens, except paupers and persons under guardianship, if resident one year in the state. To help secure acceptance of reform, Hallett addressed a mass meeting at Fanueil Hall on October 21, 1853. In his speech he said that his aim had been to remove the last relic of feudalism.[34] By a small majority, voters rejected the principle of manhood suffrage, even in state elections, demonstrating perhaps that where the suffrage had always been quite democratic in practice and where the

[31] *Boston Post*, March 18, 1843.
[32] *Official Report of the Debates and Proceedings in the State Convention* . . . [1853] (Boston, 1853), pp. 564-565.
[33] *Ibid.*, p. 567.
[34] *Boston Post*, Oct. 26, 1853.

number of foreign-born was increasing there was indifference and even hostility to democratic suffrage theory.

The opposition of Massachusetts Democrats to the abandonment of the taxpaying qualification in local elections was by no means exceptional. Demands for manhood suffrage were resisted more successfully at this level than at any other. States with universal suffrage in state elections still upheld the principle, once applied to all elections, that local government was a kind of public service corporation which either was, or should be, non-partisan and in which only taxpayers should share. Vermont, for example, had based its state elections upon manhood suffrage, its town elections upon taxpayers.[35] While this distinction was almost wholly nominal in states where most adult males were polled, as in Vermont, it was not so in states which did not impose a compulsory poll tax. In these states, a taxpaying qualification was actually a property qualification, varying in severity with the incidence and the kinds of property subject or not subject to taxation. Different property qualifications for voting in various kinds of elections, aside from different residence requirements, do not seem to have been the cause for much criticism, save in Richmond, Chicago, and New York City. Even in these cities, the grievance had been removed by 1837. When the taxpaying qualification was abandoned, it was generally by the process of passing either a general law amending the legislation or special acts applying to specific towns and cities.

The circumstances by which, gradually, the qualifications in town and city elections in most states became, by the time of the Civil War, as democratic as those for state elections are obscure. The possibility that they were purely political is indicated by the history of the abandonment of the taxpaying qualification in at least one city, St. Louis. Whigs led the

[35] Williamson, C., "Suffrage, Property and Democracy in Windham," op.cit., pp. 135-141.

attack upon the qualification when they became convinced that they had lost the 1843 elections to the Democrats because Democratic political clubs had encouraged their members to secure dog-tax certificates, which would qualify them as taxpaying voters in city elections. The payment of local taxes on local dogs by local Democrats became a cause célèbre in 1844. Whigs won the election and abolished the taxpaying qualification.[36]

The gradual removal of property and taxpaying qualifications for voting in a majority of the states led, over a number of years, to a shift of the focus of suffrage reform from the issue of who could vote to the manner of voting. Always on the periphery of suffrage reform, electoral procedures moved closer to the center, particularly from Jackson's time forward. The manner of voting involved the question of whether voting should be easy or difficult and this, in turn, involved matters of democratic philosophy and of party advantage and expediency as well. When the leaders of either major party thought they would benefit from removing obstacles to voting, they made every effort to do so.

Residency requirements were a case in point. A two-year residence, as required in South Carolina after 1810, could leave unenfranchised, or even disfranchise, the poor, migratory element of the population. In many states, both Democrats and Whigs agreed that ne'er-do-wells, the floating element of the population, or the "birds of passage" should not vote. Often they defended a residence requirement as necessary to prevent the importation of voters in such numbers as might be decisive in a local or state election. In Connecticut, Democrats endeavored in 1839 to lower to one year the residence requirement, as part of a plan to stimulate working-class affiliation with their party. Whigs opposed their efforts,

[36] Snow, Marshall S., *The City Government of St. Louis* (Baltimore, 1887), pp. 13-14.

as Democrats opposed the efforts of Whigs to get Yale students who would support them to vote in New Haven elections.[37]

The season of year in which elections were held and the number of days or even the hours the polls were open might make a great difference to the individual elector when he decided to vote. In Virginia, voters complained intermittently that the elections were held about the time farmers were busy getting in the harvest and they were obliged to forego exercising their right to vote. In Louisiana, a sharp quarrel broke out between Whigs and Democrats on the floor of the convention of 1845. Whigs, defending the interest of the wealthier classes of New Orleans, objected to holding elections in September because many "respectable citizens" left the city during this time of year in order to avoid what some called "the baptism of citizenship," yellow fever.[38] The Whigs were anxious to arrange for November elections because by that time their supporters were once again resident in the city. In this convention, Whigs concentrated their efforts upon securing this change rather than attacking universal white manhood suffrage.

Not only the season of the year but the hours during which the polls were open were of vital significance to both parties. Whigs favored keeping something approximating banker's hours at the polls. In Massachusetts, the polls were closed at sunset, to disfranchise, according to Democrats, Cambridge laborers who worked in Boston but had to vote in their place of residence. When they returned home the polls were closed.[39] The device of the Sunset Laws was much admired

---

[37] *Hartford Times*, Feb. 16, 1839; *Connecticut Courant*, Dec. 3, 1842.
[38] *Official Report of the [Mass] Debates*, pp. 20-21.
[39] Brunet, Michel, "The Secret Ballot Issue in Massachusetts Politics from 1851-1853," *New England Quarterly* (xxv, September 1952), pp. 354-362. See also Evans, E. C., *A History of the Australian Ballot System in the United States* (Chicago, 1917).

among Whigs. Those of Rhode Island placed a comparable law in their statute books. One advantage of the Sunset Laws was that employers could give their workers time off to vote under the supervision of plant foremen or other representatives of management. Under these circumstances, a secret ballot to the Democrats was no longer a device they read about in Harrington or heard debated in convention or press. As a matter of self-defense, Democrats in industrial states, particularly Massachusetts, Rhode Island, and Connecticut, fought strenuously to secure it.[40]

The use of the ballot, now less open to abuse than previously because of the decrease in illiteracy, was favored by many politicians because it simplified the problem of getting the electors to vote a straight ticket. By 1840, both parties employed printed tickets of varying colors which, unfolded or not, enabled everyone near the ballot box to know how the elector had voted. In Massachusetts, David Henshaw, the Democratic boss, perfected this device but it was exploited to perhaps even greater advantage by the Whigs, who, in 1839, passed a law requiring that the ballots be submitted unsealed and unfolded. This invasion of the right of secrecy in ballot elections led eventually to a coalition between Democrats and Free Soilers which achieved, in 1851, the passage of a law requiring that the ballots be deposited in the boxes in sealed envelopes.[41] Numerous violations of the law by Democrats led to a reaction favorable to Whigs, which caused its repeal. This issue and others led to the convention of 1853, in which the Democrats, mindful of the utility of the printed ballot in achieving party regularity, sought to apply the principle of the secret ballot in state elections, excluding its use in town elections where party regularity was not thought

[40] Albright, Spencer D., *The American Ballot* (Washington, D.C., 1940).

[41] Brunet, *op.cit.*, pp. 354-355.

so desirable as financial regularity. This effort to defend the interests of the Democrats at the same time as those of the people was not acceptable to the voters. Rhode Island used the ballot in much the same way as Massachusetts. It made the use of the sealed envelope optional. By the Civil War, however, the use of the secret ballot had become general, save in Illinois and Virginia.[42] This form of secret ballot was a step toward the elaborate and perfected form of secrecy known as the Australian secret ballot which was adopted generally in this country after the Civil War.

Opposition of the Whigs in some states to the secret ballot was matched by their enthusiasm for registration of voters,[43] a movement associated with eighteenth-century English reformers who had secured a short-lived county registration voters bill which Massachusetts imitated in 1800. Whigs espoused voter registration as the chief means of providing fair play in elections by reducing the "floating" and "repeating" vote.[44] Because Whigs of New York and Connecticut were convinced that Democrats benefited most when residency requirements were flouted, they pressed for a reform measure. The Democrats were angered and to some extent with justification. Registry laws could work against the poor neglectful Democrats if they had to make application in person for registration, particularly if it had to be done a month or so before election. The payment of a registry tax of $1 in Rhode Island almost a year before election quite naturally cut down the number who could vote, no matter how interested Rhode Islanders might have become in current political issues since the last registry day. Often, men were away at work when the assessors called at their homes or lodgings. It was not surprising, therefore, that the Registry Act of Pennsylvania,

[42] Evans, *op.cit.*, pp. 1-40.
[43] See Harris, J. P., *The Registration of Voters in the United States* (Washington, D.C., 1929).
[44] 28 George III cap. 36; 2 William IV cap. 45.

passed in 1836, cut down the size of the vote in Philadelphia.[45]

Taking their cue from Pennsylvania, New Jersey Whigs tried to secure a registry law in 1838. In 1840, New York Whigs passed a Registry Act, applying it in partisan fashion to New York City and to no other part of the state. The Democrats were furious, holding mass meetings in Tammany Hall, parading with transparencies containing the legend, "Let Dogs be Registered," and attacking the Whigs in the newspapers for having imported voters from Philadelphia at $30 a head in the election of 1838.[46] The *Morning Herald* had to confess, however, that the parties were equally to blame and that the hiring of houses for tenants and the creation of fagot voters showed that elections in New York were carried on in the "pot-walloping and fagot system that prevailed in England, previous to the wholesome cleansing of the Reform Bill."[47] So blatantly partisan was the measure that it was repealed in 1842. Not until 1859 did the legislature pass an act requiring statewide registration of voters.

With the same admixture of disinterested and self-interested motives, Connecticut Whigs successfully advocated the passage of a registry bill in 1839. It established annual registration on the day before election and for one hour on election day of all persons who claimed to be legal voters and who wished to vote. When Democrats saw that the measure did not require that registry board members be drawn from both parties, they immediately interpreted it as designed to help the Whigs. They said it was a "disfranchising law," a modern version of the old Stand Up Law and proof that Whigs were the successors of the Federalists who had opposed suffrage reform for twenty-five years.[48] The Democrats were on sound ground in

---

[45] Harris, *op.cit.*, pp. 67-68.
[46] *Morning Herald* (New York), Sept. 25, Oct. 7, 1840.
[47] *Ibid.*, Feb. 9, 1838. [48] *Hartford Times*, June 29, 1839.

attacking annual registration as not only inconveniencing 55,000 electors but also violating the rule in Connecticut of "once a freeman always a freeman" unless disqualified by the Supreme Court, and as such unconstitutional.[49] One critic declared that in a large majority of towns the bill was not necessary because every elector was known and the possibility for fraud almost non-existent.[50] Democrats repealed the law in 1842 and enacted one which placed the burden of registration on the shoulders of town selectmen and clerks, a measure which Whigs said would enable the Democrats to resume cheating in elections.[51] Whether or not this was so, it is a fact that Democrats hailed their registration bill of 1844 and the universal manhood suffrage amendment of 1845 as the attainment of the Democratic goal and as the "end of the road for the party which called itself Democratic."[52]

It was hardly so, nevertheless, in Connecticut or elsewhere. Suffrage democracy even on the eve of the Civil War was confined to the world of adult male citizens, preferably white and native-born or of Anglo-Saxon background. Excluded from the franchise generally were women and Negroes. Surprisingly enough, aliens were often permitted to vote because there was less prejudice against them. The desire of the alien to vote was met in many western states by the provision that he might do so if he had declared his intention of becoming a citizen. Although the movement against alien voting had begun long before the Civil War, a contrary movement to enfranchise aliens reached its height right after the Civil War. During the nineteenth century, twenty-two states and territories permitted aliens to vote. Alien suffrage came to an end in Arkansas as late as 1926.[53] Elsewhere aliens, particularly if

---

[49] *Ibid.*, June 29, 1839.   [50] *Ibid.*, June 11, 1842.
[51] *New Haven Palladium*, April 15, 1844.
[52] *Hartford Times*, Nov. 15, 1845.
[53] Aylsworth, Leon E., "The Passing of Alien Suffrage," *American Political Science Review* (xxv, Feb. 1931), pp. 114-115.

Catholic, were the major objects of attention of the Native-American movement of the 1850's which sought to delay their admission to citizenship and in other ways to prevent them from exercising political influence. Even Tocqueville had gloomy forebodings for the future of America if its ethnic composition should be changed drastically. In 1854 he declared that the increase in the number of people "not of the Anglo-Saxon race is the great danger to be feared in America—a danger which renders the final success of democratic institutions a problem as yet unsolved."[54]

More nearly nationwide was the desire to prevent free Negroes from voting. New York, which had permitted Negro freeholders to vote under the constitution of 1821, withdrew the privilege in 1846.[55] The well-known tendency of this small segment of the northern population to vote Whig had heightened the hostility of humble Democrats to the Negroes in that part of the country where, as much by oversight as by design, they had been allowed to vote by a literal interpretation of constitutional suffrage clauses. By 1858 the suffrage was denied to free Negroes in an overwhelming majority of the northern states. The Liberty and Free Soil parties favored Negro suffrage and raised the issue in a few states, among them Ohio and Wisconsin, thus foreshadowing an issue which the Republicans made their own after 1865.

Where Indians were present in any number, they were likely to remain unenfranchised because they were not white. The argument against allowing them to vote in the California Constitutional Convention of 1850 had a ring of authentic Blackstonianism. "There are gentlemen," declared an opponent

---

[54] Tocqueville, *op.cit.*, II, p. 276.
[55] Olbrich, E., *The Development of Sentiment on Negro Suffrage to 1860*, pp. 73-74; Weeks, S. B., "The History of Negro Suffrage in the South," *Political Science Quarterly* (IX, Dec. 1894), pp. 671-703.

of Indian suffrage, "who are very popular among the wild Indians, who could march hundreds up to the polls."[56]

Pre-Civil War America passed on to the next era not only the problem of Negro suffrage but woman's suffrage as well. The involvement of women in the anti-slavery movement and the discrimination against them by men who favored equal rights for Negroes drew a caustic comment from Harriet Tubman, famous fugitive slave, that in the South she had suffered discrimination as a slave, and in the North as a Negro and as a woman.[57] By 1848, the woman's rights movement was in full swing. State constitutional conventions from this time forward were bombarded with petitions. One sent to the Wisconsin legislature made the statement that "there is no reality in any power that can not be coined into votes."[58] Woman's rights leaders were demonstrably learning fast. Not all wanted suffrage democracy for themselves, thinking that either a property or an educational test might be desirable for women. As late as 1880 in Rhode Island, the woman's suffrage movement refused to attack the freehold and taxpaying qualifications which some Rhode Islanders appealed to the federal government to prohibit, on the grounds that the rights of the citizens of the United States, guaranteed by the Reconstruction Amendments, were being violated.[59] Arguments for enfranchising women were not in any way original beyond the declamation against the aristocracy of sex which, it was said, made an absurdity of democracy. Woman's rights leaders even attempted to seek in Anglo-Saxon and English history the precedents for women's voting and officeholding.

[56] Brown, J. R., *Report of the Debates of the Convention of California* (Washington, D.C., 1850), p. 64.

[57] Myrdal, Gunnar, *An American Dilemma* (New York and London, 1944, 2 vols.), II, pp. 1,073-1,078.

[58] Stanton, E. C., *History of Woman's Suffrage* (New York, 1881-1902, 4 vols.), I, p. 867.

[59] Williamson, "Rhode Island Suffrage Since the Dorr War," *op.cit.*

One wrote with pride that "ladies of birth and quality" sat in the Witan, that four women were members of a parliament of Henry III and ten in that of Edward I. Woman's rights leaders were aware that women had voted prior to 1807 in New Jersey.[60]

The almost total elimination of property as a qualification for voting and the adoption of democratic techniques to encourage the voter to exercise his privileges proved how successful had been the suffrage reform movement by the time of the Civil War. Although the future proved that much had to be accomplished by later generations, it was an impressive fact, of world significance, that the movement to eliminate property as a test for voting had achieved so great a degree of success by 1860. Manhood suffrage without democracy, as conceived at that time, existed in the France of Napoleon III and the German Empire of Bismarck, but not in the America of 1860.

[60] Stanton, *op.cit.*, I, pp. 30-31.

CHAPTER 15

MINORITY REPORT

On the eve of the Civil War, Europeans, regardless of whether or not they were kindly disposed toward America, considered its political institutions unique. "Against the single example of the United States," declared a British writer, "we quote the whole history of democracy, the turbulence and destruction of the Greek states; the overthrow of the liberties of the Roman republic; the confusion of the Long Parliament, followed by the iron sway of Cromwell; the horrors of the French Revolution; the feebleness of the South American Republics; we read one convincing tale, the despotism of the many occasioning the misery of all, and terminated by the absolute power of the few. It is repeated from Athens to Bogota."[1]

Despite the fearsome precedents of democracy in the past, most Americans were not apprehensive for the future of their country. On the contrary, the uniquely democratic character of their institutions was a source of pride and pleasure. Not only had they achieved suffrage reform but also rotation in office, the abolition of property tests for officeholding, the creation of many more elective offices, and the democratization of the electoral college. The majority believed as an article of faith that, in time, most of these institutions and practices would be adopted by the rest of the civilized world.

Judging from the success of the democratic program in all parts of the country, the American public heartily approved the changes with regard to the suffrage. A Whig journal as early as 1836 said truthfully that the day had passed for argu-

[1] *Fraser's Magazine* (v, April 1832), pp. 294-316.

ing the question of universal suffrage on this side of the Atlantic.[2] Seven years later Charles F. Adams, a grandson of John Adams, commented upon the eagerness of both parties to prove to the electorate that each was as democratic as the other, or more so. In a review of an edition of Madison's papers, Adams said that not a single American of his day would dare express with impunity "such sentiments of un-limited dislike of democracy as are here reported." He mar-veled at how undemocratic, in terms of the America of President Tyler, had been the political sentiments of such leaders of the early Republican Party as Elbridge Gerry.[3]

Other observers noted how greatly opinion had changed since 1787. When anyone remarked how different and per-haps how much sounder were the principles of the founders of the republic, the retort, declared Felix Grund in his *Aristocracy in America*, was "simply: that a great number of those whom an overruling Providence used as instruments in be-stowing liberty and happiness on our people, did not under-stand what they were doing. . . ."[4] So strong was the sentiment favoring a democratic suffrage, said E. L. Godkin, editor of the *Nation*, that regardless of its dangers it was impossible to convince the American people that universal suffrage had been a mistake. Criticism of democratic voting qualifications was to no avail because "all children were taught they have a right to suffrage."[5]

While it is true that majority opinion in the United States applauded the achievement of a democratic suffrage, there was nevertheless an astonishing amount of overt criticism, albeit greatly in the minority, which cut across party, class,

---

[2] *American Quarterly Review* (xx, Sept. 1836), p. 208.

[3] *North American Review* (LIII, July 1841), pp. 41-79.

[4] Grund, F. J., *Aristocracy in America* (London, 1839, 2 vols.), II, pp. 270-271.

[5] Godkin, E. L., "The Democratic View of Society," *North American Review* (CI, July 1865), pp. 103-133.

and sectional lines. According to Alexis de Tocqueville, Salmon P. Chase was convinced that there was hardly a distinguished man in America who did not believe that a very broad suffrage was harmful but none of them could struggle against the fixity of public opinion on the subject.[6] Chase exaggerated the incidence of criticism as well as the pressure of majority opinion to conform. Nevertheless, his statement is of value as an indication of the stubborn strain of criticism of universal manhood suffrage which had always existed in America.

Prior to the Jacksonian era, criticism had been confined to a considerable degree to the press, pamphlets, legislatures, and constitutional conventions. From Jackson's time forward, it began to appear in the more polite world of periodicals and books. The climax came in the 1840's because of great public interest in the Dorr affair and because people thought, quite erroneously, that the suffrage reform movement had enormously increased the proportion of adult males who could vote.[7] Probably, in any state, the smallest increase in the size of the electorate was about 10 percent and the greatest increase about 50 percent. As has been shown, the pattern of enfranchisement was by no means uniform nor did it come all at once. Unacquainted with the evidence, and confusing an increase at this time in voter participation with the separate phenomenon of increased enfranchisement, critics believed that men of substance and education were being swamped at the polls by newly qualified voters. One Whig paper wildly estimated that the electorate had been increased twenty-fold. "In plain English," it said, "the electoral character of the country goes now upon all fours," representing a real revolution.[8]

[6] Pierson, G. W., *Tocqueville and Beaumont in America*, p. 557.

[7] Warner, H. W., "The Republic," *American Review* (x, July 1849), pp. 39-56.

[8] *Ibid.*, Sept. 1849, pp. 278-295.

On firmer ground were critics' efforts to seek in history and in the spirit of the times the cause for the phenomenon they observed. By and large their analysis conformed to that of Tocqueville in his *Democracy in America*. One United States senator summed up the position economically. "The levelling system," he declared, "commenced at the very settlement of the country, and was most active during the Revolution."[9] Writing many years later, Orestes Brownson applied this theme to the America he had known before the Civil War. Since 1825, he said, "the American people had shown a marked tendency to interpret their government as a pure and simple democracy and to shift from a territorial to a purely popular basis." In his opinion, Negro suffrage would be conceded in time because it was the essence of equal rights not to draw distinctions of class or race. All distinctions of birth, race, or private wealth were "anomalies in the American system and would be eliminated," he believed, "by its moral developments."[10]

The most surprising critics of manhood suffrage were those who had at one time favored a broadening of the suffrage but who were disillusioned by suffrage reform in practice. Many came to agree with Ralph Waldo Emerson's assertion that Americans, rich and poor, were all alike. "We know," said Emerson in 1854, "that wealth will vote for the same thing which the worst and meanest of the people vote for: rum, tyranny, slavery, against the ballot, schools, colleges, etc."[11] Suffrage reform was not always an end in itself but the means of gaining popular support for other political measures. If the newly enfranchised failed to support these measures, reformers often became disillusioned. Many American reformers had espoused a democratic suffrage in the same frame of mind as

[9] Grund, *op.cit.*, II, pp. 270-271.
[10] Brownson, O. A., *The American Republic* (New York, 1865), p. 380.
[11] Emerson, R. W., *Journals* (Boston and New York, 1909-1914), VIII, p. 494.

their British counterparts, Jeremy Bentham and James Mill, who supported suffrage reform partly to gain the support of the masses for Utilitarian legislation which British oligarchs opposed. In the first issue of the *Westminster Review*, Mill commented that political factions would appeal to public opinion in their contests for power, considering such appeals means as well as ends.[12] When the people voted against them, reformers sometimes expressed their disappointment in questioning or opposing the democratic principle: majority rule whether that majority is right or wrong. Thomas Cooper, Joseph Priestley, Samuel Young, James Fenimore Cooper, Orestes Brownson, and even Walt Whitman began to have doubts about democracy after the achievement of manhood suffrage and as the country became more democratic. Federalists who had become more conservative when the people rejected their policies and voted them out of office were the first American faction, after the loyalists, to respond in this very human fashion. That prince of Federalists, for example, Harrison Gray Otis, reacted as violently to the election of 1840 as did Brownson, saying that Harrison's election had shaken his confidence as to the "ultimate result of universal suffrage & the irresistable tendency of the masses to acquire & abuse power."[13]

A few spokesmen for labor, surprisingly, criticized the results of suffrage reform. Some of their strictures anticipated Karl Marx, who entertained a low opinion of manhood suffrage as a kind of opiate for the masses. The Philadelphia *Workingman's Advocate* was not in existence early enough to be a factor in the early and more important era of suffrage reform. As a result, it did little more than acknowledge it with respect and denounce its enemies, both real and alleged,

[12] *Westminster Review* (i, Jan. 1824), pp. 1-18.
[13] Morison, S. E., *Life and Letters of Harrison Gray Otis* (Boston and New York, 1913, 2 vols.), ii, p. 300.

although it was often ignorant of who those enemies were. This paper reported in 1830 that, at a Fourth of July celebration, two toasts had been offered, one to universal manhood suffrage and one to Charles Carroll of Carrollton, that consistent enemy of universal suffrage.[14] Having won the battle for suffrage democracy, said the *Advocate*, workingmen must ask themselves what they had gained, if anything, in Pennsylvania or elsewhere. The *Advocate* was disappointed that, in such an important election as that of 1829, only a few workingmen had voted and that little had been accomplished, under a regime of manhood suffrage, to help them. "Can any one point," asked the paper on November 7, 1829, "to a single law in the statute book of this commonwealth calculated to benefit the working classes?" The future, it was hoped, would be different. "To the elective franchise, then, we must look as the redeeming power that will improve our condition," but not until laboring men sent their own kind and not members of the middle class to represent them. "The doctrine," it declared, "that learned men make our best representatives is exploded," because they "represent only themselves, and the privileged orders."[15]

Disappointment with working-class use of the vote in America was reflected abroad in the beginning of British left-wing anti-Americanism on the grounds that the United States, in the opinion of that old Chartist, Ernest Jones, was the home of "as vile a wage slavery as any in Europe." The worst evils, he said, were merely mitigated by an abundance of land.[16] American democracy was a sham despite a democratic franchise. The coming struggle in America, he predicted, would be against the monopoly of machinery and against the growing danger of a monopoly of land. In this country, recognition of the limitations of the ballot, in so complex a society, helped

[14] *Workingman's Advocate*, July 14, 1830.   [15] *Ibid.*, Oct. 31, 1829.
[16] Saville, John, *Ernest Jones: Chartist* (London, 1952), pp. 145-146.

to emphasize for labor spokesmen the necessity of engaging in trade unionism at the expense of political action or of third party activity.

The most persistent critics of suffrage democracy of pre-Civil War times and, indeed, of the movement for greater democracy on all fronts, were Whigs. In the *North American Review*, the *American Review*, the *American Quarterly Review*, and other journals of Whig opinion, writers contemplated with regret the decline of virtue and principle in American political life since the eighteenth century. Declaring that neither the Federalist nor the Republican parties had believed in universal suffrage, they asserted that the proliferation of elective offices and the like had resulted more from party impulses than from settled convictions. If any one man was responsible for the decline in the American Republic that man was Martin Van Buren. He rose to power as a democratic leader, Whigs said, by raising the ghost of Federalism and creating a democratic party. His objective was his own personal advancement and that of other party leaders.[17]

Many Whigs who would accept universal suffrage gagged, however, at the democratic theory that the electorate had the right to bind its representatives and, as Cooper wrote in *The Monikins*, make responsibility "the substitute for virtue in a politician, as discipline is the substitute for courage in a soldier."[18] John Quincy Adams dared to uphold the Burkean dicta in his first message to Congress, saying that representatives should not have their hands tied "by the express will of their constituents."[19] Whigs often pictured themselves as representing an objective, unselfish, disinterested aristocracy, the American counterpart of the British aristocracy and by right entitled to exert here the moderating influences ascribed to

[17] *American Review* (III, May 1846), pp. 455-464.
[18] Cooper, J. F., *The Monikins* (New York, 1896), p. 311.
[19] Weston, Florence, *The Presidential Election of 1828* (Washington, D.C., 1938), p. 28.

British aristocrats. But Democrats denied to Whigs even the consolation that might be derived from this conception of their place in American life. Felix Grund dismissed the idea that they played any such role, saying "from the historical aristocracy of England, to the nameless money lenders of America, there is a greater transition than from the substance to the shadow of a thing. Incorporated companies and banks are as yet the only armories that furnish weapons to the chivalrous knights comprising the aristocracy of the New World; and there is scarcely any American squire that would not be willing to sell horse and lance provided a proper price be offered him."[20]

Few northerners cared much after Jackson's time to criticize American democracy in the way southern leaders dared. Some southerners attacked universal suffrage under a system of free labor as an evil in itself and the Siamese twin of that even greater evil, abolitionism. In phrases which showed their indebtedness to Aristotle, Blackstone, and Malthus, southern critics of manhood suffrage declared that, in a society where workingmen were free and where their number was increasing rapidly, thanks to the unwise stimulants of the American System, the full consequences of evil already apparent—the power of landlords and manufacturers in politics and the increase in dependency, corruption, and demagoguery in elections—would have, in time, to be faced. They warned that America would not be exempt from the rule of history that eventually a barbarized, pauperized population would lose patience with the inequalities in the distribution of wealth and overthrow the existing order. The ownership of workers of the south under the slavery system, said these southerners, obviated all danger from this quarter by rendering harmless universal white manhood suffrage. An agricultural society, based upon a black slave labor system and composed of a

[20] Grund, *op.cit.*, II, pp. 80-81.

homogeneous white population which enjoyed equal rights, was the only social and political order acceptable to many in the south.[21]

During the Civil War, the *Southern Literary Messenger* argued, in an article entitled "Philosophy of Secession," that "cheapening" of the electoral qualification and the increase in the number of elective offices had made of northerners "a voting people." The practice of everyone voting all the time for everything had infected the north, as much so as anti-slavery fanaticism. Both suffrage and anti-slavery reform movements were denounced as tending to the same results. "To say all men are entitled to vote," said the writer, "is the equivalent of saying all men are created free and equal."[22] While George Fitzhugh and other southern leaders wished to disfranchise only foreigners and northerners, still others had already taken a stand against suffrage reform, as in Virginia in 1829-1830, or had openly advocated the disfranchisement of the propertyless whites, as did the *Southern Review* as early as 1830.[23] During the Civil War, southern critics of white manhood suffrage proposed that the president of the Confederacy be chosen by the state legislatures rather than by electors in order to "prevent mere democracy of numbers."[24] In 1830, the *Workingman's Advocate* had commented critically upon the anti-democratic suffrage views of members of the Virginia convention and those of the *Southern Review*. It informed northern working men of the unflattering opinion some southerners had of their role in politics.[25] Lincoln did

[21] See *Southern Review* (v, April 1869), pp. 249-275; *De Bow's Review* (xxii, February 1857), pp. 113-129; *Southern Literary Messenger* (v, October 1839), p. 687.
[22] *Southern Literary Messenger* (xxv, Sept. and Oct. 1862), pp. 550-558.
[23] Fitzhugh, George, *Sociology for the South, or the Failure of Free Society* (Richmond, 1854), p. 256; *Southern Review* (vi, Aug. 1830), p. 21.
[24] *Southern Literary Messenger* (xxvi, Jan. 1863), pp. 39-43.
[25] *Workingman's Advocate*, April 3, Sept. 11, 1830.

the same during the Civil War. In 1864 he remarked upon the
hostility of southern leaders to universal suffrage. More than
ever, said Lincoln, the insurrection was a war upon "the first
principles of government—the rights of the people." The
southern stand on the suffrage issue was conclusive. "In these
documents," he said, "we find the abridgment of the existing
right of suffrage, and the denial to the people of all right to
participate in the selection of public officers, except the legislature, boldly advocated, with labored arguments to prove
that large control of the people in government is the source of
all political evil."[26] Abroad, British reformers who were
friendly to the north were perspicacious enough, however, to
recognize that not all opponents of manhood suffrage were
southerners. One Briton said that the opponents of Lincoln
in the north were all who were afraid of manhood suffrage
and of the rising power of immigrants as well as those who
would surrender their own principles in order to avoid a war.

American critics of suffrage reform offered various remedies
for the dangers and evils they saw in suffrage democracy.
Many political solutions were advanced only to prove un-
realistic almost immediately. Samuel Jones of Stockbridge,
Massachusetts, an unregenerate follower of Blackstone, defended the freehold qualification concept of suffrage even
after the Dorr War,[27] as did some southerners. In 1862, John
Hale Hunt, claiming that past efforts to establish a democracy
had resulted only in an aristocracy of business, published
anonymously a work in which he attacked the foreign-born
voters and advocated a complicated plan to return to a balanced form of government in which only freeholders could
vote.[28] Otherwise, Whig and other opponents of a democratic

[26] Nicolay, J., Hay, J. (eds.), *The Complete Works of Abraham Lincoln* (New York, 1905, 12 vols.), x, pp. 50-51.
[27] Jones, Samuel, *A Treatise on the Right of Suffrage* (Boston, 1842).
[28] Dorfman, J. F., *The Economic Mind in American Civilization*, ii,
pp. 964-965.

suffrage had little to offer except vague remarks that perhaps the government needed to be changed as the country became more industrialized and urbanized. No one suggested how the change could take place without a violent counter-revolution. The *American Review* refused to endorse the statement, possibly derived from Tocqueville, that the time would come when the poor of the great cities would be restrained only by a standing army.[29]

Some critics who were less than enthusiastic about suffrage reform took comfort in the fact that the American political system contained enough rigidities, limitations on power, and checks and balances to enable the Republic to endure as James Madison had hoped. Grund quoted one who said that most people acted in politics as they did in religion. "Every doctrine," he said, "is with them, more or less a matter of faith; received, principally, on account of their trust in their apostle."[30] In other words, the American spirit in politics, no less than its institutions, provided the opportunity for leadership. Means existed to curb in practice the sovereignty assigned by the American system to the people. Alexander H. Everett thought these considerations helped to make democracy bearable. In a brilliant essay he sketched an imaginary conversation between Montesquieu and Benjamin Franklin. Wherever representative government has been introduced, he had Franklin say, the results have been the same, regardless of who was allowed to vote. "What form of election, for example," Franklin exclaimed, "would have failed to place Pitt and Fox at the head of their respective parties during the controversies of the French Revolution? The formal influence given to property is not important. If a rich man can alone vote in the county he has one vote, if all can vote he has two or three hundred." In these sketches, Everett implied that

[29] *American Review* (v, May 1849), pp. 614-629.
[30] Grund, *op.cit.*, II, pp. 239-240.

leadership was important in government, whether aristocratic or democratic, and that democracy was by no means incompatible with it. Broadening the basis of political power would perhaps require different methods of leadership but would leave unimpaired its prerogatives, duties, and responsibilities.[31]

If a counter-revolution was out of the question, the strong probability remained that free, tax-supported, compulsory education would provide the balance wheel for society. Critics of suffrage reform were fearful, in the words of James Fenimore Cooper, that the people would in time have respect for no one but themselves.[32] Because of ignorance or self-interest, dependence of the people upon themselves was as dangerous as their dependence upon landlords or employers. Dependence upon education was preferable even if legislation compelling school attendance was necessary. Rousseau-like, these reformers would force the American people to be free and democratic, to be independent of demagogues and selfish politicians. Ironically, the Democrats who had been associated most often with reform frequently opposed, as they did in Connecticut, the spending of taxpayers' money on education. One reason for Henry Barnard's becoming a Whig was his conviction that the Whigs generally were more sympathetic to his educational philosophy and would be more likely to provide, among other things, an antidote to the evils of a democratic suffrage.[33] Having been unsuccessful in Connecticut, Barnard was invited to go to Rhode Island in 1843 to establish a plan of education in the wake of the Dorr War.

Horace Mann was even more explicit in claiming social and political benefits for his educational philosophy. He believed

[31] Everett, A. H., *Critical and Miscellaneous Essays* (Boston, 1845, 2 vols.), I, pp. 382-407.

[32] Cooper, J. F. (ed.), *Correspondence of James Fenimore Cooper* (New Haven, 1922, 2 vols.), II, pp. 600-601.

[33] Curti, Merle, *The Social Ideas of American Educators* (New York, 1943), pp. 159-164.

that the schools were not only a social convenience but a necessary political institution. Universal suffrage, he thought, must be accompanied by universal education to insure that elevation of intellectual and moral faculties of the people without which there would be "universal mismanagement and calamity." He appealed to men of property to support his plan because he was convinced that they had a stake in public education of the masses. Unless their minds were enlightened "by knowledge," he said, "and controlled by virtuous principles, there is not, between their appetites and all you hold dear upon earth, so much as the defence of a spider's web."[34]

Mann's arguments that public schools were necessary because the churches were no longer in the key position they had once occupied was not appreciated by various lay and professional church leaders, who were convinced that it was their responsibility to expand their role as teachers of the great religious and social truths. The bulwark of suffrage democracy, they believed, was not the school but the church. The pious must not refrain from participating in politics, declared the Presbyterian, E. S. Ely, D.D., in 1828. If they did, he said, the country would be under rulers elected wholly by the impious.[35]

Protestants and Roman Catholics disputed which branch of Christianity would prove the most effective stabilizer. Orestes Brownson, convert to Catholicism, was convinced that Protestantism was by nature too individualistic and democratic to provide immutable standards for human behavior, and he criticized also those who, like Fanny Wright and Abner Kneeland, relied on secular education to meet the need. Only

[34] Mann, Horace, *Lectures and Annual Reports on Education* (Cambridge, 1867), p. 198.
[35] Ely, E. S., *The Duty of Christian Freemen to Elect Christian Rulers* (Philadelphia, 1828), p. 7. See also *Workingman's Advocate*, Oct. 30, 1830.

religion would be effective, Brownson said, and it must be Roman Catholicism because "it must be a religion which is above the people and controls them, or it will not answer the purpose."[36]

To other critics who were concerned with the dangers of suffrage democracy, church and school were not the only environmental factors which could provide the necessary safeguards. The Malthusian laws could be ignored safely in America, some thought, at least for the time being, because the population was not determined by sustenance. Instead, sustenance was determined by the population. In the second place, the American System of diffusing property by industrial employment and the elevation of living standards would prevent the development of rigid social classes. "How can the poor be arrayed against the rich," queried Francis Bowen, "so long as [the] son of an Irish coachman becomes Governor of State and the grandson of a millionaire dies a pauper?"[37] Talk of the dangers of a revolt against property was ridiculous where it was so widely shared and where the doctrine of self-help instead of socialism prevailed. Under these circumstances, an attack upon property by a small faction would arouse in its defense the great majority. Lastly, the character of the American people, whatever the cause, would render democracy and universal suffrage harmless. The *American Review* took comfort from the belief that an ingrained respect for law characterized a democracy.[38]

The capacity for self-restraint, self-government, and self-help inherent in Americans required rational explanation. Some attributed these characteristics to the physical environment, others to historical developments, while still others

[36] *Brownson's Quarterly Review* (II, Oct. 1845), pp. 514-530.
[37] Bowen, F., *The Principles of Political Economy*, quoted in Curti, *op.cit.*, p. 300.
[38] *American Review* (v, May 1847), pp. 614-629.

thought they might be the result of the Anglo-Saxon or British origins of a large part of the population. The increase in the number of Irish, German, and other immigrants increased the pride of many Americans in their British inheritance. In Britain, the success of American democracy was ascribed primarily to the fact that it had been a natural offshoot of the British stock.

The relation of these beliefs to the suffrage was made explicit. In 1845 the *American Review* argued against allowing foreigners to vote, claiming that the political power of the state must rest upon "homogeneity of race."[39] British reformers took pride in the achievements of their own kind overseas, assigning their success to ethnic causes. As early as 1794, Joseph Gerrald, on trial in Britain for his life for treason, declared that he had lived in Philadelphia for four years and had not found that the form of government there had been anything but good. "What has been found by experience to be wholesome for Americans," he said, "can never prove hurtful or poisonous to Britain, from the purest stock of whom Americans are descended."[40] Almost three-quarters of a century later, J. Arthur Partridge wrote that American people and the English were one because the former "drew its blood and its creed from the heart of England . . . we know the Pedigree of that great people, both after the flesh and after the spirit, and we will swear it is worth its breeding."[41]

More commentators preferred an environmental to a racial explanation of the American character. The American way of life was considered unique, with the result that democracy was, in Metternich's phrase, a "natural" phenomenon. If this were true, American democracy was not for export. The statement of an Englishman that his form of government was not

[39] *American Review* (II, Nov. 1845), pp. 437-451.
[40] Fraser, L., *English Opinion of the American Constitution and Government: 1783-1798* (New York, 1915), p. 73.
[41] Partridge, J. A., *On Democracy* (London, 1866), p. 407.

to be thought akin to a recipe for pudding which would produce the same results everywhere applied to American government also. Whigs saw the logic of this argument, but seldom Democrats. "No man in the possession of his reason," exclaimed Francis Bowen, "would wish to establish a popular government for the serfs of Russia, the *lazzaronis* of Naples, or the licentious and degraded population of Paris."[42]

Whether America's suffrage institutions could be imported and utilized as easily as American grain was the subject of considerable debate in Britain at the time of the passage of the Reform Bills of 1832 and 1867. As might be expected, reformers and their opponents saw in the United States what they wanted to see and both attempted to buttress their positions by appealing to their own conceptions of America. Jeremy Bentham, the "great legal steam engine" of the day, became during his democratic phase a warm friend of America. He cited America as a country which almost met his full approval.[43] Chartist advocates of manhood suffrage in Britain took comfort from the American example. The motto of a Chartist demonstration at Huddersfield in 1841 was: "The Glorious Revolution of America, and soon may England imitate that country, its people happy and contented."[44] A Chartist paper, published in Glasgow, stated in the issue of May 29, 1841, that the wildest imagination could not conceive of a more democratic government than that existing in the United States, and declared that if, seventy years before, anyone had asserted that it was possible for a people so widely scattered to govern themselves through delegates chosen by universal suffrage he would not have been believed.[45] The

[42] *North American Review* (LVI, April 1843), p. 397.

[43] Williamson, C., "Bentham Looks at America," *Political Science Quarterly* (LXX, Dec. 1955), pp. 531-543.

[44] Hovell, Mark, *The Chartist Movement* (Manchester, 1925), p. 226. See also Lillibridge, G. T., *Beacon of Freedom* (Philadelphia, 1954).

[45] *The Chartist Circular* (Glasgow), May 29, 1841.

growing sense of disillusionment of the Chartist, Ernest Jones, did not affect the Manchester Liberal, John Bright, perhaps the outstanding British interpreter during the Civil War of American democracy. Indeed, Bright had claimed, in a speech delivered in 1858, that the first Reform Bill had been a conscious effort to Americanize Britain.[46]

To make such a statement was to play into the hands of the enemies of British reform. Bentham had complained to James Madison as early as 1811 that opponents of reform tried to prevent his and others' efforts to clean out the Augean stables of Britain with the cry that they were trying to republicanize the country. In Bright's day the cry was heard again. In 1831, *Fraser's* demanded, apropos a demand for ballot elections, "Is the mere fact of the prevalence of a certain custom in America ground enough for its legislative adoption among us?"[47] British conservatives endeavored to forestall reform and confound the pro-American group by directing attention to certain undemocratic American institutions and practices. During the earlier phases of the nineteenth-century reform movement, defenders of the unreformed House of Commons cited as undemocratic the taxpaying and property tests for voting in some of the American states. Even the *Edinburgh Review* acknowledged in 1818 the existence of property tests in Virginia and New England.[48] The removal of these last impediments to a democratic suffrage in America forced the abandonment of this line of attack.

Descriptions of the seamy side of American elections under manhood suffrage proved an effective substitute. The *Edinburgh Review* accused Mrs. Trollope of giving a biased picture of American life "out of pure alarm for the English con-

[46] Smith, G. B., *John Bright: His Life and Speeches* (London, 1885, 2 vols.), II, p. 325.
[47] *Fraser's Magazine* (III, Feb. 1831), p. 87.
[48] *Edinburgh Review* (XXXI, Dec. 1818), pp. 165-203.

stitution."[49] A number of other works were published with the same object. One of these, by one Thomas Brothers, was published in London in 1840. It was entitled: *The United States of North America as they are; not as they are generally described: being a cure for Radicalism.* Brothers affirmed that in America debts were bigger, taxes heavier, and poverty and oppression more general than elsewhere. Other writers described, in the same spirit, the nightmare of elections in American cities, such as New York and Baltimore. According to the *Saturday Review*, Baltimore was in the hands of "a ferocious mob" for two years.[50] By a discriminating selection of facts, it was easy to prove that American democracy set a bad example for Britain. Even Disraeli, architect of the Reform Bill of 1867, felt obliged to say that the principles upon which he proceeded were "English, not American."[51]

This one-sided view of American democracy in practice was not long unchallenged. The man who helped more than any one to separate the stuff from the nonsense was William G. Ousely, at one time an attaché in the British Ministry in Washington. When he returned to Britain, he published in 1832 a splendid account entitled *Remarks on the Statistics and Political Institutions of the United States.* Ousely was convinced by his sojourn in America that the evils of American democracy had been greatly exaggerated and that American laws and institutions worked well in the American environment. As a relativist in outlook and possibly influenced by Montesquieu's assertion that no one system of laws was suitable for all people everywhere, he denied that America had any message for Europe. Over the years, Britons inclined more and more toward this opinion, partly because it could be used to confirm conservatism. Conservatives found comfort in the

[49] *Ibid.* (LV, July 1832), pp. 479-526.
[50] *Saturday Review*, Nov. 26, 1859.
[51] Hansard, CLXXXIII (1866), p. 110.

implication that what was natural in America might be a monstrous aberration elsewhere. In emphasizing the differences between America and Britain—namely, the abundance of land, the absence of feudal institutions, the infant state of manufacturing and urbanism, the predominance of the middling or intermediate classes, and the proliferation of schools—the conservatives tried to prove that America was the great exception to the general rule that democracy was a mistake. British reformers did not believe so. They were certain that the achievement of free trade, the restoration of the yeomanry, and the establishment of a free tax-supported educational system for the masses would render British democracy equally beneficial.

Whether or not Americans believed that their form of government was exportable, they took pride in their democratic achievements, among which the divorce of property from the suffrage was prominent. "It remained for the people of the United States," wrote Alexander H. Everett in 1827, in a statement taken from Jefferson without proper acknowledgment, "to furnish . . . an entirely new solution to the problem of government. . . . The object of this solution is not, as some affirm, *democracy* rejected but *democracy made easy*."[52]

[52] Everett, A. H., *America: or a General Survey of the Political Situation of the Several Powers of the Western Continent, with Conjectures of their Future Prospects* (Philadelphia, 1827), p. 81.

INDEX